Reference and Information Sources and Services for Children and Young Adults

LESLEY S.J. FARMER

ROWMAN & LITTLEFIELD
Lanham • Boulder • New York • London

Acquisitions Editor: Charles Harmon
Assistant Acquisitions Editor: Erinn Slanina
Sales and Marketing Inquiries: textbooks@rowman.com

Credits and acknowledgments for material borrowed from other sources, and reproduced with permission, appear on the appropriate pages within the text.

Published by Rowman & Littlefield
An imprint of The Rowman & Littlefield Publishing Group, Inc.
4501 Forbes Boulevard, Suite 200, Lanham, Maryland 20706
www.rowman.com

86-90 Paul Street, London EC2A 4NE

British Library Cataloguing in Publication Information Available

Library of Congress Cataloging-in-Publication Data

Names: Farmer, Lesley S. J., author.
Title: Reference and information sources and services for children and
   young adults / Lesley S.J. Farmer.
Description: Lanham : Rowman & Littlefield, [2022] | Includes
   bibliographical references and index.
Identifiers: LCCN 2022015276 (print) | LCCN 2022015277 (ebook) | ISBN
   9781538163184 (cloth) | ISBN 9781538163191 (paperback) | ISBN
   9781538163207 (epub)
Subjects: LCSH: School libraries—Reference services—United States. |
   Children's libraries—Reference services—United States. | Young adults'
   libraries—Reference services—United States. | Libraries—Special
   collections—Reference sources. | Reference sources—Bibliography.
Classification: LCC Z675.S3 F23745 2022 (print) | LCC Z675.S3 (ebook) |
   DDC 025.5/2778—dc23/eng/20220521
LC record available at https://lccn.loc.gov/2022015276
LC ebook record available at https://lccn.loc.gov/2022015277

Dedicated to
reference publishers and librarians

Contents

List of Tables and Figures

Preface

It's been eight years since I wrote my book *Introduction to Reference and Information Services in Today's School Library*. A lot has happened since then: two changes in U.S. presidents, the COVID-19 pandemic, increased polarization relative to information and disinformation, "wokeness" (hopefully), more evidence on climate change, virtual assistant tools like Siri, an explosion of streaming services, revised American Association of School Librarians (AASL) and International Society for Technology in Education (ISTE) standards, a new Advanced Placement course on research, plus thousands of revised and new print and online reference sources. It's no wonder that a colleague of mine asked if I was going to update my reference book.

And still, the need is great for young people. They still have research assignments to do and have imposed questions to answer. They still have personal research needs: choosing which game to get or ways to get them, finding a job, knowing how to care for a pet, going on a diet, helping plan a family vacation, cleaning a chocolate stain on the carpet before the parents get home, and so forth. They might even be helping a friend or a relative with an information need, especially if there is an access gap because of technology or literacy.

Libraries play an important role in providing value-added physical and intellectual access to information and ideas so that young people can become effective users of ideas and information, which competencies support educational curriculum and broader aspects of literacies for daily life. As such, youth-serving librarians need to provide reference and information resources and services now more than ever.

Some of those resources remain the same: types of reference, such as encyclopedias and atlases, although their subject might change such as selection tools for choosing apps. Likewise, formats continue to include print, but digital formats have expanded as has the concept of dynamic/changing content. Reference and information services continue to occur face-to-face on a one-to-one and group basis, but delivery modes have also expanded to include smart speakers.

Youth-serving librarians provide a unique combination of personal and professional reference and information services and provide relevant reference collections. By analyzing key features of reference and information services to young people in school and public library environments, including the research behind the trends and issues, you can make sure that those services are appropriately responsive to children and teens. This book helps you to optimize those resources and services.

Chapter 1 defines reference and information services and provides an overview of information and reference needs, resources, and standards in terms of today's realities. A sidebar exercise invites librarians to invent ideal youth-centric reference/information services.

Chapter 2 focuses on sources of research information and addresses a range of formats. As a sidebar exercise, collaborative R&I services are explored.

Chapter 3 defines reference sources generically and provides well-recognized selection criteria, tools, and policies for both print and media reference resources. In order to be relevant to the community and its youth, reference materials may be contextually specified and collected. A sidebar exercise encourages librarians to expand their collection of diverse reference materials.

Chapter 4 examines reference and information services in light of life cycles of reference materials. Special attention is devoted to subscription databases in terms of factors to consider, licensing, and digital resource management. A sidebar exercise explores resource sharing.

Chapter 5 focuses on the continued need for physical access and strategies to optimize their use. It also explores the increasing use of online sources for both convenience and timeliness, noting issues that accompany virtual space. A sidebar exercise shares the benefits of browsing.

Chapter 6 discusses different information behaviors, drawing upon current theories. Next, the chapter provides techniques for effectively researching and retrieving reference information from different types of print, nonprint, and digital resources: based on young people's actions and leading them to the next level of competence. In the process, techniques for searching visual and aural information are also provided. A sidebar exercise explores information behavior models and theories.

Chapter 7 focuses on a core reference service: reference interaction as a negotiated and partnership model. The chapter addresses reference interactive standards and strategies in different modalities and time frames. A sidebar exercise delves into the use of mediaries.

Chapter 8 discusses the process of curating and designing information packages, addressing content and format issues. A sidebar exercise provides a case study to facilitate research skills collaboratively.

Chapter 9 deals with representative legal and ethical issues that arise when serving youth. Criteria for ethical decision-making are provided. A sidebar exercise provides a case study in R&I ethical equity within a school library.

Chapter 10 notes that reference and information services for youth should be a dynamic function, responding to changing information needs and behaviors as well as changing resources and emerging technologies. A sidebar exercise imagines possible scenarios for reference and information services in Cybrary 2030, and another sidebar provides a rubric to help you plan your library's R&I future.

The book finishes with a bibliography and an index.

We all have information needs, which benefit for effective reference and information needs. Hopefully, this book will highlight how we can be good consumers and producers of such services in a participatory manner.

1

Overview

THE WORLD OF INFORMATION

The world is full of information: organized and meaningful data that can lead to understanding and knowledge. While some information is relatively stable, such as basic arithmetic equations, other information changes constantly, such as temperature. People constantly generate information, and it is disseminated more widely and in various information "channels" than ever before. In terms of data, in 2020 people created 1.7 MB of data every second. As of January 2021, 4.66 billion people were active Internet users. In 2021 alone there were 2 trillion Google searchers (Bulao, 2021).

All of our children and teenagers—youth—are true Millennials: born in the twenty-first century. What has been their world?

- New York City's World Trade Center is remembered as a tragic event rather than an economic milestone.
- Vladimir Putin has always been the prime minister or president of Russia.
- India's population has always been more than a billion.
- The euro has been the main currency in Europe since 2002.
- Mobile devices, such as cell phones and tablets, have always been around, as has Wikipedia.
- Swipe is a way to pay for something with a credit card, more than stealing a credit card.
- There was always an Oscar for the best-animated feature.
- Harry Potter books have always been banned somewhere in America.
- The Peanuts cartoons are all historical because Charles M. Schulz died in 2000.

Their most memorable event will probably be the COVID-19 pandemic.

Nowadays, people are bombarded with information, and yet people—including children and teens—lack information in order to do what they want and need to do. It's one major reason for education. For instance, this generation's children and young adults have an unprecedented complex world of information to navigate, discern, and address. For many young people, finding information is not as much of a problem as finding the *right* information that is comprehensible. Whom can youth trust to help guide them through this morass?

LIBRARIES AS A GATEWAY TO THE WORLD OF INFORMATION

Libraries are centers of information, facilitating people to access and use the recorded information. You can think of information and its carriers—books, canvases, computers, and so on—as material input. Library workers are the human "input." Libraries, both physical and virtual, constitute the environment in which those resources are acted up; librarians select and organize recorded information in support of the intended users, who then retrieve and use that information for personal and intellectual growth and enjoyment. The library environment also enables users to generate and share their own information. The results can be inspiring!

So where do reference and information services fit into this picture? The short answer is, where there is an information need or gap, the librarian as an information professional is there to help bridge that gap, facilitating the connection between persons and information. The reference part deals with referring persons to needed sources of reliable, relevant information. In this age of disinformation, libraries are uniquely positioned to provide high-quality reference and information (R&I) services. Libraries are trusted institutions and places of inclusion, librarians build collections of authenticated information, and librarians are leaders in teaching information literacy (Sosulski & Tyckoson, 2018). Focusing on services to children, the International Federation of Library Associations and Institutions (IFLA) (Rankin, 2018) stated that "the purpose of the children's library is to provide resources and services in a variety of media to meet the needs of children of all ages and abilities for the education, information and personal development" (p. 4). In terms of collections, IFLA's guidelines explicitly include reference materials in a variety of formats and state that "libraries should be a place where children can both use technology access resources, and information and learn how to critically evaluate such information" (p. 10).

Just as information has expanded in content and format, as have information questions, so have R&I services. While some R&I services still occur at a reference/information desk, they now occur online as a roaming duty and as an embedded presence. R&I services have expanded their instructional role, and variations thereof, and their curation responsibilities. Increasingly, R&I services also include research partnership with their constituents: from locating grant opportunities to conducting literature reviews, coauthoring, and managing research data and publications. Even burgeoning youth are doing research projects, which could actively involve librarians.

Nevertheless, the basic features of R&I services for children and teenagers endure the following:

- They are youth centered. You should start by identifying young people's information and literacy interests and needs in order to identify services that can respond to those interests and needs.
- They leverage the library's material and human resources. For instance, librarians teach media literacy so young people can understand how streaming video (that the library subscribes to) communicates messages.

Everyone benefits from good R&I services; they build trusting and meaningful relationships and partnerships, and they foster literacy and learning.

DEFINING TERMS

Information can vary from a single fact to a broad academic domain of knowledge. Sometimes the general notion of information may be parsed into:

- Data: symbols, signs, signals, and "raw facts," such as "0" or an arrow.
- Information: meaningful, functional, organized, or structured data, such as $1 + 2 = 3$.
- Knowledge: information connected in relationship and accumulated synthesis of multiple sources of information over time, such as the ability to explain, calculate, and apply mathematical functions to solve problems.

The source of information is ultimately the creator of information; humans are the de facto originators. For instance, Einstein is generally considered the originator of the general theory of relativity. Creators represent information in words, numbers, images, print artifacts, videos, games, audio files, deep fakes, sculptures, and so on. Continuing the example, Einstein represented the general theory of relativity in the form of equations and an explanatory book. Information resources, therefore, may be considered as information that is recorded (made more or less permanent) in "containers." Libraries focus on recorded information, and school libraries focus on recorded information that supports the curriculum and the broader conditions that support student success (which can address personal interests).

Reference resources can be considered as any resource that is used to answer an information need. However, the general notion of reference resources tends to think of "ready reference," that is, those materials that contain and are arranged to locate quickly specific facts. Such resources are intended for consultation and referral, rather than for continuous reading. They are also intended for frequent use, often across curricula, and may be costly. Encyclopedias exemplify the concept of a reference source, but many subject-specific reference sources exist, such as chemical formula tables, timeline references, and gazetteers (RUSA, 2008). It is important to note that format is less important, except possibly in terms of timeliness because digital "native" resources do not undergo the added process of printing.

Likewise, reference services range from looking up a specific fact, such as a country's highest mountain, to providing dissertation research consultation and can vary from a single individual transaction to a self-contained graduate course. The underlying function, in any case, is intellectual access to information. In the strictest definition of a reference transaction, the librarian uses information resources to help people meet their information needs (RUSA, 2000). More broadly, then, reference work encompasses reference transactions as well as other activities that "involve the creation, management, and assessment of information or research resources, tools, and services" (RUSA, 2000, p. 1).

Information services in libraries encompass even more forms: reader's advisory and other information assistance, signs and other dissemination of information, and the more general concept of access to information, both physical and intellectual (RUSA, 2000). Think of all the information services that youth-serving libraries provide daily: helping a child find a "fun poem to recite," labeling shelves, finding a review of *To Kill a Mockingbird* the year that the book was published, collaborating with a teacher on developing a lesson on using atlases, researching evidence-based practice on the whole language approach to reading, suggesting a novel to help a teen deal with a friend's suicide, developing a list of CAD software to teach architecture, showing how to use the library catalogue, creating social bookmarks of websites for third graders on China, publicizing the newest Caldecott Award winner, conducting a workshop for parents on choosing magazines for their children, and referring a high school junior to a college counselor. In short, R&I services comprise a vital part of the total library program.

As exemplified previously, youth-serving libraries provide physical access to information resources through the organization of the library facility itself, classification schemes, the library catalogue, the library web portal, webliographies, directional signs and posters, magazine racks, book displays, reserve shelves, directories, files, Internet-connected computers, and other equipment such as audio players, 3D printers, and assistive technologies.

Intellectual access includes teaching youth and staff how to gain competence in information literacy: the ability to locate, select, evaluate, share, manage, use, communicate, and generate information. Again, the options are many and diverse: showing how to use encyclopedia indexes, providing thematic pathfinder research guides, creating screen-capture videos to demonstrate how to find a magazine article in a database, conducting a webinar on copyright fair use, developing customized searching engines, acquiring bilingual dictionaries, coaching teachers on creating online timelines, co-teaching how to take Cornell notes, providing citation style links on the library web portal, demonstrating how to use advanced searching options such as reading-level filters, and collaboratively designing instruction on fake news evaluation.

In educational settings, all instructors ideally have the same purpose in helping youth become effective information users, but each of them has a specific "lens" in this regard. For instance, elementary grade school teachers tend to frame curriculum in terms of age-appropriate content and interaction, in contrast to secondary grade teachers who use an academic domain as their lodestone so that their students learn how to "think like a mathematician," for instance. Recreational instructors might focus on procedural skills such as swimming or playing an instrument, while interest club advisors tend to encourage youth to dig into their subject area. Service group leaders, such as Girl Scouts, are likely to facilitate their members' locating and advancing social issues. Information literacy spans age and curricula at the same time that instruction in intellectual access is particularized for the information task. In that respect, school librarians are most effective when they collaborate with these educators because they can bridge information across curricula and age levels, making for an articulated approach to information literacy and general lifelong learning.

REFERENCE AND INFORMATION SERVICES WITHIN THE INSTITUTION

To some extent, library programs as a whole might be conceptualized as R&I services. Theoretically, the entire collection exists to meet information needs, and library services seek to help youth physically and intellectually access and use the collection. Such services can be described along several dimensions (Dumler & Skinner, 2008):

- How R&I services deal with resources: from processing to facilitating intellectual access.
- The degree of user contact: from backroom cataloguing to one-to-one reference guidance.
- The degree of labor intensity: from clicking on an online encyclopedia article to providing reading advisory service.
- The skill needed by the service provider: from a ten-minute training of a secondary school volunteer to a master's degree preparation for leadership skills.

R&I services exist within the context of their library-information environment. Library and information services for young people typically occur within the contexts of school libraries and public libraries. Each of these settings has unique and overlapping aspects in terms of mission, educational perspective, governance, staffing, access, and user support. By comparing these contexts, librarians can better determine how they impact services.

As an example, school librarians must facilitate the physical and intellectual access to a wide variety of information resources that support the curriculum, first and foremost, and meet the individual needs of the school community. Formal education does realize that students' social and emotional needs should be considered, including independent reading, but the library program of resources and services mostly aligns with and supports the school's and district's mission. In terms of physical access, students are most likely to use the library facility in groups, as scheduled by their teachers. Independent use tends to occur outside class time, such as recess and lunch, as well as before and after school. Similarly, the instructional aspect of R&I services is often expected as part of those class visits and involves some degree of planning and preparation ahead of time. Of course, small group and individual R&I service occur routinely as needs arise throughout the day, and some school librarians offer virtual R&I service outside of school hours. School librarians also produce and maintain instructional documents such as portals and subject resource guides that either support curriculum or reading promotion.

On the other hand, public libraries have a broader mission and serve a wider clientele, although most children expect that the public library will also fulfill their academic research needs, especially since the public library constitutes the default type of library in most

Table 1.1. School and Public Library Comparisons

Criteria	School Libraries	Public Libraries
Mission	Support the school mission	Support community information needs
Governance	School, school district, and state department of education	City government (sometimes under recreation) and state library
Legal Issues	Loco parentis responsibility, required content filtering software, acceptable use policy, FERPA, COPPA, data security, and privacy and confidentiality	COPPA, data security, and privacy and confidentiality
Number of Potential Users	School population and possibly family members	Community population
Facility	Part of the school (room, floor, or separate building)	Usually a separate building, but may be a separate floor; note that school/public libraries may share a facility
Access Convenience	For students, physical access is convenient whenever the library is open and permission is given within the school; depending on the library portal's existing access rights, access may be available 24/7 (dependent on youth's Internet connectivity)	Physical access depends on the library's opening hours, youth's availability, distance from youth's location, and transportation availability; depending on the library portal's existing access rights, access may be available 24/7 (dependent on youth's Internet connectivity)
Open Operating Hours	Ideally, the entire school day Monday to Friday (35–45 hours/week); can vary: only during courses or only between courses	Ideally, every day for at least 8 hours daily (56+ hours/week); can vary: 1–7 days/week, 0–12 hours/day; each day may have different hours, and staffing patterns may vary
Library Staffing Patterns	Ideally, at least one school librarian and one library assistant; sometimes student and adult volunteers; can vary from one part-time adult volunteer to several librarians and other library workers	Depends on the size of the library: from one adult volunteer to dozens of librarians and other library workers; student workers are usually paid shelvers; the library may have a youth specialist, a children's specialist, and/or a YA specialist (the latter being the least common)
Librarian Qualifications	Usually school librarian and teaching certification	Usually library/information science degree
Education Orientation	Mainly formal	Mainly informal
Curricular Support	Curriculum-centric	Minimally provide curriculum-based resources
Reference Collection	Support school curriculum and may support other personal interests	Support entire user community interests; may be more extensive than a school library's collection; may have a separate children's reference collection
R&I Services Users Grouping	By class (usually scheduled by teacher), small group researchers, and individual (usually by same age grouping)	Individual, by family, small group researchers (usually by same age), and event group (same or mixed ages/gender)
Instruction Type	Possible library scope and sequence curriculum as course or unit; scheduled visit by class/subject/club, just-in-time, reader's advisory, library aides/club, and workshops	Just-in-time, reader's advisory, events (e.g., workshops and presenters), and library club
Instruction Modality	Face-to-face at librarian's desk, presentation area, roaming; less virtual (videoconferencing, Facebook, email, texting, Twitter, link to virtual ref desk service); print documents (bibliographies, bookmarks, and posters); multimedia tutorials posted on library portal, school learning management system, and school communication (newsletter, newspaper, and PSA)	Face-to-face at librarian's desk, presentation area at events, roaming; virtual (virtual ref desk service; email, texting, Twitter, Facebook, online chat, and videoconferencing); print documents (bibliographies, bookmarks, and posters); multimedia tutorials posted on the library portal

communities. Other obvious distinctions between school and public libraries are different (and sometimes longer) operating hours, location, and staffing. As a result, youth are more likely to use the library independently or in small groups. Instruction consists mainly in terms of just-in-time help, or as a formal program offering such as a "Getting a Job" or an anime "con." Library guidance documents are typically more generic or facilitate readers' advising.

Table 1.1 shows how school and public libraries are compared by several criteria.

STANDARDS FOR R&I SERVICES

What standards exist for R&I services? The Reference and User Services Association (RUSA) of the American Library Association (ALA) is the key association for developing R&I service standards. They have developed R&I service standards for specific subject areas and populations, service modalities, reference collections and documents, and competencies. Focusing on school libraries, the American Association of School Librarians (AASL) has developed standards for learners, librarians, and library programs (2018). In her study of R&I services internationally, VanScoy (2019) found that conceptualizations of such services crossed cultural boundaries and had a global agreement, which is heartening as librarians serve increasingly diverse youth populations.

In the final analysis, the most meaningful measure is the impact on users: children and teenagers. Did they get the information they wanted or needed? Did the R&I service satisfy them both in terms of process and product? To that end, some standards focus on generic positive outcomes for youth, which can be contextualized in terms of R&I services. For instance, relative to R&I services, AASL's 2018 learner standards include the foundational standards of inquiry processes, addressing a variety of perspectives, collaborating (including with librarians), engaging with information ethically, and curating resources. Similarly, in 2016, the International Society for Technology in Education (ISTE) identified several standards for students that R&I services can contribute to empowered learner, digital citizen, knowledge constructor, innovative designer, computational thinker, creative communicator, and global collaborator.

For youth to acquire these knowledges and competencies, R&I services should be of high quality. As noted earlier, RUSA has specific standards for various contexts. In terms of overall R&I services, RUSA's guide for measuring and assessing reference services and resources is the most germane; it focuses on reference transactions (excluding formal instruction), the creation and management of information resources, and R&I assessment activities. Focusing on R&I services in school library settings, AASL's 2018 library program standards apply: providing a welcoming educational environment with a rich and relevant curated collection of developmentally appropriate reference/information resources in various formats; offering multiple opportunities for youth to access, use, and generate information; collaborating with the school community to facilitate learning; and modeling and instructing youth in ethical information practices.

R&I LIBRARIAN COMPETENCIES

To optimize the positive impact of R&I services for youth, standards also apply to the effectiveness of librarians themselves as they help youth access information. RUSA's standards for professional competencies for reference and user services librarians are the most relevant. For reference transactions to be effective, librarians need to be visible and approachable, show a high level of interest in user queries, accurately identify the user's information needs in a comfortable manner, search effectively, and follow up to ensure user satisfaction. More holistically, librarians need to offer service that is responsive to expressed information needs, curate high-quality, relevant information from diverse sources, collaborate to guide information use, use information literacy and instruction skills, market and advocate for library services, and assess and address diverse user needs and preferences. To that end, the ALA provides the gold standards for librarian competencies in working with children and teenagers.

In 2020, the Association of Library Service to Children (ALSC) updated its list of competencies and broadened its scope to include all library settings. The following factors inform and impact R&I services.

1. Commitment to client group: understand human development and the environment in which children live; respect diversity and inclusion; assess and respond to needs; and provide an accessible and enjoyable library environment.
2. Reference and user series: model respectful and developmentally appropriate R&I services, instruct and support children's information skills and use of library resources in various formats, and conduct inclusive reference and readers' advisory transactions.
3. Programming skills: incorporate literacy development and technology in developing and implementing library programs.
4. Collection knowledge and management: develop and manage diverse, current, relevant children's collection in different formats and languages that considers users' input.
5. Outreach and advocacy: use effective media public relations techniques to promote awareness and support of children's information needs.
6. Administrative and management skills: plan and deliver, represent and support R&I resources and services to children and their families; follow legislation when developing and maintaining R&I policies and procedures.
7. Professionalism and professional development (PD): comply with ALA codes of ethics and standards, support and participate in PD and relationships, and demonstrate cultural competence.

Similarly, the Young Adult Library Services Association (YALSA) 2017 teen services competencies also cross library setting borders. The standards address dispositions and content areas, and most indicators apply to R&I services. Teen librarians should the respectful and caring, using an asset-based approach that values diversity and its impact. They provide accessible, responsible, responsive R&I services with curiosity, creativity, flexibility, and perseverance. They communicate, engage, support, and collaborate with teen-serving stakeholders. Teen-serving library staff apply teen development knowledge as they interact with and support teens. They provide accessible, positive learning environments and experiences. They also cultivate teen engagement and leadership. They also assess and improve their R&I services, and continuously learn in order to provide high-quality R&I services.

Focusing on school librarians' role in R&I services, AASL's librarian standard states the importance of collection development, curriculum-based instruction and collaboration, and information engagement. Increasingly, attention to social-emotional learning (SEL) and the soft skills that support caring and responsive interactions with youth have been promoted. In her study of emotional-social intelligence (ESI) of reference and user services librarians, Summey (2017) found that Bar-On's 2004 ESI model reflects RUSA's behavioral standards well. That is, the librarians who rate high on self-perception, self-expression, interpersonal relationships, decision-making, and stress management are predicted to provide more effective R&I services.

Food for Thought: Inventing Reference and Information Services

What if reference and information services didn't exist? Would they need to be invented? Try this mental exercise.

1. Put yourself mentally in the shoes of a young person. What is your everyday life? Write down possible information needs (e.g., Where can I find a gas station? Why am I having stomach pains? Where can I learn Japanese? How do I remove dirt stains? What can I do to stop cyberbullying?)

2. Brainstorm possible information that you might need: How to solve equations? How to double-space a text document, facts such as chemical formulas or Cabinet members? Why seasons exist? When nuclear energy can be safe? What is the reason for religion?

3. Imagine that libraries and librarians don't exist. How do you find information? Where do you go?

4. Whom do you ask? Whom do you trust?

5. How do you evaluate the information you find?

6. Assume you have very little money. You have no Internet access. You cannot afford to buy books or other information resources. What do you do?

7. What if you want to learn how to be more self-sufficient or more effective in meeting your information needs? How would you go about it? Whom would you ask?

8. What might be conditions that would optimize meeting your information needs? Somewhere along the way, you probably would like to have credible information conveniently located, and free to use. You probably would like to contact a dependable, easily available set of people to help you with your information need.

9. In the end, the answer to your information needs might not be the Internet, largely because it is so hard to sort out all the results and determine the quality of information. Most online experts have narrow specializations.

10. In most cases, the best "bang for your buck" is probably the library, and the librarian is the most likely person to help you become an information expert for yourself.

REFERENCES

American Association of School Librarians. (2018). *National school library standards for learners, school librarians, and school libraries.* American Library Association.

Association of Library Service to Children. (2020). *Competencies for libraries serving children in libraries.* American Library Association.

Bar-On, R. (2004). The bar-on emotional quotient inventory (EQi): Rationale, description, and summary of psychometric properties. In G. Geher (Ed.), *The measurement of emotional intelligence: Common ground and controversy* (pp. 115–145). Nova Science.

Bulao, J. (2021, May 18). How much date is created every day in 2021? *Techjury.* https://techjury.net/blog/how-much-data-is-created-every-day/

Dumler, M., & Skinner, S. (2008). *A primer on management* (2nd ed.). South-Western.

Sosulski, N., & Tyckoson, D. (2018). Reference in the age of disinformation. *Reference & User Services Quarterly, 57*(3), 178–182.

Summey, T. (2017). Emotional intelligence: A framework for the competencies and traits of reference and user services librarians. In M. Matterson & S. Hines (Eds.), *Emotion in the library workplace* (pp. 127–142). Emerald Publishing.

VanScoy, A. (2019). Exploring reference and information service in a global information context. *ALISE 2019 proceedings* (pp. 219). Association of Library and Information Science Educators.

Young Adult Library Services Association. (2017). *Teen services competencies for library staff.* Chicago: American Library Association.

FURTHER READING

Anderson, K., & Cvetkovic, V. (2015). *Reinventing reference: How libraries deliver value in the age of Google.* American Library Association.

Cassell, K., & Miremath, U. (2018). *Reference and information services in the 21st century: An introduction.* American Library Association.

Gottfried, J., & Pennavaria, K. (2017). *Providing reference services: A practice guide for librarians.* Rowman & Littlefield.

Hicks, D., & VanScoy, A. (2019). Discourses of expertise in professional competency documents: Reference expertise as performance. *The Library Quarterly, 89*(1), 34–52.

Hirsch, S. (2018). *Information services today: An introduction.* Rowman & Littlefield.

Reference & User Services Quarterly. https://journals.ala.org/index.php/rusq

The Reference Librarian. https://www.tandfonline.com/journals/wref20

Reference Services Review. https://www.emeraldgrouppublishing.com/journal/rsr

Riedling, A., & Houston, C. (2019). *Reference skills for the school librarian: Tools and tips* (4th ed.). Libraries Unlimited.

Rod-Welsh, L. (2019). *Improving library services in support of international students and English as a second language learners*. American Library Association.

Summey, T. (2017). Emotional intelligence: A framework for the competencies and traits of reference and user services librarians. In S. Hines & M. Matteson (Eds.), *Emotion in the library workplace* (pp. 129–146). Emerald Publishing Limited.

Wong, M., & Saunders, L. (2020). *Reference and information services* (6th ed.). Libraries Unlimited.

2

Sources of Information

SO MUCH INFORMATION AND SO LITTLE

Information is all around us, but sometimes it is hard to find, rather like "water, water everywhere but not a drop to drink." Sometimes we need to solve a problem such as a certain ache in the body but have a hard time finding out the reason for the pain or a way to heal the body. Sometimes we encounter information, such as a news event, and we want to know the background story, which might be hard to uncover.

In providing reference and information services, librarians try to help youth find and access the information they want: providing the right information at the right time to the right person. This is a core function of the library program. Yet all the parts are dynamic: youth have some intrinsic characteristics and needs but those also vary by time, culture, environment, situation, and personal attributes. Likewise, some information is relatively universal and stable, such as the chemical composition of a diamond, but other information changes constantly, such as tide tables. Information too can vary by time, culture, environment, situation, and personal/creator attributes. Moreover, the medium that transmits the information may have existed for millennia such as speech, but languages and words have varied tremendously. The written word has been expressed on stone, papyrus, and calves' hide, as well as microfiche and electrons. Images are "real" but may be socially defined, and they have been recorded on stone, as well as on celluloid. Some numerical concepts are universal, but numbering systems vary, and those numbers have been expressed as notches on a stick, knots on a string, and pixels on a computer monitor. Over the centuries, new media have been created, and certainly the last century has seen a great expansion in the possible formats for conveying information.

This said, librarians focus on collecting and organizing recorded information, which does not capture much tacit information that tends to be shared only as needed and even then may be transmitted only orally. At the same time, the first source of information that people consult is often another human being: more specifically, a trusted expert with particular knowledge such as the family doctor or the parish priest. Librarians are usually not the first experts contacted, probably because their expertise is more process-based (i.e., *finding* information more than *knowing* information), with breadth outweighing depth. However, librarians can help identify those human resources and refer youth to them, especially local people such as social service agencies, hobbyists, tutoring services, and so forth.

In short, the youth's information task becomes the librarian's information task and finding the "right" information that meets the young person's wants can be daunting.

REFERENCE SOURCES BY FORMAT

What's the first image that comes to mind when imagining a reference resource? It is probably a thick tome or set of printed books with short entries arranged in some logical order: alphabetically, chronologically, or thematically. Lots of information is provided in one spot and is quickly retrieved. Nowadays, such "default" reference sources may well be available digitally as an ebook or a website with its own internal hyperlinks and search tool for easy information retrieval. The digital format may duplicate the print version or it might take advantage of its digital format by including sound and motion, pop-up glossary links, translation features, simplified English options, and even links to other reference sources. Some digital versions of reference documents even permit customization, which is particularly useful for English language learners (ELLs) and individuals with disabilities: font style and size, spacing between lines, different background colors, read-aloud text, and simple translation.

Sometimes a periodical may be considered a reference source, especially if it is a specialized publication such as a sports newspaper or events magazine. More typically, newspapers have separate sections that each may be used as reference sources, such as stock market figures, sports statistics, and movie times.

Online reference databases constitute another cluster of reference sources. These resources may comprise a collection of stand-alone, existing reference monographs or series (such as Gale's products); database aggregators of articles, research, proceedings, images, sounds, or multimedia from different publishers (such as EBSCO products); or repositories of disparate reference materials (such as MERLOT). These databases may be open source, such as government websites (e.g., usa.gov) or subscription-based websites. The good news is that databases curate, collate, and index dispersed information into an easy-to-use central location. The bad news is that databases are typically pre-packaged so that librarians cannot pick and choose which publications to include in the database. Nowadays, most databases are online, but in the past, they could be produced as print documents, microforms, or optical disc products.

At the other end of the spectrum are individual reference materials such as informational posters, maps, and charts (e.g., types of plants or cross-sections of the human body); pamphlets (e.g., travel brochures or earthquake preparedness tips); reference sheets (e.g., software program tips or basic vocabulary and grammar for "tourist" language); realia (e.g., globes and other models); single videos (e.g., instructions for home repairs or Internet use); and specialized Internet websites and apps (e.g., weather conditions or translator tools). It should be noted that multimedia, including digital reference resources, require the appropriate device and usually some kind of connectivity in order to access the information.

Regardless of the format, reference sources should be easy to use and search through so that the wanted information can be retrieved quickly and accurately. In addition, if timeliness or currency is important, reference sources need to be kept up to date. In the past, yearbooks or supplements updated or added information; nowadays, such reference materials have been digitized and provided online for near-instantaneous updating and revising. In many cases, the past versions should be kept to track changes.

MATCHING REFERENCE SOURCES AND USERS

Remember librarian Ranganathan and his five laws of library science, including this one: "every reader his or her book"? This law is easily adapted to "every young person his or her reference resource." In most cases, the chief criterion is relevance: Is it the information wanted? Second, is it physically accessible; not only should the appropriate device be available, but for sensory differences? Materials may need added features such as alt-text or closed captioning. Third, is it comprehensible linguistically: by language, structure, and vocabulary? Fourth, is it intellectually accessible; does the user have the background knowledge or experience to understand the information, such as a calculus equation? Fifth, is the information and its representation aesthetically pleasing; is it interesting and pleasurable to look at and feel, is it new and clean, and is it novel and engaging? Beyond these criteria, personal factors come into play: convenience, choice of format, dimensions of the resource, popularity of the resource, and likelihood that the teacher will approve (e.g., some teachers dismiss Wikipedia).

Note that this section focuses on reference resources, but no reference on human interaction; that topic is covered in a later chapter.

Developmental Issues

A few factors have more general considerations. Particularly with regard to young people, a significant issue is developmental appropriateness. The same topic may be handled differently, such as bodily functions. Choosing the most appropriate reference source depends on the cognitive development, emotional maturity, physical development, reading ability, preexisting knowledge base, past experience, and support agents (such as family and educators). Even the format choice may depend on developmental factors; for instance, a simple diagram might be more appropriate for younger audiences but a graphic depiction of a disease progression might be inappropriate for those younger eyes. This issue is particularly pertinent in public libraries; undivided reference collections can result in some awkward browsing choices, yet separated reference collections can be too restrictive. That situation may be mitigated when children come with their parents or guardians, but even then librarians may want to give some guidance based on what they know about the resource and its typical use. It should also be noted that young people do not develop congruently; that is, their reading ability might not be as developed as their emotional maturity; girls may need information about menstruation that is easy to read but thorough enough to discuss pregnancy and birth control.

Probably the best advice in addressing developmental issues in order to provide developmentally appropriate resources is for librarians to get to know the youth they serve. Nevertheless, some general rules apply: progress from simple to more complex vocabulary and concepts, progress from more visual to more textual format, progress from more general to more specialized information, progress from short to longer entries, and progress from a single source to a variety of sources and perspectives.

Language Issues

As noted earlier, language and linguistics (the study of language) constitute another important aspect when providing appropriate reference materials to young people. Language needs to be considered both orally and in written form. Young children typically have a larger oral vocabulary than a written one, so materials that are sound-based or can be read aloud may be more suitable. Sometimes ELLs may also have an easier time comprehending spoken language rather than written language, especially if their first language uses a different written system (e.g., pictorial/symbolic versus letter-phoneme system). The writing system difference is especially challenging for immigrants because even with Roman-based alphabetic systems, keyboard characters and their arrangement differs between countries. Also, note that ELL youth may have been born in the United States but learned how to communicate in another language.

Fortunately, the Internet provides information in increasingly numerous languages, and search engines have country-specific variations, Google being a prime example (http://www.genealogyintime.com/articles/country-guide-to-google-search-engines-page3.html). Library portals can also provide links to directories of non-English search engines such as http://www.searchenginesindex.com/ and http://www.searchenginecolossus.com/. Furthermore, online translation tools are improving their ability to translate text and even entire websites. Even online videos (at least in YouTube) increasingly have translation options. Nevertheless, librarians should provide reference materials in the language of choice, as appropriate and needed. Sometimes print titles are hard to find for some languages, as well as hard to evaluate, but they are detailed in the next chapter. In the meantime, here are some tips to provide reference resources that are more supportive of English language users.

- Look for resources with simpler vocabulary and sentence structure.
- Look for resources that include visual representations of information. It should be noted that some images may be unrecognizable, demeaning, or have different meanings to different cultures.
- Encourage the use of digital reference resources as they are more likely to include multimedia features and have the capability of being customized.
- Encourage the use of https://simple.wikipedia.org.
- Install http://rewordify.com on computers; this free tool simplifies English to a lower reading level.
- Adjust search engine reading level in its settings.

- Show how to use text-to-speech features on computers, and consider installing more sophisticated software programs such as JAWS, which was originally developed for people with visual impairments.
- Remember that reading level does not equate to concept level.
- Take into consideration that immigrant children may have additional barriers as their culture may have different communication styles and different connotations to language.

These tips can also inform your choice of resources for young people who are emerging readers as well as youth with disabilities, especially those with cognitive delays or learning differences.

Youth with Disabilities

Youth with disabilities, be they chronic or temporary, constitute possibly up to 20 percent of the U.S. population. The Individuals with Disabilities Education Act identifies fourteen types of disabilities, which include different sensate and physical impairments, learning disabilities, emotional disturbances, communication disorders, and other health issues. These young people face a variety of access and processing barriers as they seek information. They may have physical limitations that make it harder to engage with the material, or they may have internal processing differences, such as dyslexia or neural disorders that cause difficulties in comprehending the information. Some may have problems asking for help because of language or social interaction challenges. Others may feel that they will be stigmatized if they self-disclose their disabilities so choose not to. At the same time, they may feel isolated or need to depend on others in order to achieve.

Their information needs echo the needs of their typical peers—academics, personal interests, and issues—and they also want specific information that addresses their unique disabilities, showing them ways to succeed (e.g., Wrightslaw Yellow Pages for Kids with Disabilities: https://www.yellowpagesforkids.com/). Librarians need to match resources and services to specific needs while aiming for inclusivity. For instance, communication should include simple step-by-step directions and routines, combined with visual scaffolding as appropriate. The library itself needs to optimize physical access through reachable shelving, adaptable computers, appropriate assistive technology, and open traffic areas. The American Library Association (ALA) has several recommendations on using assistive technology in support of effective and inclusive R&I services (http://www.ala.org/rusa/assistive-technology).

Be they language and developmental, linguistic, or other differences, each young person is a unique combination of physical, mental, emotional, and social attributes and experiences, so reference choices need to be as informed as possible. A good framework to use is universal design for learning (UDL). Young people should be afforded multiple means to engage with reference information, access information representations that they can choose from, and access and use reference sources.

SCANNING FOR INFORMATION

Already, it is obvious that youth-serving librarians need to know the persons they potentially serve. Reference and information services should be both responsive and predictive. That is, sufficient reference sources need to be available to satisfy most of the youth's information wants and able to refer youth to other sources of information, be they material, institutions, or people. The goal is to have the resources that are most likely to be relevant to those youth. Considering that over half a million books are published yearly in the United States alone, even if reference books constitute a small percentage, no library has the purchasing power to buy all the possible titles—and even then, probably it would be hard for young people to ferret out those reference materials that would be appropriate and appealing to them.

Therefore, to optimize the reference collection, librarians need to gather information themselves about the youth population whom they potentially support. With that information, librarians can then select reference materials that are the most likely to be used and valued by those youth. This process may be called an environmental scan.

This scanning process involves gathering data and information about several aspects of young people and their community:

- Young people themselves and their families: demographics (age, gender, ethnicity, language, citizenship status, disabilities, religion, ZIP code, household size and configuration, household income), family education level, youth groups, volunteer opportunities, employment, home reading materials, technology, and connectivity.
- Formal and informal educational institutions: population, governance (e.g., public, non-public, homeschooling), mission, standards, curriculum, teaching styles, assignments, co-curriculum, technology, student and faculty demographics (age, gender, ethnicity, language, citizenship status, disabilities), retention rate, graduation rate, standardized test scores, Title I eligibility, financial aid, and libraries' characteristics and usage.
- Community characteristics: demographics (population, ethnicity, gender, socioeconomic status, employment and main employers, housing) including changes over time, geographic features, transportation, health care, social services, places of worship, recreation and cultural centers, communication channels/media outlets, technology infrastructure, and services.
- Other reference information organizations' collections: museums, historical societies, bookstores, hospitals, nonprofit and government libraries, company libraries, media outlet libraries, religious libraries, travel agents, and Little Free libraries.

Typical sources of information include census tracts, school documents such as annual reports, local and state education websites, other government websites, chamber of commerce records, realtor websites, community websites and directories (remember phonebooks?), interactive maps (e.g., Google maps), surveys, focus groups, and observation.

DATA ANALYSIS

The data that librarians gather inform their decisions about reference collection development and service. Here are several scenarios, with implications following in italics.

Johnson Elementary School is situated in a poor residential part of a city in the agricultural part of the state. The area once was highly black, then was populated largely by Southeast Asian immigrants. Now the majority of the neighborhood is Latinx, and blacks are returning. Many students are still learning English. All students are eligible for free or reduced lunch, unemployment is about 8 percent (pre-pandemic), and a fifth live in poverty. About a fifth of adults did not finish high school; most local jobs are in the service sector, such as food services. About a third of households are headed by single parents. No public library or bookstore is within walking distance of the school. Home Internet connectivity is uneven, with the most often used digital device being a cell phone. The student population is low-performing relative to the rest of the state. The school library has the only class set of computers and only recently gained access to state-funded databases. The library is open at lunch but not before or after school because of safety considerations. The reference collection includes about 200 titles, which supports the curriculum, and is somewhat current. Reference service is also integrated into the curriculum. *The school library's reference and information service plays a vital role in these students' lives, so regular visits to the library are needed so students can have frequent opportunities to learn and gain information literacy and research skills using reference materials in a variety of formats. The reference collection needs to include Spanish, highly illustrated materials, and topics that address the students' personal interests since they have little access elsewhere to reference sources. Some reference materials should be updated, and slightly older titles should probably be in the general circulating collection. The library portal and databases should be mobile- and ADA-accessible so that students can access them from home. The librarian can provide just-in-time reference service via video conferencing and texting to classrooms. Texting reference service might be a possibility, especially if it can be provided by the public library.*

Grant Middle School is situated in a prosperous suburban "bedroom" community, close to two universities. The average income is $80,000 in white-collar jobs, but about 10 percent live in poverty. About two-thirds of residents are renters about half of the community population is white, a third are Asian/Pacific Islander, and next in ethnicity is Latinx. About 40 percent are foreign born, and almost half speak English at home; the school has an ELL program. Almost all local adults have a high school diploma and about three-quarters earned a bachelor's degree. Eighty percent of the children live in two-parent families. Internet access is ubiquitous. There is a chain store bookstore nearby, but public libraries are some distance away and most transportation is private; high schoolers can use one of the university libraries. The school is state and nationally recognized for its excellence, and its students are high performing. The library is open from 7:30 a.m. to 4 p.m. on weekdays and has a class set of computers; in addition, the school has a 1:1 laptop program. The print reference collection is "lean" and supports the curriculum; it needs weeding. The school has several databases, including an online encyclopedia. Modifications and accommodations are provided for ELLs and students with special needs through a variety of print materials as well as websites researched and linked as needed in collaboration with their teachers. The librarian has a chat account to facilitate just-in-time reference queries. Collaboration with teachers is uneven, mainly because of little joint planning time. Because middle schoolers are unlikely to use university libraries and public library use is mainly dependent on getting car rides, this library continues to serve as the most useful place for R&I services. Because of the technology accessibility, the librarian can focus on digital sources and services. For example, as the librarian weeds the reference collection, he/she can spend most of the reference budget on subscribing to online reference materials and can promote the existing online reference databases. The technology can also serve as a good selling point for collaborating with teachers: showing those online resources, virtually co-planning learning activities, instructing classes via video conferencing, creating custom online tutorials, and continuing chat-based reference service. The librarian can also encourage students to get public library cards to access their databases and get other public library online R&I services.

Polk High School is one of five high schools (grades 9–12) in a high-density, urban industrial, mid-size city. About a third of the residents are Asian/Pacific Islanders, another third are white, and another fifth are Latinx. About a quarter of residents are foreign born, mainly from Asia, but fewer than 5 percent of the population do not speak English well. Two-thirds of voters are Democrats and mainly Catholic. About a third of married couples have children. About half of the adults earned a bachelor's degree, and unemployment is only 4 percent (doubled to 8 percent during the pandemic). Major employers include technical services, health care, education, and machinery. Private cars are the main mode of transportation. Two public libraries are within walking distance of the school and bookstores are available in a couple of the shopping malls; nevertheless, most students would buy books rather than borrow them from the library. The school has about two thousand students, of which about a fifth are eligible for free or reduced-price lunch, and about a tenth have identified disabilities. Career technical education and sports are very important to the school. The high school graduation rate is about 95 percent, with 90 percent enrolling in post-secondary education, and almost a third of the students take an honors or advanced placement (AP) course. Suspension rates are less than 2 percent. The library is open from 7:30 a.m. to 3:30 p.m. on weekdays, and a student store is also housed in the library. The library has fifteen computers, and the computer lab is next door (no throughway). Teachers schedule time for students to do work in the library but do not co-plan with or ask the librarian to instruct. Teachers will sometimes check out a book cart of books for students to use for research projects in their classes, but reference books stay in the library. The reference collection is outdated because of budget limitations; to compensate, the library portal lists free online reference sources. However, materials are not available for students with disabilities. The librarian is smart to provide online reference resources but should check that digital material is accessible. The librarian probably needs more administrative support to increase the budget for reference materials, to facilitate professional development training about the library's research resources, and to encourage more collaboration between teachers and school librarians. A systematic information literacy and research skills curriculum would be useful, especially because AP students conduct more research and need more reference materials.

Taylor Public Library is situated in a lovely pocket suburban town; it is part of a complex comprised of the town hall, an elementary school, and a middle school. There is plenty of parking and has regular bus service nearby. The immediate neighborhood is well-to-do but is surrounded in two directions by lower-middle-class towns. Fortunately, people in the region can get free library cards, and the library is open daily, including four evenings. The library subscribes to several databases, including a Chinese digital library (since about 60 percent of the population is Asian—mainly Chinese); the website notes databases for youth, but the link is broken. Instead, a different tab for homework help links to some standard reference tools. The library is quite spacious but has a traditional atmosphere, even in the children's area. Two reference areas exist: one in the corner of the children's room by the children's librarian desk and one by the main reference desk. Both collections are very limited and out of date. The YA collection is in a separate room by the bathrooms and has no reference collection; a YA librarian is on staff but has no public area desk. However, some YA program is academic (i.e., college testing) and a teen council exists. No reference guides exist. It does not appear that face-to-face R&I services have a high priority; leisure reading seems to be its main purpose. Even the one link with local schools consists of an accelerated readers book list for the nearly elementary school. The library has great potential to expand and improve its R&I services: updating and expanding its print reference collection, including YA titles; involving its teen council in providing R&I-related programming and reference sources; and working more closely with local school librarians, including those in nearby needed neighborhoods.

Food for Thought: Collaborative R&I Services

As you read about these examples of collaboration, think about what R&I resources and services are locally available and have the potential to be shared in order to serve your community.

Data collection and analysis can be optimized if conducted collaboratively with stakeholders. The most obvious collaboration exists within the same agency: the school library and the school site's administration, the public library and its community government supervisor. Probably each entity already has valuable data that they can share. In the process, each entity can cooperate to make more inclusive and interdependent decisions that can result in more effective practice.

School librarians sometimes collaborate with their counterparts within the school district, potentially with peers at the same grade range level as well as with their neighborhood feeder and higher-level school libraries. In the first case, school librarians can compare their neighborhood characteristics, their school's curriculum and student body, and their R&I program of resources and services. In the latter case, school librarians can see how their students mature, how the curricula are—or can be—articulated, and how their reference collections and service can also be articulated so that information literacy skills can progress seamlessly.

Occasionally, schools and public libraries share facilities and staff, so that the data collection can be more comprehensive. Even with separate governance and location, school and public libraries overlap in their potential youth population, so it makes sense for their librarians to collaborate in gathering and analyze data. They should also consider working with post-secondary librarians. In this way, they can coordinate both reference collections and information services to optimize their respective budgets. Furthermore, such collaboration also facilitates articulation of information literacy instruction and application.

In all of these scenarios, the libraries can do joint purchasing at a discount and can use interlibrary loans and digital sharing for occasional reference source needs. They can provide joint staff training in R&I services, promote both libraries' R&I services more effectively, and evaluate their R&I more comprehensively.

Virtual reference service is one example where differences and deeper discussions are needed. To begin with, children, in particular, are likely to assume that the online librarian is either their school librarian or knows that librarian and the school's curriculum. To improve services, public librarians should connect with school librarians to find out more about school assignments and overall curriculum or target curricular areas such as STEM (science, technology, engineering, mathematics). On their part, school librarians need to keep in touch with classroom teachers about forthcoming assignments and alert local public librarians ahead of time if possible. More fundamentally, school and public librarians should discuss and compare their reference service approaches. For instance, public librarians are more likely to find and give the information wanted, such as the local water quality while the school librarian is more likely to focus as much on working with the children to determine search strategies on getting the answer. Furthermore, the school librarian is more likely to contact the teacher who made the assignment to discuss the rationale for the assignment or ways to explain to the class how to find such kinds of information in general.

RUSA's Cooperative Reference Service Committee developed guidelines for cooperative reference services (2008), which provide advice on clarifying each library's purpose and scope of services, their individual and joint R&I structures and organization, their funding sources and expenditures (including possible consortium memberships and fees), and details about their R&I services and methods of transmission.

REFERENCE

Reference and User Services Association. Cooperative Reference Service Committee. (2008). *Guidelines for cooperative reference services*. American Library Association. https://www.ala.org/rusa/resources/guidelines/guidelinescooperative

FURTHER READING

Buckland, M. (2017). *Information and society*. MIT Press.

Cassell, K. (2021). *Public libraries and their communities: An introduction*. Rowman & Littlefield.

Cooke, N. (2016). *Information services to diverse populations: Developing culturally competent library professionals*. Libraries Unlimited.

Del Castillo, M., & Ball, M. (2018). *The myth of the declining reference statistics: Revealing dynamic reference services through digital analytics.* FIU Libraries. https://digitalcommons.fiu.edu/glworks/83/

Mehra, B., & Davis, R. (2015). A strategic diversity manifesto for public libraries in the 21st century. *New Library World, 116*(1/2), 15–36.

Reference and User Services Association. (2021). *Children with disabilities.* American Library Association. https://www.ala.org/rusa/children-disabilities

Reference and User Services Association. (2007). *Measuring and assessing reference services and resources: A guide.* American Library Association.

Smallwood, C., & Becnel, K. (2013). *Library services for multicultural patrons: Strategies to encourage library use.* Scarecrow Press.

Developing Reference Collections

WHAT IS A REFERENCE RESOURCE?

While the entire library serves as a central place to access information, a vital subset of that place is access to reference materials. But what constitutes a reference resource? One simple operational definition is "a resource that is referred to in order to answer an information question." More formally, the American Library Association (ALA) defines a reference book as a "print or electronic book designed by the arrangement and treatment of its subject matter to be consulted for definite items of information rather than to be read consecutively" (2013, p. 212). This definition may be broadened to include reference sources in various formats. These materials offer invaluable information for librarians and other users, including children and teenagers.

The typical reference resource has the following characteristics:

- Locates facts
- Is arranged for quick retrieval of information (e.g., alphabetical, chronological, tabular)
- Is used for consultation rather than for continuous reading
- Is used frequently
- May be unique in coverage
- May be costly
- Is usually restricted to library use

Additional optional criteria for reference materials might include timeliness, access points (e.g., indexes and cross-references), and substantive unique features (e.g., charts and diagrams). For instance, a current yearbook of consumer product reviews might be considered a reference book while older editions might not be as useful as a reference tool but could be interesting for a historical review. On the other hand, a dictionary of literary terms might be old but still a valuable reference tool.

Usually, the first kinds of resources that people think of as reference resources include encyclopedias, dictionaries, atlases, and almanacs. Other types of resources that might be considered as reference, but may have more general use, include statistical compendiums, handbooks, indexes, and directories. Biographic and geographic sources comprise a range of possibilities, from series of individual people or places to specialized bibliographies.

One could make the case that "reference is in the eye of the beholder." For instance, a book of paintings might be considered a reference resource to see an example of an artist's work, but for another person, that same book might be a "coffee table" book to browse through. That same book of paintings might be shelved in an elementary school library's reference collection but be shelved in a public library's general collection. In another situation, that same book might be placed in a high school library's general collection, but when the art teacher asks each student to create a picture in the style of a specific artist, that book might be placed in the reference collection during that time period. In short, youth's characteristics and their usage impact the designation of a reference source.

Reference resources are further defined and collected institutionally. While libraries are usually governed by a community-based board of trustees, the level of governance differs. Public libraries tend to report to their local town or city and may report directly to a division of that governmental entity such as the department of parks and recreation. School libraries report to the school's administration, which reports to its legal educational agency such as a school district with its board of trustees. Nonpublic schools may be stand-alone entities or they might report to a larger organization such as a Catholic diocese. This governance is important because the library's mission and charge must align with, and support, the governing body's mission. As such, the public library's reference collection usually has to address the educational, recreational, and inspirational needs of the entire community—of all ages. In contrast, school library collections have as their first priority to support the school's curriculum, which is a much narrower charge. As a result, reference collections are likely to look different in public and school libraries.

Policies can also impact the reference collection as a whole. For instance, a general overview of the book, such as a fancy art history volume, might be found on the reference shelves, largely because of its cost or size. Librarians could just as easily have an oversize and/or restricted use set of shelves in order to differentiate the materials' intended use. Increasingly, libraries are migrating to a small "lean" ready reference section, integrating multivolume series such as animal encyclopedias into the general shelves. In some cases, the books may be marked as "in-library" use only, which may result in some confusion at the circulation desk for youth who equate general collection with circulating collection. On the other hand, too often large reference sections are underused, so librarians would prefer users finding the materials and being disappointed that the items must stay in house than not finding the resources at all. Furthermore, some librarians have liberal circulation policies relative to reference and reference-wannabe items, particularly if users have limited access to the library. For those cases when many youngsters would want to consult the same volume, the librarian simply places that item on a reserve shelf. All of these issues point out the need for clarification of reference materials and policies about their arrangement and use.

EVALUATING REFERENCE SOURCES

In the final analysis, a good reference source is one that answers questions accurately and adequately for the young person, and a poor reference source is one that fails in that effort. But the devil is in the details. Nevertheless, evaluating reference resources builds upon general collection development selection policies and practices. The more granular evaluation depends on the type of reference source, subject matter, format, and community characteristics.

Generic Reference Selection Criteria

As with other library materials under consideration, reference sources need to be evaluated in terms of a number of criteria, which should be delineated in the library's selection policy.

- Scope or coverage. A statement of purpose can state what subject matter and concepts are addressed, although the ensuing materials sometimes do not fulfill the purpose well. Scope also includes geographic and time frames. In some cases, currency is not as important, such as a mathematics source, but other sciences need up-to-date information. Biographical sources can be problematic in that an older title might be useful for historic individuals, but a title such as *100 Greatest Women* could be misleading if the copyright date is 1990; youth might assume that it includes contemporary names such as Michelle Obama, Angela Merkel, or Malala Yousafzai and be disappointed to not find them there.
- Authority and accuracy. Because reference materials are acquired with the assumption of authority, the credentials of the authors should carry academic, experience, and writing weight. Some publishers focus on reference works, such as Gale Group, Macmillan, and Salem Press, and their reputation almost guarantees that the reference work will be authoritative, accurate, and objective. This directory of reference publishers can serve as a useful guide: https://www.publishersglobal.com/directory/subject/reference-publishers. Especially since reference information can be highly specialized, librarians often have to rely on subject expert reviewers for validation.
- Arrangement and organization. Reference resources need to be arranged for easy retrieval and use, so typical arrangement orders include alphabetical, chronological, or classification (e.g., Dewey Decimal Classification and genrefication). Tables of content and indexes are usually mandatory, and specialized indexes (e.g., by genre and geographic region) add value. The resource might also have tabs or color-coding to facilitate usage.
- Presentation. What is the overall look of the resource: its layout, typeface, headings, and guiding features? What is the length of each entry, and are entries consistent in the type of sequence of information? How are sidebars, charts, tables, and images used to clarify or add information?

- Special features. Several items can make the research resource unique: image quality or quantity, case studies, tutorials, hyperlinks, sound, video clips, help features, interactive elements such as polls and quizzes, and accompanying tools.
- Bibliographies. Most reference resources include bibliographies, either for each entry, chapter, section, or at the end of the work. The bibliographies help verify the accuracy of the resource's information and guide the reader to further study. If possible, bibliographies themselves should be checked for accuracy, perspective, and currency.
- Developmental issues. Librarians need to consider the reading level and developmental stage of the materials, including the needs of English language learners (ELLs) and youth with special needs. Remember that youth develop at different paces, even within themselves; a teen with intellectual delays may be physically mature and may have adult sexual interests. Therefore, a "kiddie" reference book would usually be inappropriate for a teenager; instead, an easy-reading or highly visual reference resource would be more relevant.
- Comparison with similar sources. More than one resource is likely to cover the same topic, so librarians need to compare the potential resources whenever possible. All of the above criteria need to be considered: scope, arrangement, features, ease of use, and accessibility (including issues of inclusion). It may be useful to provide several similar reference materials in different formats in order to offer different approaches. Of course, the current collection should be a starting point for comparisons.
- Physical condition. Reference resources can get heavy handling so librarians should look for library binding and sturdy paper for print materials. Posters and charts should be laminated. If the resource is in good physical condition, sometimes librarians can acquire used titles.
- Curriculum support. The school library's first priority is to support the curriculum so the librarian should map each reference source onto that curriculum. Resources also support professional practice so reference materials on counseling and administration, for instance, would be appropriate. Public librarians should also be aware of the local schools' curriculum to supplement school libraries' collections, even though the public library can focus more on complementing school curricular-centric reference sources with sources on recreational and personal topics.
- Demand and usefulness versus cost. Ideally, reference sources provide valuable information that addresses youth's varying interests and needs. On the other hand, one expensive title might fill a unique information niche, and worth the price. Making the situation more complex in school libraries, a teacher might want the librarian to buy a personal favorite reference source; while it is important to be responsive to faculty needs, the overall collection and funding need to be taken into account.

Evaluating Electronic Reference Sources

Increasingly, reference sources are available in both print and digital formats; in fact, some publishers have abandoned print versions altogether (including *Encyclopedia Britannica*). Theoretically, digital sources can be updated quickly and can include multimedia features. However, it is important to check those assumptions carefully. Some digital sources are merely scanned versions of print editions, with no added value such as internal search engine, multi-media features, hyperlinks, or even assurance of readability for users with visual impairments. Nor does online format ensure lower cost. Many online reference sources are available only on a subscription basis, which gives users access for a specified timeframe; usually, the library cannot download the entire product to store on a local server. Therefore, if the library lacks funding some year, it no longer has any access to that resource, and so is left with nothing. For that reason, among others (e.g., the quality of hands-on use and the need for electricity and equipment), school librarians should maintain print copies of core ready reference sources: one or two encyclopedias, dictionaries, a thesaurus, atlases, and almanacs.

Digital reference sources should stand up to the standards for evaluating reference sources of any format. However, they are held to a higher standard because their digital aspects must also be discerned. However, instead of examining paper and binding quality, librarians need to examine the digital properties as well as the equipment required to access them. These additional criteria should be included in the library's selection policy. These factors follow.

- Content. Today's users expect full-text resources, not just indexing or abstracts. Furthermore, the content needs to be ADA (Americans with Disabilities Act)-compliant (e.g., readable via software for people with vision impairments). Increasingly, content may be available in more than one language, which could be useful depending on the community's needs.
- Storage. Increasingly, content is stored remotely, in the "cloud," which saves local server space and, hopefully, eliminates worries about theft or maintenance. Resultingly, librarians must ensure that the vendor's storage is stable and dependable. Typically, then, the library is paying for access, not ownership, so that in poor budget years, that access might be eliminated even if subscriptions had been paid for years before. Few vendors permit local-archiving options, but librarians can still ask about that possibility; disadvantages of local storage include storage space, corruptibility, possible crashes, and security and authentication procedures if accessed remotely. In the past, a few references were available as CD-ROMs, which the library might install onto a local server, but this format is now considered outdated. The one notable exception is juvenile hall libraries for incarcerated youth who usually are not allowed Internet access.
- Interface. Digital resources *should* be so simple and intuitive to use that no guidance is needed. Producers should aim for a consistent look and layout to facilitate access and use; for instance, icons should have instant meaning and avoid culture-specific connotations. Librarians should test web-based products on several browsers and devices; amazingly, the layout may differ, particularly between Mac and P.C. operating systems. Increasingly, reference resources are available in mobile mode (sometimes at extra cost). However, not all mobile-ready products have equal interface quality, especially as the user needs to drill down through page "layers." Sometimes a special plug-in or application program is needed to read the file, especially if it is an ebook. Most digital products should incorporate searching and browsing features so users can locate the needed information in several ways. That said, products should include online help such as a starting tutorial and feature-specific tips.

Certainly, resources should include documentation for technical administrative purposes. As noted earlier, the content and interface must be ADA-compliant. If possible, content should be represented in more than one medium, such as sound and text; similarly, users should be able to access content in more than one way (e.g., via keyboard or touch screen). These days, librarians should also look for customization options such as "branding," differentiated reading levels, or even user-specific tracking features. Furthermore, social media features such as the ability to make comments or use interactive features should be considered.

- Output. What is the result display: how much information is shown, and how complete is it; how many clicks are needed to retrieve the information? Can users download, save, and print content? In some cases, information must be viewed and printed page by page rather than as a whole file. On the other hand, a few products do not allow the user to print or save just a selected portion of a file. Even the file format needs to be ascertained: is it saved as a .pdf, .jpg, or .rtf?

- Hardware. At this point in time, most digital resources are stored and accessed remotely, but librarians might check on possible local server options. Nevertheless, digital products usually do require certain technical specifications such as processing speed, RAM, bandwidth, sound, and video cards. Often, online plug-ins such as JavaScript and media players may be required—and updated—as the vendor also upgrades the resource. Can thin clients access the resource? In most cases, products are usually P.C./Mac neutral, but mobile operating systems now need to be considered. Savvy librarians should have one sample of several mobile devices: an iPad, at least one e-reader, an Android, or other popular phone-scale device. In that way, library workers can test products for flexible accessibility.

- Software. Technically, the operating system is software. As mentioned earlier, where librarians had to consider P.C. and Mac systems, they now have to think about mobile operating systems as well. Also noted earlier, librarians have to make sure that required plug-ins and other applications can be installed in whatever equipment is used to access the reference resource. With the need for ADA-compliance, software is also increasingly interoperative so that assistive technology software (e.g., read-aloud software) can interface with the resource's programing. Librarians should also ask about network software, especially in terms of authentication and other protocols for remote access.

- Cost. Digital resource pricing can be complex. Subscription rates can depend on the total number of potential users or the number of simultaneous users, in-library or remote access, server options, customization options, single- or multi-site use, single- or multiyear licenses, premium features, service and support options, and so on. Sometimes librarians can get discounts by choosing multiyear agreements or subscribing through a consortium. No standard exists, so each license agreement needs to be negotiated. Database aggregators and, increasingly, general reference publishers can be especially challenging because of packaging options; especially if the company has several product lines, those collections of resources may overlap considerably, so librarians must examine the resource lists carefully. Beyond the vendor costs, librarians also need to factor in technical support costs, along with equipment costs.

- Vendor. Librarians tend to use well-known, stable resource vendors with good reputations, such as EBSCO, ProQuest, Cengage, and Oxford University Press. Nevertheless, reference products do change over time, and publishers do get bought out, so librarians should continue to keep an eye on the reference publishing market.

Other non-digital multimedia reference sources have format-specific criteria. For instance, video resources must have high fidelity and clear imagery, and the videotape quality itself must withstand heavy use. That said, videotape resources have seldom served as reference sources, except for specialized uses such as local archives. Likewise, realia such as skeleton models tend to serve as subject-specific references and are seldom held by the library, although cataloging these items would facilitate their retrieval as needed.

Factors in Choosing Formats

In sum, reference resources may be produced in several formats, not only books but also pamphlets, periodicals, online, video, and audio. As with other resources, librarians need to match content, delivery mode, and the needs of the community. As noted earlier, multiple formats are usually a good idea for important reference sources. Increasingly, reference resources are available in both print and digital format, sometimes with the online version offered as a free product when a print copy is purchased. Here are some other specific criteria to address when choosing formats. Library selection policies should also include a section on format choice in order to ensure consistent and appropriate decisions.

- Access versus ownership. Increasingly, libraries pay for access to digital resources rather than ownership rights. If ownership is important, then print sources should have priority.
- Degree of access. Online access usually extends access in terms of distance, simultaneous use, and timeframe convenience. If a resource is available only on one machine, a print version might be more convenient.
- Ease of use. Depending on their experience, the print might be easier to navigate for younger users, while digital resources might be easier for online aficionados. It should be noted that even regular computer users might be inefficient keyword searchers.
- Features. Digital resources often include sound and motion and provide more linkages than print resources. On the other hand, print resources might include tables and charts that are easier to read and copy than online ones. Increasingly, database aggregators provide value-added features such as visual searching, citation formatting, personal saving options, federated full-text locating and linking, and advanced delimiters. Some of these features may cost additional money, so it is important to determine if the potential users really have a need for these added functions.
- Need for supporting equipment and staff. As noted earlier, digital and multimedia resources require equipment and usually electricity. On the other hand, books per se are often not ADA-compliant without assistive technology. Users may also need staff help to navigate the

source, with different kinds of help depending on the format; for instance, youngsters need to learn how to use a print index and how to use an online navigation bar.

- Need for timeliness. Theoretically, digital resources can be updated continuously, but reality may be a different case. Librarians need to examine sources carefully to determine the frequency of changes. Sometimes a print resource is complemented with online updates, which is not very convenient for the user.
- Stability and archiving requirements. No matter the format, over time the material will become worn or deteriorated. Digital resources can be hard to archive—or illegal, depending upon the licensing agreement.
- Special needs. Throughout this chapter, the requirements of individuals with special needs are mentioned. If possible, reference sources should be available in several formats to accommodate the physical and psychological learning needs and preferences of users.
- Cost. Pricing remains a bottom-line consideration. Again, librarians need to weight onetime costs with annual subscriptions.

TYPES OF REFERENCE SOURCES

Reference sources tend to be categorized by their type of usage, as detailed in the following subsections. As such, they have unique characteristics. Reference sources are also considered in terms of scope: either general (such as a generic dictionary) or subject specific (such as a gazetteer).

Each library contains a core set of reference sources that are consulted daily, particularly to answer quick factual questions such as "What is the flag of Malawi?" (which is an example of a question that would be hard for Siri or Alexa to answer). These materials are known colloquially as "ready reference." As a librarian, you need to familiarize yourself with these basic tools so you can use them efficiently. Increasingly, reference collections consist solely of ready references rather than deep references such as specialized encyclopedias. Of course, what is a ready reference in a public library might be considered a deep reference in a school setting. Furthermore, online reference collections may include more specialized resources, including database aggregators; a reference website may serve as a directory, with one web page to ready reference, another for databases, and a third set listed by curricular areas.

The major types of reference tools are described in the following subsections, along with specific criteria for evaluating them. Each section notes typical types of questions that are well addressed by each type. Representative titles are also listed, including a few popular free websites.

Encyclopedias

Encyclopedias constitute the most obvious reference source. They provide background information, sometimes with sub-topics and cross-references. Most encyclopedias are arranged alphabetically, with quick access through indexes found either at the end of each volume or as a separate volume. Furthermore, some publishers may intermix the terms "encyclopedia" and "dictionary" for alphabetically arranged references with entries that may be one to several paragraphs in length. Most encyclopedias are multivolume, but a few, such as subject-specific encyclopedias, may consist of a single volume. Such resources may be underused if not actively promoted by librarians. Representative titles follow. Note that popular free reference websites are also included.

- *World Book* (also available in Spanish)
- *Encyclopedia Britannica* (also available in Spanish)
- *G.O.: Grolier Online*
- *D.K.* encyclopedia versions
- *Catholic Encyclopedia*
- *Gale Encyclopedia of Science*
- *Oxford Music Online* (gateway to *Grove Music Online*, *Oxford Dictionary of Music*, and *Oxford Companion to Music*)
- http://wikipedia.org and https://simple.wikipedia.org/ for language/reader learners
- *Encyclopedia of Life*, https://eol.org/

Typical questions answered by encyclopedias include the following:

- What is Shakespeare's impact?
- What were the causes of the Cold War?
- How does television work?
- What is the life cycle of a butterfly?
- What were the main features of each major music movement in history?

When evaluating and using encyclopedias, look for some of these added criteria:

- How is article content sequenced? Some give a summary and then go into more depth. Some have a gradated reading level, starting with simpler language and progressing to more complex text. Still others start with an overview and then treat the topic chronologically.
- Are articles signed?
- Do articles include a bibliography? If the encyclopedia is online, does it link to the bibliography entries?
- How often is content updated? What is the basis for updating an article?
- How searchable is the encyclopedia: cross-references, one or several indexes, online search tool?
- Does the encyclopedia include user tips or research tips?
- Do digital encyclopedias have hotlinks, including news or other content updates?
- Do digital encyclopedias include sound and video?
- Is the encyclopedia available in non-English, or does it include a translation tool for digital versions? It should be noted that Spanish vocabulary and grammar practices vary among countries. Mexican publishers and editors are probably a better match for U.S. readers.

Dictionaries

A dictionary is an alphabetical list of words. Generally, each entry includes definitions, pronunciation, origin (etymology), and usage. Some dictionaries include charts, diagrams, maps, or other illustrations. Some dictionaries include added facts, such as lists of higher education institutions, rhymes, or grammar rules. Along with subject-specific dictionaries, other types of specialized dictionaries include synonym/antonym, slang, and abbreviations. Dictionaries also vary in terms of depth, varying from pocket size to one-volume desk size to multivolume. Unabridged dictionaries are supposedly word inclusive; the most popular U.S. dictionary is *Webster's Collegiate Dictionary*, and the most comprehensive dictionary is the *Oxford English Dictionary*, particularly for etymologies and historical usage. Other representative titles include the following:

- *Merriam-Webster Dictionaries* and http://Merriam-Webster.com (free)
- *Webster's New World Children's Dictionary*
- *Roget's Thesaurus* (note that the original version was arranged thematically, similarly to an ontology; most thesauri are arranged alphabetically)
- *Webster's Dictionary of English Usage*
- *McGraw Hill American Slang Dictionary*
- *Brewer's Dictionary of Phrase and Fable* (note that it has a British bias)
- *Random House Webster's Compact American Sign Language Dictionary*
- *Webster's Office Crossword Puzzle Dictionary*
- *Gale Acronyms, Initialisms, and Abbreviations Dictionary*
- *Facts on File Visual Dictionary*
- *Columbia Gazetteer of the World* (dictionary of geographic terms)
- *Glossary of Literary Terms*
- https://www.dictionary.com/
- https://www.wordreference.com/ (includes more than a dozen languages)
- https://www.netlingo.com/
- https://kidshealth.org/en/kids/word/
- https://www.rhymezone.com/

Typical questions answered by dictionaries include the following:

- What is the origin of the word "kowtow"?
- How do you pronounce "chiaroscuro"?
- What is the plural form of "radius"?
- What does the acronym NOAA stand for?
- What English words starting with Q do not have a U immediately following?
- What is another word for "mice"?
- What rhymes with "blanket"?

When evaluating and using dictionaries, look for some of these added criteria:

- Reading level (note that a dictionary for primary grades should differ from one targeted to adult ELL)
- Variant spellings
- Pronunciation keys
- Grammatical information
- Inclusion of sample sentences
- Synonyms and antonyms
- Images
- Order of definitions: some dictionaries list definitions in order by popularity, while others order them chronologically, so it is best to read the preface to ascertain the order.

Non-English dictionaries have additional properties that should be considered. Several publishers are known for their foreign language and bilingual dictionaries: Cassell, HarperCollins, Harrap, Langenscheidt, Larousse, Longmans, Merriam-Webster, Oxford University Press, and Vox. England produces several good bilingual dictionaries (e.g., Harrap); however, they use British spelling, which can confuse U.S. students. Currency is particularly important for bilingual dictionaries because formal and informal vocabulary vary and can make the communicator sound dated or pedantic if the wrong word is chosen. For high school collections, single language dictionaries, such as *Larousse Petit Dictionnaire Francais* and *Diccionario Espasa de la lengua española* can be useful for more advanced students. Foreign language dictionaries should provide simple definitions and examples of use in a sentence. When locating a word in another language, it is a good idea to then verify the word choice by looking at the word in the target language and see what English word it references. For instance, the French word for "disk" is "disque" (no surprise), but three words are associated with the word "disque" (in French): "disc," "disk," and "record"; a one-to-one correlation cannot be guaranteed.

Almanacs and Yearbooks

Almanacs and yearbooks are usually annual publications with fast facts and figures in an easy-to-find format. Almanacs are more likely to provide long-standing data, such as award winners and geographic statistics, as well as show current trends such as economic data. Yearbooks tend to focus on topics for a specific year. Sometimes chronologies are included in this category of reference sources. Almanacs and yearbooks are typically arranged topically, with detailed index to facilitate information retrieval. Most have tables and charts that succinctly present statistical data. Increasingly, online almanacs are used more than print ones; however, middle school libraries should keep a class set of print almanacs to teach data analysis skills—and see how almanacs are organized. Typical titles include the following:

- *Information Please Almanac* and http://www.infoplease.com
- *World Almanac*

- *Statesman's Yearbook*
- *Chase's Calendar of Events*
- *African American Almanac*
- https://www.guinnessworldrecords.com/
- *Internet Movie Database* http://www.imdb.com
- https://www.baseball-almanac.com/

Typical questions answered by biographical resources include the following:

- Which is the most air-polluted city in the world?
- What is the world cell phone use by nation?
- What were the most important events of the last year?
- What movies did Chloe Zhao direct?
- Who has won the Nobel Peace Prize?
- What percentage of the U.S. population is obese?
- Who are the all-time National Basketball Association statistical leaders?

When evaluating and using almanacs and yearbooks, look for some of these added criteria:

- Currency and time frame of statistics
- Granularity of statistics
- Sources of data
- Use and readability of tables and charts
- Quality of indexes and table of contents
- Physical durability

Atlases

An atlas is a systematic collection of maps covering one or more topics. Several types of maps exist: physical, political, thematic, and historic. It should be noted that atlases may focus on animals, astronomy, and even imaginary places. Besides maps, atlases may include glossaries, statistics, illustrations, comparative maps, and text; online atlases may include video and sound clips as well. Information is typically accessed via tables of contents and indexes. Globes are not as popular as they once were, but they can serve as a useful teaching tool in schools; the main limitation is their quick obsolescence. Some indexes refer to places by map coordinates (e.g., G2), and others reference by latitude/longitude. Atlases exemplify the need for currency, except for historical atlases. Indeed, *Shepherd's Historical Atlas*, though dated, remains a valuable source of information. It should be noted that gazetteers (geographical dictionaries) and guidebooks serve as useful complements to atlases for geographic information. It should also be mentioned that online maps have become the preferred format for map information because of their timeliness, flexible scale, and ability to be enriched through customizable features. Nevertheless, libraries should maintain a core collection of print atlases. Indeed, it is a good idea for middle schools to have a class set of a student version of a print atlas (e.g., Merriam-Webster's *Student Atlas*) in order to teach map reading skills. Key map publishers include National Geographic Society, Oxford, and Rand McNally. Other representative titles include the following:

- *Times Atlas of the World*
- *Rand McNally Road Atlas*
- *Oxford Atlas of World History*
- *National Geographic Historical Atlas of the United States*
- *Historical Atlas of Native Americans*
- *Ocean: An Illustrated Atlas*
- *The Atlas of Mars*
- *Atlas of Endangered Species*
- *Atlas of Imaginary Places*
- https://earth.google.com/
- https://www.mapquest.com/

Typical questions answered by atlases include the following:

- What is the distance between Buenos Aires and Sao Paulo?
- What is Afghanistan's terrain?
- Where was the silk route?
- Where are the highest underwater mountain ranges?
- What is the relationship between the presence of rivers and the location of cities?
- What is the migration pattern of different birds?
- What does Narnia look like?

When evaluating and using atlases, look for some of these added criteria:

- Projection: Mercator can be misleading; some people prefer Gall-Peters projection, and several other projection models exist.
- The order of the maps and their scale usually reflects the perspective of the publisher; for instance, U.S. publishers usually start with the Americas and have detailed state maps, unlike British publishers who may favor European countries.
- Spelling preferences such as variants from U.S. spelling; the preface usually explains the usage.
- Keys and legend quality.
- Measurement scale: metric versus English/American.
- Use of color: differentiation should be made by additional methods (e.g., labels and line quality) in order to be accessible for people with color blindness.

Handbooks and Manuals

Handbooks and manuals provide concise facts, often technical, and guides to a specific topic. Manuals, in particular, focus on procedural knowledge and often include diagrams and other illustrations. Access to these sources is usually through the table of contents or index. Representative titles include the following:

- Chilton's car manuals
- Peterson and National Audubon Society nature field guides
- *Masterplots*
- *Emily Post's Etiquette*
- *Bartlett's Familiar Quotations*
- *American Red Cross First Aid and Safety Handbook*
- *CRC Handbook of Chemistry and Physics*
- *MLA Handbook for Writers of Research Papers*
- http:// usgovernmentmanual.gov
- http://weather.com
- https://kidshealth.org
- Purdue Online Writing Lab https://owl.purdue.edu/

Typical questions answered by handbooks and manuals include the following:

- How do you troubleshoot a printer problem?
- What is the chemical formula for ammonia?
- How do you address a senator?
- How do you make a batik?
- Who said, "Beauty is in the eye of the beholder"?
- How do you differentiate between safe and poisonous mushrooms?
- What is the correct way to cite a website using the American Psychological Association style?

When evaluating and using handbooks and manuals, look for some of these added criteria:

- Expertise: Authority, expertise, and current knowledge are often critical, especially in the areas of health and repairs; company manuals are usually a good choice.
- Currency: Some sources are not time-sensitive, such as drawing manuals, but even artist handbooks need to be current as materials and ways to handle them have changed. Other niches change frequently: government officeholders, computers, cars, first aid advice, and so on.
- Safety factors: Handbook and manuals may involve issues of safety, such as dealing with electric or toxic materials, applying practices in the outdoors, or following questionable diets; safety issues should be identified with measures to keep safe.

Biographical Sources

Reference sources about people can vary from short dictionary entries, which might give just vital statistics and contact information, to long essays. As with encyclopedias and dictionaries, biographical reference sources can be universal or subject-specific, as well as be contemporary or historical. Similarly, some biographical sources have a bias (usually favorable) while others are more objective and fair-handed. Representative titles, besides the encyclopedia and dictionary mentioned earlier, include the following:

- Marquis' Who's Who series
- *Current Biography* (the cumulative index is a vital part of the source)
- *McGraw-Hill Encyclopedia of World Biography*
- Gale group biography series, especially for literature
- Rosen *Black American Biographies*
- *Encyclopedia of Associations* (technically a directory)
- *Congressional Biographical Directory of the United States Congress* https://bioguide.congress .gov/
- http://scienceworld.wolfram.com/biography

Typical questions answered by biographical resources include the following:

- What was the legacy of John Lewis?
- Who are some notable Indian mathematicians?
- Who were the most influential leaders of Women's Liberation Movement?
- How can I contact Rami Malek?
- Who can I network with about model making?
- What are some literacy criticisms about Toni Morrison?

When evaluating and using biographical resources, look for some of these added criteria:

- Criteria for selection. Because most biographical sources are exclusive, it is important to find out the editor's criteria for selection. Indeed, some directories (i.e., lists) of people may be considered "vanity" publications for which the publisher requires that the listed person pay for the privilege of being included.
- Source of information. Most biographical reference sources draw upon other sources of information, which should be cited.
- Authorship. In some cases, one person writes all of the entries, while in other cases, numerous contributors write the entries so each one should be evaluated in terms of his or her authority.
- Currency. Particularly when contact information is listed, currency is important because people move and change jobs.
- Context. Individuals are impacted by their environment and times, just as they impact others. Therefore, it is useful for biographies to include such contextual information.

Guides to Other Sources

Locating high-quality relevant reference sources, and the resources within, can be challenging. School librarians should teach high school students (and their teachers) how to use indexes, abstracts, concordances, and bibliographies. All of these tools point to other reference sources, similar to a library catalogue and aggregator databases.

Indexes. Most reference books have indexes (which might be considered as search engines). Multivolume reference sources normally have a separate volume for the next, which sometimes has to be purchased separately. *Current Biography* and Gale series exemplify titles that need indexes for users to find the information they need. Magazines also use indexes, such as *National Geographic* and *Scientific American*, and aggregator databases are built on the idea of indexing.

Abstracts. Most aggregator databases include abstracts for the documents they index. Such abstracts help users determine the content and quality of the information, and the abstract may suffice for some research.

Bibliographies. Lists of vetted sources can give users a good research starting point. Some reference sources include selective bibliographies for each entry or at the end of the volume. Whole volumes can be bibliographies, such as professional collection development selection tools. In any case, bibliographies need to be evaluated in terms of their scope, accuracy, currency, organization, means of selection, and information included for each entry. Librarians routinely create bibliographies, often in the form of pathfinders, which detail research strategies: key terms, background information sources, key reference sources, relevant periodicals, and relevant Dewey Decimal Classification System numbers. Mindspring is a subscription-based application that enables librarians to produce professional-looking bibliographies that can embed multimedia. Free and open-source options for creating subject guides are listed at https://journal.code4lib.org/articles/47.

Concordances alphabetically list the location of significant words that occurred within a work. The best-known concordances list terms for religious works and Shakespeare's writing. Concordances can be valuable aids for the content analysis of texts.

Reference Databases and Collections

While periodicals themselves are often not considered reference materials, per se, largely because their use varies greatly, a strong case can be made that aggregator databases such as EBSCO's Academic Search or SIRS should be considered reference tools because they serve an indexing function, facilitating retrieval of resources used in research. Unlike such index tools of the past, such as the *Reader's Guide to Periodical Literature*, many of today's digital indexes are embedded within the aggregator database itself, which includes the full text of the targeted resource. Moreover, library catalogs, which may be considered as indexes, increasingly provide interfaces that incorporate these databases so that the user can search both entire products (e.g., a book or DVD) and articles within a resource from a single search "bar." Aggregator databases demand special attention because of their cost and complexity. In addition, they tend to package together hundreds of periodical titles, with varying timeline runs, and the librarian does not have the right to pick and choose which periodical to subscribe to. Here are some guiding questions to ask. However, the most important question is this: What information is needed by the target population?

Interface:

- How easily can the user find needed information?
- What browsers does it support?
- Is the database mobile-friendly?
- What navigation tools are available?
- Is searching intuitive and accessible?
- To what depth can the user search for information?
- What HELP function is available?
- Does the source employ an open URL standard?
- How does technical format impact action?
- Can content be downloaded/printed/saved/sent?

Readability:

- How clear is the layout?
- Are text and images easy to view?
- Are plug-ins necessary?
- Is content, including the searching process, ADA-compliant and accessible for individuals with special needs?
- Can viewing options be changed or customized?

Technical requirements:

- What kind of system requirements (e.g., operating system, platform, speed, RAM, video, sound) and connectivity are needed?
- Can the resource be networked?
- Can the resource link to other resources, such as locating articles in a different database?
- Do multiple simultaneous user access impact performance?

Licenses:

- What is the scope?
- How complete is the content?
- What is the license duration?
- What warranties exist?
- What indemnification exists?

- What kind of access is available?
- What confidentiality is guaranteed?
- What sharing and archiving are available?
- Is the product disability compliant?
- What statistics are available?
- Is there "leasing with an option to buy"?

CORE REFERENCE COLLECTIONS

Here are starting checklists of reputable popular core reference titles, which are likely to be useful for most libraries serving youth. The "as needed" portion is included to address possible subject niches or to consider if budgets are plentiful.

Elementary School Age

Notes: for dictionaries and encyclopedias, examine the content to match them most closely with your youth population; when several publishers are included for the same kind of reference, all of them are satisfactory.

- *American Heritage First Dictionary*, *Children's Dictionary*, and *Children's Thesaurus*
- *Merriam-Webster Children's Dictionary*, *Elementary Dictionary*, and *Visual Dictionary*
- *Oxford Primary Dictionary*, *Junior Illustrated Dictionary*, and *Primary Thesaurus*
- *Scholastic First Dictionary* and *Scholastic Children's Dictionary*
- *Webster's New World Children's Dictionary*
- *World Book* (also available in Spanish) (also online subscription)
- *DK First Children's Encyclopedia*, *New Children's Encyclopedia*, and *Children's Illustrated Thesaurus*
- *Britannica All New Kids' Encyclopedia*
- *National Geographic Kids Beginner's World Atlas* and *Kids U.S. Atlas*
- *Wide Eyed Editions 50 States*
- *Kingfisher Nature Encyclopedia*
- *DK First Earth Encyclopedia*, *First Science Encyclopedia*, and *Animal Book*
- *National Geographic Kids Science Encyclopedia*, *Kids Animal Encyclopedia*, and *Kids Wild Animal Atlas*
- *National Geographic Kids Almanac*
- *World Almanac for Kids* (online subscription)
- *Phaidon Ultimate Art Museum*
- *Scholastic GO: Grolier Online* https://emea.scholastic.com/en/grolier-online (subscription)
- http://www.factmonster.com
- http://www.refdesk.com/kids.html
- https://kids.wordsmyth.net/
- https://kidshealth.org/en/kids/, https://kidshealth.org/en/kids/word/

As needed:

- *Firefly My First French/English Visual Dictionary* and *My First Spanish/English Visual Dictionary*
- *Kar-Ben My First Hebrew Word Book*
- *Lonely Planet Kids Flag Book* and *Travel Book*
- *Routledge Math Dictionary for Kids*
- *DK First Dinosaur Encyclopedia*
- *National Geographic Kids Extreme Records and Encyclopedia of American Indian History and Culture*

Middle School Age

- *American Heritage Student Dictionary*
- *Britannica Student Encyclopedia*
- *National Geographic World Atlas for Young Explorers, National Geographic United States Atlas for Young Explorers*
- *Merriam-Webster Student Atlas*
- *Kingfisher Atlas of the Ancient World*
- *Usborne Encyclopedia of World History*
- *D.K. History Year by Year, Timelines of Everything,* and *Timelines from Black History*
- *Omnigraphics Holidays* and *Festivals and Celebrations of the World Dictionary*
- *UXL Encyclopedia of World Biography*
- *Visible Ink African American Almanac*
- *Guinness World Records,* https://www.guinnessworldrecords.com/
- *National Geographic Animal Encyclopedia*
- Macauley, D. (2016). *The Way Things Work Now.* HMH Books for Young Readers
- *D.K. The Arts: A Visual Encyclopedia*
- *D.K. Sports Book*
- EBSCO or ProQuest school database subscription
- Virtual Middle School Library, http://www.sldirectory.com/virtual.html
- https://simple.wikipedia.org/
- http://www.visualdictionaryonline.com/
- http://www.infoplease.com
- https://www.50states.com/
- http://www.rhymezone.com
- Encyclopedia of Life, https://eol.org/
- http://weather.com

As needed:

- *D.K. 5 Language Visual Dictionary*
- *Merriam-Webster Illustrated Spanish-English Student Dictionary*
- *Random House Webster's Compact American Sign Language Dictionary*
- *Scholastic Dictionary of Idioms*
- *D.K. Ciencia!* (general encyclopedia in Spanish)
- *Smithsonian History: From the Dawn of Civilization to the Present Day*
- *UXL Encyclopedia of U.S. History* (eight volumes)
- *Junior Worldmark Encyclopedia of the States* (four volumes)
- *Junior Worldmark Encyclopedia of the Nations* (ten volumes)
- *Worldmark Encyclopedia of Cultures and Daily Life* (five volumes)
- *Illustrated Dictionary of the Muslim World*
- *Interlink Pocket Timelines of Islamic Civilizations*
- *Usborne Encyclopedia of World Religions*
- *Cavendish Atlas of Endangered Animals*
- *D.K. Encyclopedia of Ocean Life* and *Elements Book*
- National Audubon Society, National Geographic Society, or Peterson nature field guides
- *Firefly Sports Book*
- *Human Kinetics Sports Rules Book*
- *Ferguson Encyclopedia of Careers and Vocational Guidance*
- Draw upon elementary titles

High School Age

- *Merriam-Webster Collegiate Dictionary, Collegiate Thesaurus*
- *Scholastic Dictionary of Synonyms, Antonyms, Homonyms*
- *Oxford Visual Dictionary*
- *Encyclopedia Britannica* (also available in Spanish)
- *World Almanac*
- *Oxford Atlas of the World, New Concise World Atlas*
- *Times Comprehensive Atlas of the World*
- *Rand McNally Road Atlas*
- *D.K. History of the World Map by Map*
- *Culture Grams*
- *Gale American Decades*
- *Current Biography*
- *Gale Encyclopedia of Multicultural America*
- *Rosen Black American Biographies*
- *Rosen Respecting the Contributions of Asian Americans*
- *Opposing Viewpoints*

- Giesecke, A. (2020). *Classical Mythology A to Z*. BlackDog & Leventhal.
- *Merriam-Webster's Encyclopedia of World Religions*
- *Bartlett's Familiar Quotations*, http://www.online-literature.com/quotes/quotations.php
- *Collins Dictionary of Literacy Terms*
- *Brewer's Dictionary of Phrase and Fable*, https://www.infoplease.com/dictionary/brewers
- *McGraw-Hill Dictionary of American Slang and Colloquial Expressions*
- *Benet's Reader's Encyclopedia*
- *Facts on File Guide to Research*
- *Great Source Writers Inc.*
- *Gale Encyclopedia of Science* (and online subscription)
- *National Geographic Visual Encyclopedia of Earth*
- *CRC Handbook of Chemistry and Physics*
- *Walch Real-Life Math*
- *National Geographic Human Body Atlas*
- *College Board College Handbook*
- *Oxford Concise Dictionary of Art and Artists*
- *Sports: The Complete Visual Reference*
- *Rules of the Game*
- http://wikipedia.org
- http://ReferenceDesk.org
- http://www.reference.com/
- http://www.nysl.nysed.gov/reference/readyref.htm
- http://itools.com/tag/reference
- http://Refdesk.com
- http://www.refseek.com/directory/
- https://www.encyclopedia.com/
- https://www.jstor.org/site/reveal-digital/independent-voices/
- http://www.credoreference.com
- Digital Public Library of America, https://dp.la/ (includes selective National Archives and Records Administration, Smithsonian Institution, Internet Archive, HathiTrust, ARTstor, federal and state archives, J. Paul Getty Trust, etc.)
- http://usa.gov
- http://copyright.gov
- http://cia.gov, especially https://www.cia.gov/the-world-factbook/
- http://usgovernmentmanual.gov
- https://bioguide.congress.gov/
- Library of Congress http://loc.gov, especially https://www.loc.gov/collections/
- https://www.nasa.gov/
- Centers for Disease Control and Prevention, https://www.cdc.gov/
- Smithsonian https://www.si.edu/
- https://www.archives.gov/

- Occupational Outlook Handbook, https://www.bls.gov/ooh
- http://www.un.org/en/documents/
- http://data.un.org
- https://www.bartleby.com/quotations/ (links to Roget's)
- Purdue Online Writing Lab, https://owl.purdue.edu/
- https://www.linguee.com/
- National Science Digital Library, https://nsdl.oercommons.org/
- http://scienceworld.wolfram.com/biography
- https://kidshealth.org/
- https://www.mayoclinic.org/
- https://medlineplus.gov/encyclopedia.html
- http://www.greeninfoonline.com
- Dictionary of Computing, https://foldoc.org/
- https://www.sports-reference.com/
- http://www.imdb.com
- http://www.edmunds.com

As needed:

- *Catholic Encyclopedia*
- *American National Biography* (online subscription)
- *Gale Biography in Context* (online subscription)
- *EBSCO Biography Reference Bank* (online subscription)
- *Chase's Calendar of Events*
- *Statesman's Yearbook*
- http://www.columbiagazetteer.org/ (online subscription)
- *Encyclopedia of American Facts and Dates*
- *Houghton Mifflin Harcourt Encyclopedia of World History*
- *Diagram Group New Weapons of the World Encyclopedia*
- *Encyclopedia of Associations*
- *Gale Who's Who among African Americans*
- *Salem Press Great Lives from History: Latinos* (three volumes)
- *Salem Press Asians and Pacific Islander Americans* (three volumes)
- *Salem Press African Americans* (five volumes)
- *Random House Historical Dictionary of American Slang*
- Foreign language dictionary publishers: HarperCollins, Larousse, Oxford University Press
- *Gale Literature Resource Centers* (online subscription includes): *Contemporary Authors, Contemporary Literary Criticism, Dictionary of Literary Biography, Novels for Students, Shakespearean Criticism*, and *Poetry Criticism*
- *Granger's Index to Poetry*
- *Salem Press Masterplots*

- *Atlas of Imaginary Places*
- *Merck Manual*
- Papadakis, M. et al. (2022). *Current Medical Diagnosis & Treatment*. Lange.
- *The Atlas of Mars*
- *Atlas of Endangered Species*
- *Atlas of Imaginary Places*
- *Oxford Music Online* (subscription gateway to *Grove Music Online, Oxford Dictionary of Music*, and *Oxford Companion to Music*); the dictionary and companion may be bought separately in print
- *Robert's Rules of Order* and http://www.rulesonline.com/
- *Consumer Reports*
- *Emily Post's Etiquette*
- *SIRS Researcher*
- Foreign language dictionaries: Cassell, HarperCollins, Harrap, Langenscheidt, Larousse, Longmans, Merriam-Webster, Oxford University Press, Vox
- Draw upon younger titles

Professional

- *Sear's List of Subject Headings* or Library of Congress's *Children's Subject Headings*
- *Abridged Dewey Decimal Classification*
- http://www.worldcat.org
- http://www.ala.org/
- http://www.libraryspot.com/
- http://www.sldirectory.com/
- http://www.libraryresearch.com
- http://www.teacherreference.com

SELECTION TOOLS

The preceding lists can serve as a selection tool when developing and improving a reference collection. Indeed, the list itself was generated by examining sources firsthand and using a variety of selection tools to help evaluate the quality and relevance of the reference sources.

Just as been said that humans can be a valuable information source, so librarians and reference collection users can testify as to the quality and benefit of reference resources they have handled. Another good practice is to visit libraries that serve youth: observing what materials are collected and used (including noting the wear of the items) and getting advice from staff about reference collection development. To an extent, bookstores can also provide opportunities for inspecting potential reference sources, although their target audience is usually home use.

However, it is unlikely that you the librarian can experience every possible reference resource. Especially as librarians can focus on reviewing their areas of interest, they can complement each other's expertise. While face-to-face sessions provide rich insights, online chat and written reviews can serve as a good basis for most selection purposes. Sharing professional insider information about resources saves time and money and offers a reality check about possible acquisitions. In some cases, joint reviewing can lead to resource sharing of seldom-used but still worthwhile items. You might also consider developing a review group that includes teachers and students in order to broaden the base for consideration.

Published professional reviews further expand the knowledge base. Most reviewers of library materials are not paid, although they may be able to keep the item they review (which increasingly consists of digital galleys), and their reviews are likely to be well substantiated. Reviews of individual works can be found via *Book Review Index,* standard subscription databases, and EBSCO's Library, Information Science and Technology Abstracts, which is a free research database that facilitates access to these reviews. Professional and trade journals such as the ALA's *Booklist* (and its associated *Book Links* for children's materials) focus entirely on reviewing and making special note of reference materials. *Library Journal* and its affiliated *School Library Journal, Horn Book, Bookbird, VOYA, Kirkus, The Bulletin of the Center for Children's Books, Reference & User Services,* and *School Library Connection* keep librarians up-to-date on library materials, including reference sources. Journals from other professional organizations and the publishing industry also offer good advice: for example, American Association for the Advancement of Science's *Science Books & Films,* International Literacy Association's website (https://www.literacyworldwide.org/), *Publishers Weekly, New York Times Book Review,* and *Foreword Reviews.*

Another good feature of *Booklist* is its annual list of best reference books, based on the collected reviews over the year. Curated lists offer a great jumpstart on substantive reference collection assessment. The ALA and its divisions provide the most relevant, reputable lists. H. W. Wilson is another gold standard publisher of core collection lists, which are generated by professional librarians; their most relevant selection tools—with include reference book titles—are *Children's Core Collection, Middle & Junior High School Core Collection,* and *Senior High Core Collection.* Their online versions are provided by EBSCO and Libraries Unlimited's *American Reference Books Annual* and *Recommended Books for Small and Medium-Sized Libraries and Media Centers,* as well as ALA's *Reference Sources for Small and Medium-Sized Libraries* (now a bit outdated), which are mainstay volumes that include titles for youth. Several online websites also focus on book reviews that include reference titles for youth: https://www.thechildrens-bookreview.com/, Cooperative Children's Book Center (https://ccbc.education.wisc.edu/), and the Internet Library for Librarians (http://www.itcompany.com/inforetriever/).

Circling back to bookstores, several major book vendors provide their own lists of recommended resources, which sometimes include reference books: for example, Baker and Taylor, Brodart, Follett, Ingram, Mackin, Amazon, and Barnes & Noble. Some lists cite or extract reviews, although these notes may be cherry-picked. While these lists can be informative, they may also be skewed; vendors are in the profit-making business, and they might favor those publishers who offer a better price point for sales.

Reviews of nonprint reference resources are harder to find. AudioFile, *Video Librarian*, and https://www.commonsense.org/education/edtech-reviews-resources are good starting points; in addition, *Booklist, Library Journal*, and *School Library Journal* have AV sections. Since digital resources require hardware to access them, selection tools can help in determining the best fit for those electronic reference resources. AV-iQ (https://www.av-iq.com/) consists of an international database of audiovisual products, which includes specifications, options to compare products, and vendor information. CNET http://www.cnet.com is a reputable source for electronics reviews. Another good source for comparative shopping is http://Lustre.ai

Food for Thought: Diverse Reference Resources

More than ever, youth-serving librarians need to provide an inclusive reference collection. That means addressing the needs of youth of different ethnicities, languages, abilities, and self-identities. Not only should reference collections reflect all users but they should also provide a window to expand knowledge to all users. As you read this section, consider auditing your own reference collection to determine areas for growth.

Languages

Youth from other cultures may want to see reference sources about their first culture or in their home language. For several populations, resources in the dominant language (usually English in the United States) should be available in a simple grammatical style with basic vocabulary. In that respect, visual dictionaries and other reference sources with explanatory visuals are very welcome; clear images with white backgrounds (a Dorking Kindersley signature look) are usually the easiest to comprehend. Youth who are fluent in languages other than English can take advantage of translation tools such as Google Translate, which can translate websites. In addition, Wikipedia is available in several languages as well as in simple English (http://simple.wikipedia.org). Print references in non-English languages can be daunting to librarians who are not fluent in those languages. One workaround is Google in different languages, which can link to resources of publishers in the associated languages (https://support.google.com/websearch/answer/873?hl=en&co=GENIE.Platform%3DDesktop). The disadvantage is that the results might not link to high-quality reference resources. Finding print reference resources in non-English languages can be daunting even if the librarian is fluent in the target language, as the reference publishing situation can vary widely across countries. Furthermore, acquiring those resources can be difficult because of publication challenges as well as banking and shipping obstacles. Spanish is the most accessible; both *World Book* and *Encyclopedia Britannica* are available in Spanish, and a few other general encyclopedias are published in Spanish (e.g., *Enciclopedia Universal*). Creighton University's LibGuide (https://culibraries.creighton.edu/c.php?g=163412&p=1074215) lists a number of Spanish reference resources in Spanish and about Spanish populations; it should be noted, though, that reference materials produced in Spain may use a slightly different version of Spanish than materials produced in Latin America. Wikipedia lists general encyclopedias by language (https://en.wikipedia.org/wiki/List_of_encyclopedias_by_language). Other languages can be more challenging, so librarians should check with those library systems that serve non-English populations as well as librarian ethnic associations such as Reforma and the Chinese American Library Association.

Ethnicities

Librarians need to model and promote appreciation and inclusion of cultural knowledge, including ensuring that reference collections reflect and enrich their communities. Starting from early childhood, young people should have opportunities to experience cultural knowledge, and the library provides an open venue for such exposure. Even within the English language, significant differences in terms of cultural perspective. Ethnic-centric library associations, such as the Black Caucus American Library Association and the American Indian Library Association, provide advice on relevant reference resources. In locating appropriate biography reference resources, it was difficult to find current resources for K–12 readers. Titles such as *100 greatest . . . by ethnicity* had not been updated for over a decade. It was easier to find ethnic-centric collections by career (e.g., entertainers), but these titles were more likely to be targeted to adult audiences. With the increased awareness of ethnicity and associated inequities—and the need for materials that support self-identity—it is important for youth-serving librarians to find ways to help youth to engage with ethnic-relevant reference resources. One way to leverage this particular issue, particularly for school librarians, is to provide a learning activity whereby students identify and research significant individuals of different ethnicities and then create an e-publication of those individuals to be added to the library's digital library collection.

Disabilities

Youth with disabilities are likely to want to know about themselves and others with similar—or different—disabilities. The options for reference resources are disappointingly slim. Reference sources are typically targeted to adults who work with youth who have disabilities such as ACB-CLIO's *Disability: A Reference Handbook*. Instead, websites are probably better reference sources. A few representative ones include https://www.mentalhelp.net/, https://youth.gov/youth-topics/disabilities and https://thinkcollege.net/.

In terms of using generic reference resources, some youth with physical disabilities may need customized reference sources such as spiral bindings or other means to ensure a flat surface, board books or other books with stiff pages, large-print books, textured books for sensory needs, or audiobooks. Youth with disabilities may also need assistive technology in order to access reference sources such as scanners and text-to-speech software. The American Library Association has a good starting list of assistance technology tips (https://www.ala.org/rusa/assistive-technology) that are applicable to reference collections.

Gender Fluidity

As with other under-represented groups, youth with non-typical gender identities have few developmentally appropriate reference resources to consult. Furthermore, the standard reference sources need updating. A couple that would be useful are BenBella's *Queers in History* (which is somewhat dated: 2009) and Gale's three-volume set *Global Encyclopedia of Lesbian, Gay, Bisexual, Transgender, and Queer (LGBTQ) History* (which is targeted to academic readers). This topic is another area of reference need. Again, reference websites are probably the best approach; representative metasites for teens include https://youth.gov/youth-topics/lgbtq-youth/references, https://libguides.usc.edu/lgbtq/links, and https://www.apa.org/pi/lgbt/resources.

REFERENCE

American Library Association. (2013). *ALA glossary of library and information science* (4th ed.). American Library Association.

FURTHER READING

Fraser, E. (2020). *Young adult nonfiction: A readers' advisory and collection development guide.* Libraries Unlimited.

Goldsmith, F. (2016). *Crash course in contemporary reference.* Libraries Unlimited.

Gregory, V. (2019). *Collection development and management for 21st century library collections: An introduction.* American Library Association.

Houston, C. (2016). Reinventing your reference collection. In IASL Annual Conference Proceedings. https://journals.library.ualberta.ca/slw/index.php/iasl/article/download/7195/4194

Hughes-Hassell, S. (2020). *Collection management for youth: Equity, inclusion, and learning* (2nd ed.). American Library Association.

Jensen, K. (2020, October 26). Collection diversity audits. *Teen Librarian Toolbox.* https://www.teenlibrariantoolbox.com/2020/10/in-my-mailbox-questions-i-get-about-collection-diversity-audits/

Lee, S. (2019). *Electronic resources and collection development.* Routledge.

Sowards, E., & Chenoweth, J. (Eds.). *The reference librarian's Bible: Print and digital reference resources every library should own.* Libraries Unlimited.

4

Life Cycle of Reference Resources

As already discussed, the line between the general collection and reference collection is increasingly fading, and the differences may well be determined as much by the young user as the librarian. Nevertheless, as with the rest of the library collection, youth-serving librarians need to approach reference collection management strategically, considering the entire information cycle: from selection relative to access options, acquisition, processing, maintenance, preservation, reallocation, and withdrawal. As part of this management process, librarians also need to develop policies and procedures to streamline and standardize practice, including specific provisions for reference materials. This chapter addresses both print and digital resources, noting key factors for each.

REFERENCE RESOURCES LIFE CYCLE
Selecting reference materials is only the first step in reference collection development, as figure 4.1 shows.

ACQUISITION
Ideally, librarians think strategically about reference collections as with other areas of the collection, keeping current with reviews in order to keep a running list of desired titles and looking out for special offers. Librarians should also keep an inventory list of their reference collection titles and dates for easy referral come ordering time.

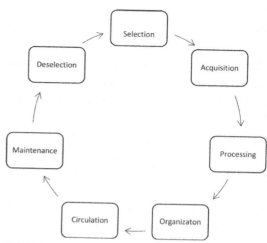

FIGURE 4.1
Reference Resources Life Cycle. Source: Created by the author

Furthermore, reference publishers sometimes offer discounts when purchasing multiple titles or multiple copies of the same title, so coordinating reference resource acquisitions across sites is a valuable practice. Another money-saving tip is checking if the publisher offers a digital version of the reference resource free if a print version is bought. Especially as reference resources can be substantially more expensive than the general collection, they may be subject to more budgetary scrutiny so advanced planning that results in cost savings can be fruitful.

Generic Ordering

Core reference materials are often ordered separately from general collection items such as fiction. For instance, encyclopedias are usually ordered directly from the publisher. Reference publishers are also likely to offer standing orders; that is, whenever a new edition of a publication is published, the library agrees to buy it automatically. This practice ensures currency in the collection for needed titles such as Wilson/EBSCO core collection publications, almanacs, and series such as *Current Biography*. In addition, database vendors such as ABC-CLIO, Gale, and EBSCO increasingly offer package deals for reference resources. This practice can reduce the number of purchase orders and may result in greater discounts, but as with other packaged deals of multiple titles, not all the resources are useful to the clientele so savings might not be as great as supposed. Therefore, such packaged deals should be scrutinized carefully.

As with any other library collection order, librarians need to keep a copy of the purchase order and subsequent communication (e.g., out-of-stock and back orders) for accuracy and date stamps, noting any special handling. When the order arrives, librarians need to check the packing slip or other fulfillment document (say for digital materials) to make sure it matches the received product; they should also inspect the physical state of the item since occasionally the resource might have printing problems (e.g., missing pages or wrong cover) or be physically damaged. If processing is included as part of the purchase, then each item needs additional inspection for those details such as the call number, correct barcode, security magnet, and covering. In any case, any shipping material needs to be saved until all the items therein are accounted for, especially since some vendors will accept returns only in the original container.

Part of the purchase order process may include options for processing, which can be worth the price for busy librarians or systems that do not provide central processing. Vendors who provide this added service typically provide a specifications profile template to stipulate how to handle each item. Even if you do not choose to use this service, completing and keeping such a profile document helps to systemize and standardize processing. A couple of templates to use are https://www.mackin.com/hq/wp-content/uploads/mackin-spec-form_10-19-20.pdf and https://www.perma-bound.com/static//forms-and-flyers/Library_Processing_US_2014.pdf.

Acquiring Digital Resources

Increasingly, librarians are replacing print reference resources with digital ones and acquiring digital resources, which usually means that the library can provide access to the resource but does not own the resource. Therefore, if the access subscription lapses or is canceled, the library is left with nothing. Nevertheless, acquiring digital reference resources sounds great:

content timeliness, remote access, greater accessibility, saving of shelf space—and sometimes computer space if saved in the cloud. However, there are several caveats. Just because a digital resource can be updated quickly does not mean that it will be. In addition, digital reference resources are more likely to be dynamic; that is, content may change at any time so that one's favorite entry might change or disappear without notification. Occasionally, remote services "crash" because of power outages, viruses, or other disasters. Remote access requires additional authentication and is not available if the user does not have the equipment and connectivity to access the resources; furthermore, some licenses restrict access to one user at a time. Some digital resources are pdf files, which might not be universally accessible or might not be customizable for easier viewing. Nor can librarians assume that digital resources are cheaper than print ones; in fact, some licenses state that the library has to resubscribe or "buy" another copy after a certain number of uses online. Even the issue of access may be problematic; how will the library catalogue or otherwise organize and make available digital reference resources? Interlibrary loans and other sharing of the content may also be restricted since the "first sale doctrine" does not apply to access-only subscriptions. In short, each license agreement needs to be carefully scrutinized and negotiated, especially because each vendor has a unique contract. More fundamentally, several reference publishers are moving to digital-only format so there is not an option to acquire some titles in a print version.

Dealing with Vendors

Vendors are business people; they want to make a profit. Even though it would seem that digital resources would be cheaper because there are fewer printing and shipping costs, but they are counterbalanced by more technical processing and labor costs. Vendors also need to comply with intellectual property law, which entails paying authors royalties each time a resource is accessed. Nevertheless, vendor quality and service vary, so librarians need to evaluate the vendor as much as the reference resource itself.

- What is their financial stability?
- Does the vendor own the data itself or just its compilation and organization? Where is the service located?
- What is their reputation in terms of long-term product and service record?
- What is their governance, decision-making process, and transparency?
- What is their technical quality in terms of access, usability, security, and technical support?
- What are their support services, and what is their quality: contacts, communication, documentation, training, and help desk?
- What is their cost-effectiveness? Is the library getting its money worth?

License Agreements

The term "digital rights management" refers to the use of technology to control and manage access to copyrighted materials. As noted earlier, one of the challenges of subscribing to digital reference resources is negotiating the license agreement, which specifies the costs, timeframe, rights, and responsibilities associated with accessing and using the vendor's/grantor's product and services. Also noted is the fact that each agreement is unique, although most agreements address common factors. Therefore, librarians need to consider several details as they review and negotiate this kind of contract.

- What does the vendor own: the data itself, the data compilation, the data organization, and the retrieval tools?
- What is the scope, extent (e.g., citation and full-text), and formats of the content? Are they universally accessible?
- Where are the data and services held?
- Who manages the digital rights?
- What are the usage rights in terms of number of simultaneous users and time frame of use?
- What is the cost basis: number of potential or actual users, number of hits, number of uses?
- What are the services and the quality of those services? Are they included in the base service contract or required additional cost?
- What are the browsing and searching features? How easy are they to use?
- What file transfer features are available?
- What cross-database features and rights are available, include interlibrary loan?
- What are their technical features: system requirements, platform availability, IP options, access protocols, authentication, security, privacy, and support?
- What are the access parameters and protocols?
- What training and support are available, and what is the additional cost, if any?
- What data and statistics are available?
- How customable is the database interface?
- What are warranties and indemnities conditions?

PROCESSING

How will reference resources be classified and catalogued? Will digital resources be catalogued? MARC metadata needs to include a subject indicator in the 600s fields (e.g., atlases) and a designation of REF (reference) in the call number, which is usually indicated in the MARC 852 field for holdings information ($k call number prefix). Particularly when a children's non-fiction chapter book is labeled as a reference work because of its usage, librarians need to add analytics in the catalogue record to optimize search results. Depending on the integrated library management system (ILMS) and vendor, individual ebooks and databases (and sometimes the articles therein) may be catalogued to provide one-step discovery. An easier solution for the librarian is to provide a link to a digital resource list web page within their library portal, which does entail possible added training for the user to access.

As with other print materials, reference books need to be marked and labeled for easy identification and retrieval (e.g., a red stripe or REF label). Reference materials must stand up to heavy usage, so preventative measures such as reinforced spine and corner protection should be done. Dust jackets also provide protection.

As for digital reference resources, librarians need to install and test those resources before they are accessed by their users. Furthermore, authentication, proxy server setup, and supported protocols need to be set up and tested ahead of time. From the starting date (which should be noted), all equipment should be tagged and inventoried. Installed software should also be inventoried. Security software should be installed to minimize viruses, hacking, and occasional file- and program-deletion accidents. To prevent theft, desktop computers and their peripherals should be locked down.

ORGANIZATION

How are materials organized and arranged in the library? Most libraries have a ready reference area, usually close to the R&I service desk. In elementary schools or children's section, librarians might consider having some of the reference sources such as Wilson's core collection titles placed behind the R&I for easy retrieval, but that placement limits access by educators and other adults who seek that information. Even less convenient is backroom, office, or even off-site storage of little-used reference materials; such decisions need to be carefully considered, and policies should be developed to ensure equitable access. Increasingly, many reference resources such as multivolume sets are being shelved with the general collection to foster more use.

As for shelf arrangement, most libraries arrange materials by call number. Occasionally, librarians may have an oversized shelf for very large materials such as large art books. Similarly, libraries may have an atlas stand or a dictionary stand to facilitate material handling. Similarly, sometimes non-print reference materials such as videos or realia (e.g., globes) might be located on separate shelves, again, close to the rest of the reference materials. These specialized areas should be located by the core collection. Sometimes reference pamphlets or booklets are stored in vertical files, although they could just as easily be placed in Princeton files and then interfiled with the rest of the reference collection, which would optimize their access.

In the final analysis, librarians need to help youth navigate the library and its holding, even to the point of explaining reference materials and their role in information seeking.

One reason to shelve all reference materials in one area is that interfiling reference sources in the general collection may confuse users who try to borrow those volumes only to find out that the materials are for in-house use only. To address that issue, some libraries permit overnight or two-to-three-day check-outs. Another reference circulation option is teacher check-out, the idea being that the entire class can use the materials in the classroom during the research project. A variation of teacher check-out is department check-out for cross-class access. The risk with that practice is that sometimes one or more volumes in a set might get lost, and it may be hard to replace those missing volumes or even pay for replacements. Sadly, students have been known to steal reference materials and even try to remove all the library labeling to hide their theft. Furthermore, if students are likely to have an assignment that draws upon a specific reference resource, then if those volumes are not returned in a timely manner (sometimes deliberately to advantage a competitive user) or are lost, the rest of the class(es) suffers. In those cases, librarians sometimes establish a reserve shelf for temporary in-house use, which optimizes access, especially if more than one class is likely to use the resources.

MAINTENANCE

As with other print items, reference materials need to be kept in good physical condition so that they stay attractive and useable. To that end, library workers should peruse reference shelves regularly to look for spine damages and other signs of wear so repairs can be made quickly. As noted earlier, items that are likely to be handled frequently may need added reinforcement or need to be placed on stands or separate surfaces (e.g., the top of counter-height shelving) for easier manipulation. Indeed, more spacious libraries sometimes put all of their reference collection on counter-height shelves.

Maintenance issues are more likely to target equipment used to access digital reference materials. Cords and cables should be out of sight to prevent possible pullouts. Keyboards can get dirty quickly, so ideally should be wiped daily. Likewise, monitors should be wiped weekly, and computers should be disc-scanned weekly. Computers should be cleaned annually. When equipment needs troubleshooting and repairs, those actions should be noted in the inventory; this practice can help signal defective equipment and otherwise provide the basis for equipment replacement. Software should be updated as necessary, although most software is now cloud based, and updates are usually automatically signaled. In any case, the library's ILMS should be backed up nightly. The following website provides valuable checklists and tips for computer maintenance: https://us.norton.com/internetsecurity-how-to-computer-maintenance.html, https://www.process.st/checklist/computer-maintenance-guide-2/, and https://www.techlila .com/computer-maintenance-tips/.

Reference-related maintenance also involves risk management. Even with the best intentions, natural disasters can strike: hazardous weather, fire, earthquakes and volcanoes, and biological agents (e.g., microorganisms, insects, and vermin). Man-made disasters can also occur: building deficiencies, power failures, water leaks, vandalism, fire, explosions, and chemical spills.

Even lighting, temperature, humidity, and storage practice can damage reference materials. Risk assessment is the first step: identifying possible hazards, determining the library's vulnerability and impact, and monitoring risks. To that end, libraries should survey their neighborhood, their building, and the collection for their physical conditions, safety practices (e.g., fire detection and suppression and alarm systems), and vulnerability to disaster. American Institute for Conservation and the Foundation for Advancement in Conservation have several useful risk assessment tools: https://www.culturalheritage.org/resources/emergencies/ risk-evaluation-and-planning-program.

What happens when emergencies occur and disasters strike? As a librarian, you should develop and maintain an emergency plan to help you act quickly and appropriately. For instance, how valuable is your reference collection and associated equipment? How easy and how expensive would it be to replace them? The answers to these questions can help you prioritize your actions in case of an emergency. The California Preservation Program has a template for writing a library disaster plan (https://calpreservation.org/wp-content/ uploads/2015/10/CPTF-Disaster-Plan-Generic-2003.doc), and the National Park Service has a useful primer to help plan for, salvage, and care for library resources (https://www.nps.gov/

museum/publications/primer/primintro.html). Another excellent source of free resources to guide library collection conservation is the Northeast Document Conservation Center (https://www.nedcc.org/free-resources/overview).

DESELECTION

The same criteria exist for reference withdrawals as for the rest of the collection: wear and other physical deterioration, outdated information, available newer replacement editions, lack of use, lack of relevance, and inappropriate reading level. Occasionally, a worn volume is worth rebinding if no other copy or similar resource can replace it. Usually, digitizing the volume is not cost-effective for many libraries, and they may run into copyright infringement issues. Librarians should keep an eye on reviews of new reference editions to find out if enough changes warrant replacement; sometimes it makes more sense to buy a different resource that covers approximately the same content. Johnson (2018) suggested some weeding timeframes for specific types of references:

- Almanacs: yearly
- Encyclopedias: five years
- Atlases: five years
- Dictionaries: five to ten years (depending on the subject)
- Computers (to access resources): four years (for client computers for simple access that timeline can be extended, depending on the RAM and possible plug-ins that are needed when digital resources are updated)

In those cases, where the information is still accurate, such as in some sections of an atlas, the item that is replaced by the newest edition may be reassigned to the general collection or given to a teacher for classroom use. In the latter situation, the volume needs to be formally withdrawn from the library catalogue inventory, with all library markings removed if possible. On the other hand, reference materials that are removed because of inaccuracies (e.g., new countries) should not be given to others; such practices would result in misinformation perpetuated by the library. The following websites provide useful guidance when weeding the reference collection:

https://www.tsl.texas.gov/sites/default/files/public/tslac/ld/pubs/crew/crewmethod08.pdf

https://cdstacked.blogspot.com/2013/01/tips-for-weeding-your-reference.html

https://help.oclc.org/Library_Management/GreenGlass/Weeding_and_deselection_bibliography?sl=en

ASSESSMENT

It should be noted that at every step in the life cycle, librarians need to assess the individual resources in light of the entire library collection and the community that they support. For instance, decisions about acquisitions need to assess the current collection and its use (including in-house use), user needs, budget, space, and vendors. Processing assessment involves cataloguing decisions based on existing resources and possible new ILMS features as well as processing costs, including staff and turn-around time. Organization of reference resources requires assessing facility and online use. Circulation policies and procedures need to assess availability and convenience of access as well as security and loss of inventory. Maintenance and deselection involve assessing the use and physical condition of resources, replacement costs, and risk of damage. At each step, associated procedures and policies need to be assessed for their effectiveness and efficiency. More fundamentally, assessment through the life cycle has to consider the users' satisfaction, based on the use of statistics, observation, anecdotes, interviews, focus groups, surveys, and outcomes such as self-efficacy and achievement.

Of course, assessment is its own first step as librarians need to analyze the assessment data, make conclusions and recommendations based on the findings, and then plan and implement targeted actions that improve the reference life cycle. As noted in previous chapters, librarians should start with their community as they assess R&I services and then examine their own resources and services.

The prior chapter focused on selecting high-quality reference resources and provided recommendations for core reference collections. The needs assessments help select which resources to add to the existing collections, what extant materials need to be reconsidered and may be withdrawn, and what reference resource gaps remain to be addressed.

Assessing the reference collection as a whole may be approached in several ways (Johnson, 2018), as shown in figure 4.2.

1. Quantitative collection-centered assessment: using statistical data such as collection size and growth, budget size and growth, title:user ratio, benchmarking holdings to comparable libraries, and state/national library standards.
2. Qualitative collection-centered assessment: checking comparable library's catalogues and bibliographies to compare collection titles and mapping the reference collection by subject area to identify the relative depth of coverage.
3. Quantitative user-centered assessment: using statistical data such as circulation and in-house use, interlibrary loan statistics, Internet "hits" and download statistics, cost per use, and user research paper citation analysis.
4. Qualitative user-centered assessment: user observation, surveys, focus groups, interviews, and suggestion input (e.g., via box, binder, and social media); reference collection mapping to school curriculum and assignment use.

When all these approaches are used, the librarian has on hand a rich set of data points that can inform and justify collection development planning to stakeholders.

1. 1K print reference titles out of 25K collection titles; 1 ref. title/1K students; $5K budget that is decreasing; average © date 20 years old; % of reference titles comparable to local libraries; provides state-funded databases, but has no reference web page in the library web portal.

2. Reference collection largest and oldest in 800s & 900s, thinnest in 500s & 600s; titles are comparable to local libraries but deficient compared to TitleWave and Blue Ribbon Award winners.

Evaluation:

Create a reference webpage with free reference resources, focus on adding new science references & core Spanish references, week outdated 900s; increase instruction and outreach.

3. Reference collection used only in-house; history & art assignments use collection the most; science uses Internet & database (ProQuest) the most; sample student research papers indicate online sources and circulating books the most.

4. Reference collection used when classes visit the library and librarian instructs (history & art); English curriculum focuses on close reading; Spanish teachers want references in their language.

FIGURE 4.2

Four-Way Reference Collection Evaluation. SOURCE: CREATED BY THE AUTHOR

Food for Thought: Resource Sharing

Reference sources can be expensive. Libraries can leverage their budgets by acquiring and sharing materials collectively. Resource sharing can also serve as a solution when storage space is tight. Which of the following strategies might be beneficial—and feasible—for your setting?

For instance, most states pay for at least one aggregator database to be accessed by public school libraries. School districts and library systems (both single and multitype) do joint purchase orders as a way to get deep discounts on print and digital resource materials. In addition, some school libraries within a district, or within close geographic proximity, collectively do reference collection development and divide reference areas by curriculum specialty among the sites so that one school might focus on the arts and another might concentrate on science-specific reference materials. A joint index of reference sources, or simply the use of union online catalogs, helps librarians keep track of other sites' holdings, although it is a good professional practice to notify participating libraries about new acquisitions so they can be better informed when making their own purchasing decisions.

When an information need cannot be fulfilled at one site, the library staff can contact the site with a deeper reference collection to get the information. With scanners and faxes, this service can be an effective alternative to purchasing a seldom-used reference volume. Materials might even be loaned between sites. Of course, copyright needs to be observed; if an item is required multiple times, that is probably a good indication that the borrowing library needs to acquire its own copy of the resource. Especially for database resources, librarians need to check license agreement details to determine if such copy-sharing complies with the contract agreement. Indeed, when those agreements are initiated, library systems that routinely participate in interlibrary loan (ILL) services should negotiate ILL options before signing such agreements.

Of particular interest is resource sharing that allows federated searching across databases. In this scenario, each library might subscribe to one unique database aggregator with the license agreement that includes the full text of the cited sources. They could then subscribe to additional aggregator databases at the citation-only level. All the libraries in the system would pay for an OpenURL link resolver such as SFX that would enable users to retrieve the full article from the database aggregator located at another library within the system. Again, this practice requires careful license agreement negotiations as well as determining if such cross-database source retrieval is technically feasible.

One promising practice is termed "floating collections." As a beginning effort, librarians— especially in school districts—can coordinate with their teachers to schedule major projects such that a deep subject-specific reference collection can circulate among schools as those topics are addressed in the classroom. This practice works best when subject teachers within the district can coordinate their schedules accordingly. In this scenario, school librarians in the district can then collaboratively select and purchase reference materials that they would not be able to get at their one site. The funding for these floating collections could then come from district budgets, taking just a small percentage from site budgets to maximize the joint acquisition that can benefit all sites. Public libraries typically practice another version of a floating collection whereby a requested book from a borrowing library branch stays at that branch rather than being returned to the lending library, and that item is then circulated to the next requesting user in the system (Saponaro & Evans, 2019). This practice can increase circulation and reduce the need for multiple purchases within the system. However, this practice does not work as well for reference resources, especially if user needs occur simultaneously.

Resource sharing also optimizes collection conservation, preservation, and storage. For instance, if libraries have little space, they might consider providing a common storage facility to house important but little used reference materials. In addition, as libraries weed reference collections, they can ensure that one copy is saved in storage if appropriate. Similarly, librarians can coordinate emergency plans and supplies to help each other in terms of disasters through off-site recovery areas and temporary space. Librarians can collaboratively acquire digitalization equipment and contract preservation services as needed.

In any case, another benefit of resource sharing is joint training and troubleshooting. Vendors appreciate conducting one-time training for multiple sites, and librarians appreciate the fact that their peers are getting the same information, which can facilitate later mutual support. Vendors might also assign one point person to support the group, thereby building a more informed relationship within the region.

These resource-sharing practices require up-front time and effort to coordinate logistics and other planning details. How will funding be handled? What happens when a site abuses the services? What if a site administration does not agree to joint resources and spending? First, the librarians and their institutions have to see the benefits of resource sharing before any action can occur; in some cases, some compelling advocacy might be in order. Next, site librarians and associated staff need to have the skills and capacity to participate in resource sharing, even at the point of preparing and transporting the resources themselves.

All the librarians and their institutions probably need to develop and agree to memos of understanding for creating policies and procedures to resolve issues of governance, decision-making processes, budgets, resources, resource life cycle, processes, and accountability. Therefore, before you as a librarian jump into resource sharing, you should consider the options and efforts needed to determine the optimum return on investment.

REFERENCES

Johnson, P. (2018). *Fundamentals of collection development and management* (4th ed.). American Library Association.

Saponaro, M., & Evans, G. (2019). *Collection management basics* (7th ed.). Libraries Unlimited.

FURTHER READING

Alvarez, B. (2015, January 2). Shelf life: The balancing act between physical and digital books. *Public Libraries Online*. http://publiclibrariesonline.org/2015/01/shelf-life-the-balancing-act-between-physical-and-digital-books/

Goldsmith, F. (2015). *Crash course in weeding library collections*. Libraries Unlimited.

Mardis, M. (2020). *The collection program in schools: Concepts and practices* (7th ed.). Libraries Unlimited.

Moran, B., & Morner, C. (2017). *Library and information center management* (9th ed.). Libraries Unlimited

Newsum, J. M. (2016). School collection development and resource management in digitally rich environments: An initial literature review. *School Libraries Worldwide, 22*(1), 97–109.

Pattee, L. (2020). *Developing library collections for today's young adults: Ensuring inclusion and access* (2nd ed.). Rowman & Littlefield.

Wilkinson, F., Lewis, L., & Lubas, R. (2015). *The complete guide to acquisitions management*. Libraries Unlimited.

Access

Reference materials are worthwhile only if they are accessed. This chapter dives deeper into access issues at each step of the reference life cycle, particularly in light of young people. In today's world, the options—and issues—are greatly expanded. Therefore, both physical and virtual access are addressed.

PHYSICAL ACCESS STARTING WITH THE USER

Getting access to the information you want in the library can be trickier than you might think.

First, imagine yourself as a fourth-grade student. You are supposed to compare the anatomy of an earthworm and a caterpillar, including an image of each animal's cross-section. The library is closed after school, and your parents don't have a car to drive to the public library, which is 3 miles away. The only computer in the house is a cell phone, and the screen is so small that you can't make out the details of the images. Fortunately, you can get to school early, and the library is open; otherwise, you would be stuck. The library has six computers, but they are already being used. You know that the library has encyclopedias, and looking around, you see where there are some multivolume sets that seem promising. You look up the two animals, and you find a picture of cross-section of an earthworm but not of a caterpillar. You go to the library's catalogue and type the animal names with no success, then you type in "animals" and there are too many titles. Time is getting short. You ask the librarian for help, and he shows you the animal encyclopedia set and points out the need to use the index volume in order to find the animals. He explains what the Roman and Arabic numerals mean (III = volume 3, and *45* in italics means an image). Success! But the books can't be checked out, and there's not enough time to draw the pictures. Fortunately, you see a photocopier, but you also see a slot to put in money. There goes part of your lunch money, but it is worth it to make a copy of the pages by class time.

Next, imagine yourself as a middle schooler. It is the last class of the day, and the teacher reminds the students that they need to hand in a bibliography of the resources that they are going to use for their research report on local native plants: no more than two online resources. You have 15 minutes between classes to dash to the library because you have to take a bus to get home after school. You quickly type in California plants in the catalogue and find two titles, but they are not on the shelf. You ask the librarian, only to find out that they are checked out. You can probably copy down the citations, but there is no guarantee you can get your hands on them in time to submit the report by the deadline. Fortunately, the librarian mentions that the reference shelf includes a field guide to North American wildflowers so the book will always be available and gives you the call number, pointing to the reference area. You rush to the book-shelf and flip through the book. The flowers are arranged by plant family, and it is hard to fig-ure out where the plants are located; nevertheless, when you have a little time, you can use the book, so you copy down the citation and the call number so you can find the title again. Now that you know about reference books staying in the library, when you get home, you go online to the local public library's catalogue, type in California wildflowers (since you have decided to narrow down the topic), and you find there is a reference book on San Francisco Bay area wildflowers. Bingo! You check that the library is open on Saturday so you can take a bus to get there. Once you get to the library, you're not sure where the reference collection is. First you try the teen section because you are not a child, but it is hard to find. You ask a person who is shelving books, and they say it's the room next to the bathrooms on the second floor. But there is no reference collection. You guess, rightly, that the reference area you need is in the adult area near the adult's reference desk, which is a bit intimidating. There you find the book, and it is just what you need. You take a few pictures with your smartphone, hoping that the battery will last. When you get home (after waiting for the bus a half hour because it is on the weekend schedule), you do a Google search, which provides some relevant hits. You are happy that you can hand in an OK bibliography and have a start on the research you have to do as well.

You've grown! Now imagine yourself as a high school senior. You have been accepted into your first-choice college, but there is a matter of finances. Your drama teacher announces a state drama competition with the theme "Drama for Democracy." It involves reciting a mono-logue from a play on the topic, and the winner gets a $1,000 scholarship. You are psyched! But how are you going to find a good monologue, and in time, since the competition is in two weeks? The Internet lists mainly speeches, not play excerpts. You check the school library's catalogue with no success; there are some sections that include plays, but none jumped out at you, and you don't have time to read a bunch of plays and the public library doesn't seem to have anything either. You ask the school librarian, and she mentions the *Play Index*, which is a reference series that locates plays and even monologues by several factors, including themes. She thinks it is available at the local university, and she checks online to make sure. You check to see when the university library is open, and you get a friend to drive you there. You look up the title, but the call number is strange: PN1655.P539. What does that mean? You go to the front desk, and they say that the library is arranged by the Library of Congress classification system. They briefly explain how that works, so you go to wander through the stacks and can't find them. You go down to the front desk again, and they point to the reference room around the corner. There you find the volumes. Sure enough, you find a couple of monologues on democracy, and it lists the play, but the library doesn't have the play according to the catalogue so you are stumped. Crossing your fingers, you go with index in hand to the reference desk where the librarian is helping someone so you wait, hoping your friend isn't too impatiently waiting. The librarian becomes available, and he shows you that plays are also available in anthologies, listed elsewhere in the index, but the library doesn't have the one you want; it is available at a metropolitan public library a couple of hours away. Again, you are stumped. The librarian says you can interlibrary loan it (and explains how to do that), but when he finds out that you are a high school student, he says that you can't use that service—but that your school librarian can provide that service. Thank goodness your school has a librarian! (although the university librarian says that the public librarian can also provide that service). You copy down all the information; you are armed to go to the library at lunchtime, since it isn't open before school, and get that service. The school librarian compliments you on your efforts and says it will probably take a week, but since it is a monologue, the borrowing library can probably scan the pages and email them more quickly. It's taken much more time to locate and access the monologue than to memorize the monologue, but you figure that most high schoolers wouldn't have gone to all this trouble, so there might be fewer competitors, which increases your odds to win. And you already have a head start on how a university library works so you have added self-confidence for next year's college experience. Bravo for you!

Each of these young people was successful, but it wasn't easy for them, and these were go-getter students with some library smarts, as well as a librarian or two to help. Several factors had to be in place for them to get the access they needed: enough time to go through the steps to access the information, some content knowledge, a computer/device with Internet connectivity and a sizeable screen, knowledge about different kinds of libraries, an open library—when they could go to it, transportation to get to the library, a library catalogue that they could access, knowledge of the library catalogue's navigation and operation, knowledge of library classification systems, knowledge of reference sections and policies about reference use, access to a printer or photocopier (and usually money to print a document), knowledge of reference sources and how they are organized, ability to locate a library worker who can help—and the ability to ask appropriate questions, citation skills, and knowledge about borrowing from other libraries through interlibrary loan.

What about other young people? What if they don't plan enough lead time—and the persistence—to access the information they need? What if they have little background knowledge? What if they don't have relatives or other adults to help? What if they have never used the library to find information? What if they get lost in a large library and can't figure out how it is organized? What if no one showed them how to use a library? What if they use key words that are not recognized in the library catalogue and database? What if there is no librarian—or the librarian is not available (or worse yet, the librarian is not knowledgeable or helpful)? What if there is little space to use the material while at a computer, such as tiny surface work surfaces? What if they use a wheelchair and the aisles are too narrow or the sources are too high? What if the type is too small to read comfortably or the vocabulary is too difficult? What if they have visual impairments? What if they need assistive technology to read or view the material? What if they don't speak or read in the available languages?

Librarians also need to consider the social aspects of access. Students are often asked to do group projects so the library needs to provide group working spaces so students can examine materials together. This joint access is particularly important with regard to physical access to digital resources. Even in the face of one computer per child, children may work together online. Therefore, each computer station should have enough table surface to accommodate two chairs and school supplies for two students.

Too often the library is configured and organized for the library workers' convenience rather than for the user. It is easy to complain when one has to adapt to a technology tool rather than the technology tool adapting to the user, but sometimes librarians forget that this complaint might be analogous to young people's perceptions of libraries. The general rule is to approach access issues with the mindset of the user. Identify ways to facilitate access. Identify possible barriers and ways to lower them. Ideally, you should interview users, and have them walk through their process of accessing reference materials with you to identify "stuck points" or bottleneck situations (e.g., inadequate signage, queues to computers, and reference desk staffing gaps). Teenagers, especially, should be involved in planning how to improve access to reference materials: be it extending operating hours, providing an inclusive learning environment, reconfiguring reference collection and use of work space, improving signage (including LARGE font, raised Braille characters, and information in users' languages), reconsidering policies about reference circulation and fines, encouraging input for reference collection development, optimizing access to high-demand reference materials for assignments, expanding wifi connectivity, providing more Internet-connected computers, providing more outlets and charging stations, improving the portal and catalogue interface—and ensuring that they are mobile-friendly and Americans with Disabilities Act (ADA)-compliant, offering online reference access tutorials and real-time online reference help, troubleshooting access problems, facilitating getting public library cards, and working more closely with teachers and other libraries to maximize access.

VIRTUAL ACCESS

Increasingly, libraries use online sources to provide timely reference information. Indeed, talking about a library's collection can be misleading in that today's libraries increasingly focus as much on subscription-based access as they do on ownership, certainly for reference materials. Academic libraries, for instance, are likely to budget more for subscriptions than for print materials overall. Quite frankly, most youth do not realize the cost of those subscriptions; they just want the information in the format that works for them. Even the idea of purchasing a DVD copy of reference resources is outdated so most publishers store their products "in the cloud," using either static IP addresses or login procedures for users to access those products. Therefore, both on-site and remote virtual access has become the normal practice.

In that respect, digital reference materials may be more attractive to youth because e-resources are likely to be accessed from home, they may be timelier, they may be easier to search through, and they are easier to copy-paste. On the other hand, digital resources also reveal digital inequities. While some schools provide devices for every student, other schools have computer labs or movable carts of laptops. Both school and public library computer inventory may range from a handful of computers to a couple of computer labs; some libraries also allow users to borrow laptops. If a young person has limited access to—or no—Internet-enabled devices at home and limited or no Internet connectivity, then they have to rely on neighborhood resources for out-of-school time access, which may also be limited or fee-based. In some cases, especially since the pandemic, public agencies have installed more community wiki hotspots, which helps lower one digital barrier, but many rural areas are still under-connected. In some communities, libraries are the sole public place that provides Internet connectivity, computers, and digital resources for free, hopefully with convenient operating hours. In that respect, the pandemic significantly hurt young people who had to learn from home and could not even go to the library because of lockdowns.

Accessibility

Having access to an Internet-connected device does not guarantee access to the library's e-resources. Library equipment, software, and files that are available to the public, particularly if the library is a public agency, must be in compliance with the Americans with Disabilities Act (ADA). Libraries should have accessible procurement review policies and procedures that follow Sections 504 and 508 guidelines that align with the Web Content Accessibility Guidelines (WCAG) 2.0 AA (https://www.w3.org/TR/WCAG20/). Fortunately, authoring tools such as MS Office and Adobe Acrobat have built-in accessibility checking features, with tips on how to make digital documents accessible. The U.S. government General Services Administration has useful guidelines on building accessibility into the procurement process (https://www.section508.gov/blog/Building-Accessibility-into-your-Procurement-Process/).

At least one computer station for every thirty stations should have optimum accessible features such as an adjustable table and seating, and the computer should have a large monitor, trackball, accessible keyboard (e.g., raised letters or larger keys), and other assistive technology peripherals such as scanners and assistive technology software (e.g., JAWS, Voiceover, Dragon Naturally Speaking, Kurzweil products, and Read and Write Out Loud). At the least, a regular computer scanner with OCR (optical character recognition) software can be used in conjunction with the computer's built-in text-to-speech program. These dedicated computers can also have installed free programs such as Rewordify, which simplifies text to make it easier to understand, and TalkTyper, which is a simple online dictation tool. Built-in computer operating settings can also be adjusted to increase accessibility, such as their "ease of access" options, such as speed and size of cursors/pointers, magnifier tool, high contrast screen, keyboard and mouse shortcuts, and screen reading.

In terms of remote access, for many youth the only such device is a smartphone, and many libraries do not check to make sure their databases, catalogues, and even their library portals are mobile-friendly, as well as being universally accessible. For that reason, website frames and tables should be avoided, lists should be bulleted or numbered, and all images need alternative text. Several websites can check for ADA compliance. The following websites provide valuable advice.

- https://libguides.ala.org/libservice-disability/General-Overview
- http://www.usability.gov/how-to-and-tools/index.html
- http://www.w3.org/WAI/gettingstarted/, especially the section on evaluating accessibility

Library Portals

A library portal offers the most convenient and efficient way to provide access to digital reference sources. Most youth-serving libraries maintain a library portal, which often serves as the library's "front door" and provides access points to resources and some services; it often sets the tone for the user's experience. At the least, the integrated library management system (ILMS) can serve that purpose with its online public access catalogue (OPAC). Even if the library catalogue and databases can be accessed only on-site, the library portal can provide access to generally available relevant reference sources as well as offer information service in the form of research guides.

Most library portals include the following information:

- Library location, hours, and staff contact information
- Library services and procedures
- Link to the library catalogue (which sometimes serves at the library portal)
- Links to library databases
- Links to library social media sites
- Links to other libraries
- Library news

Other features include bibliographies and pathfinders such as LibGuides, new acquisitions, reviews, R&I blogs or wikis, citation style help, research guidance, reference help, reference FAQs, web tutorials, Internet safety tips, library contests, R&I apps (e.g., the fact of the day, the weather of the day, the day's newspaper articles, and online map tools), group visit scheduling calendar, R&I video or webinar archives, translation tool, alternative interface for ADA compliance, and links to the rest of the overarching institution or agency as well as to counterpart libraries. In addition, the library portal should provide the youth community with ways to participate, such as interest polls, and ways to contribute, such as reference website recommendations and sample youth products related to R&I services. The school library's web portal should also showcase the librarian's instructional role: through research guidance, reference help, and online tutorials.

Youth-serving librarians should also consider incorporating web conferencing options in order to provide a richer R&I experience to individuals or groups at the point of need.

Whiteboard and sharing features can enable the librarian to give presentations, demonstrate useful websites, or even show actual pages from print reference sources using a document camera. In addition, users can show their information issues for the librarian to help solve.

Even with the best resources and participatory potential, the library portal may be ignored if it is not well designed. In fact, website development now is often labeled user experience design. The overall appearance of the library portal should reflect the philosophy and approach of the library. For instance, an elementary school library portal might have bright colors and sans serif font, use simple vocabulary, provide family-friendly websites and videos, and include a parent web page. On the other hand, a high school library can look more sophisticated to convey a college-prep attitude, or the portal can use teen-generated graphics to invite student participation. In fact, some library portals such as youth-specific portal web pages or social media sites are designed by students themselves. In any case, it is a good idea to have teens pilot-test and review the library's portal to make sure it is clear, useful, and engaging.

In that respect, school library web portals have a relatively easy time explicitly addressing R&I because of their focused mission and clientele. In contrast, public libraries serve the entire community and have a broader mission. Many public libraries include separate web pages for children and teens, but even then they usually provide more programing so that R&I can get lost in the listings. Even if public library portals have a separate tab for education, they typically need to have a drop-down menu for different age groups, including adults. A good practice in these cases is to include links to different aspects of youth resources and services to optimize access to needed R&I. On the other hand, because schools act as loco parentis, school libraries have to incorporate filtering software, which may restrict access to many useful reference resources; public libraries have more freedom to link to a wider range of online reference resources.

In any case, the following criteria should be considered in optimizing access to the library web portal and its information.

- Content. Is all content accurate, relevant, and developmentally appropriate? Does the portal provide an accurate, engaging sense of library's program and the use of library web portal? Are all digital resources described adequately?
- Layout. Does the home page attract and engage the user? Are the web pages clear and organized? Does the order of the web pages seem logical? Do visual elements and text work well together effectively and esthetically? Do pages have a consistent look to facilitate finding the needed information?
- Navigation. Does a navigation bar guide the user to the relevant pages? Is it easy and logical to go from one page to another? Is it easy to keep track of consulted pages? Is there a help feature?
- Text. Is the text easy to read and comprehend? Is the writing engaging? Is the writing free of mechanical errors? Is the vocabulary developmentally appropriate? Is font use appropriate and consistent? Are library jargon and abbreviations kept to a minimum (e.g., ILL)?

- Technical aspects. Do all technical elements work properly in all browsers and typical devices, including mobile phones? Does the site make good use of hyperlinks? Do all links work? Do multimedia resources work properly?
- Accessibility. Does the library portal comply with ADA website standards?

It should be remembered that the most important aspect of the library web portal is information, so a clean, organized look without lots of graphics (especially animated ones) should be the goal. Especially since some families continue to have dial-up Internet access or use mobile devices to access the library portal, images should be kept to a minimum. A solid light-colored background can serve as a visual attraction. St. Mary's College of Maryland has a useful LibGuide on user experience design (https://libguides.smcm.edu/ux/libraries), which also includes recommended guidebooks to consult. Sabrina Unrein (2019) offers a thorough guide on the elements of a good library website (https://ischool.syr.edu/wp-content/uploads/2020/06/2019_What_Makes_a_Good_Library_Website.pdf).

Increasingly, librarians aim for community access to reference materials from school, home, or another remote site. This option is possible with dynamic IP addresses in conjunction with login and password procedures to authorize and authenticate eligible users. A good practice is to establish one login and password for all library digital reference products, if possible, through the library portal; that option may depend on the vendors' own set-up requirements. In any case, the login and password can be made available on library posters and handouts (such as bookmarks) and in the school newsletter. Librarians should NOT provide the login/password on the library portal; that information invites strangers to use the digital products, and the librarian could find himself or herself liable for contract agreement infringement. Especially if the license limits the number of simultaneous users, outsiders could well preempt rightful users from accessing the needed information.

It should also be noted that many libraries do not have control of the appearance or access parameters of the library portal but rather have to adopt the interface of their umbrella institution or agency. For these reasons, youth-serving librarians need to participate in decision-making processes when determining what website products and features to choose.

Catalogues

Library catalogues can be challenging for young people to use. While the library's OPAC may be regarded as just another online application for the Internet user, its scope is extremely limited compared to the Internet. Increasingly, the library home page features a single search "bar," paralleling most current search engines' default display. In the end, many young people wonder why not all library materials in full text cannot be accessed directly. As a result, young people may feel frustrated, or give up, when they find out that access to some reference materials requires an additional step or a different process within the library portal.

The first question is this: What reference resources are catalogued? Obviously, books are listed, but their entries might not include detailed analytics. Parsing reference ebooks from other ebooks is more problematic, but that issue can be solved with a searchable REF call number field designation. Typically, aggregator databases are handled similarly to a serial or continuous item. Some libraries catalogue multimedia products that serve as reference materials; other libraries merely provide a separate bibliography or web page of those sources. Some librarians catalogue individual reference websites as they would other reference resources, while others handle them as they do multimedia products. Regardless of their location, any item that might be considered to be on the reference "spectrum" should be thoroughly catalogued in order to facilitate its retrieval and use, particularly for school collections. Thus, features such as bibliographies and indexes, maps, charts, and tables should be noted. Here are some applicable MARC fields to consider using:

300: Illustrative matter

490: Series statement

500: General notes, such as the index, and description of the nature and scope of the item

504: Bibliography

505: Formatted contents notes (e.g., tables of content)

520: Summary

526: Curriculum-based study

590: Local notes

Sometimes librarians use a separate web page on the library portal to list digital reference resources such as encyclopedias and almanacs, especially if the library's OPAC does not have a way to link the full text easily within the search function. Additionally, most aggregator databases require a separate interface, which might not be linked with a small public or school library ILMS.

Fortunately, today's ILMSs have the capacity to provide the links to full-text reference products, not just the bibliographical information. For instance, libraries increasingly subscribe to online reference books and integrate them into their catalogue. However, ebooks may have confusing downloading and viewing processes. Indeed, idiosyncratic license agreements may hinder access altogether if a certain number of users access the same resource simultaneously, or a certain number of hits or downloads altogether have been reached, requiring librarians to repurchase access to the same material.

Follett's Destiny program has the flexibility of providing a separate menu for digital resources or combining all types of resources into one search field with the advantage of being linked to the database from the basic catalogue and then searching within that database. Some university libraries with high-end ILMSs now provide the capacity for users to truly do one-stop access; their key words generate entries *within* individual aggregator databases so that the user doesn't even have to decide which database to access. On the other hand, when students type in "Saturn," they may end up with 50,000 entries for all sorts of resources, resembling an overwhelming Google search.

On the other hand, most library catalogues seldom include a separate interface or vocabulary for children. For instance, the Library of Congress uses a different set of subject headings for children's literature (but not nonfiction titles). Some OPACs do not provide a children's interface version, and those who do may charge more for that extra feature, which impacts libraries' often limited budgets. Furthermore, even if separate interfaces are available, libraries usually have to "lock" the catalogue search page by interface type and separate adult OPAC computer stations from children's stations, in order to prevent confusion between patrons' usages. While most OPAC platforms with two or more interfaces try hard to make it obvious and easy to switch between them, young readers often do not have the ability to follow those directions.

New cataloguing standards such as RDA and BIBFRAME can help address vocabulary and searching limitations through linked data that can connect different aspects of a catalogue record. However, public and school libraries might not have the funding to acquire the newest ILMS versions, and even some ILMS vendors may be wary to update their products to emerging standards.

Nor do software developers, who are mainly adult males, design cataloguing products with youth as the main audience except for those systems targeted at school libraries. Even then, they tend not to focus just on primary grades, and teenagers typically do not want a "kiddie" interface. Furthermore, adults are likely to serve as catalogue mediators for youngsters, especially for emerging readers and youth who do not read in the dominant language. As noted earlier, linguistic differences can be a barrier to virtual access, including to the library catalogue. Even now, most school library OPACs are available only in English. One work-around is the use of a website translation tool (such as Google's app), but that requires one more skill for youngsters who find the basic catalogue hard enough as is to use.

Other Access Tools

Aggregator databases, as seen earlier, can pose access challenges for both the librarian and user. Most states in the United States pay for public and school library database subscriptions for at least a couple of aggregator databases such as Academic Search or eLibrary. These databases then are likely to be accessed via the state's portal, so the local library has to set up the protocols for login and linkage to the appropriate website. School districts and public library system may pay for database subscriptions across locales, so the same site-based issue of linkages have to be established; this problem is often sidestepped because these same districts or systems are likely to provide a union ILMS that incorporates the database access protocol. Nevertheless, even if these other sources of database subscriptions exist, a library might still subscribe to a unique aggregator database. If possible, all the databases should be accessed from one web page since the end user usually does not care where the database resides but just wants access to the specific information. Since a file or URL can be linked from several places within a website, librarians should err on the side of providing several access points as appropriate. If librarians want to emphasize the reference collection, they can include a link from the library portal home page to a reference webpage with the list of options: aggregator databases, reference physical and ebooks, and reference websites or directories.

It should be noted that young people like federated searching, that is, a one-stop search "box" that can search across databases. Sometimes libraries will subscribe to several aggregator databases but opt for different levels of access depending on the database. This situation arises because major vendors, or a vendor with several products, might have considerable resource overlap; because vendors tend to offer a package of resources rather than letting the library choose individual titles, the library may end up with a couple of aggregator databases from competing vendors that include the same sources. Rather than paying twice for the same periodical article, the librarian might subscribe to the full-text version of one major aggregator database and the citation-only version of another overlapping aggregator database. OpenURL link resolvers interface with these databases, enabling the user to access the targeted resource from any of the databases subscribed to. Ex Libris is the most widely used link resolver, and is fee-based; the Library of Congress Portals Applications Issues lists several other OpenURL resolver products and vendors (https://www.loc.gov/catdir/lcpaig/openurl.html). School libraries and smaller public librarians tend to subscribe to just a handful of aggregator databases, so this option is usually not used. Nevertheless, as ILMSs become more sophisticated, it is useful for librarians to keep abreast of such developments.

Website-specific reference resources demand separate attention in terms of access. Traditionally, libraries have provided a web page directory of linked reference websites, usually arranged by curricular subject. This practice reflects the concept of information organization by format. Alternatively, librarians can create their own customized search engines that include a list of library-identified reference websites from which to choose; the most popular generator is Google Custom Search Engine. This approach enables students to search across websites, much like other search engines, but is limited to curriculum-relevant and developmentally appropriate resources. While major reference-centric websites tend to have stable URLs, librarians still need to check them periodically to avoid broken links; this task sometimes can be delegated to library aides. Another option is to provide links to a few existing library reference directories, which lessens the maintenance burden. Representative reference directories follow, which are best used in libraries serving teens.

- American Library Association: http://gws.ala.org/category/reference-desk
- Internet Public Library: http://www.ipl.org/IPLBrowse/GetSubject?vid=13&tid=6996&parent=0
- Internet Library for Librarians: http://www.itcompany.com/inforetriever/index.htm
- Breitlinks: http://www.breitlinks.com/my_libmedia/online_ready_reference.htm
- Fact Monster: http://www.factmonster.com/

An interesting practice to facilitate access to reference materials is to use computer tablets, such as iPads, as point-of-need kiosks to point to subject-specific reference sources, FAQs, and pathfinders. For instance, a kiosk could be located by signs in the science area; this kiosk screen would provide links to science-related reference materials. Similarly, a QR code could be embedded in a subject-specific sign, serving as a one-stop website for science references.

PUBLIC RELATIONS

As mentioned already, the library can have the best collection of appropriate reference materials in various formats, which may be accessible on-site and virtually. However, that is no guarantee that youth will use them. Both physical and digital reference sources may be underutilized because of the community's lack of awareness, lack of time, their locale, disabilities, language issues, or intellectual issues. Furthermore, digital reference materials may be underutilized because of digital divide issues. So how can reference sources be promoted?

For instance, traditional questions of separate versus integrated shelving have resurfaced, especially in light of bookstore influence. Similarly, policies on circulating reference materials are debated. What cataloguing add-ons can enhance reference and information services? How can guides to resource use be provided and linked? How can a teacher get connected when assignments benefit from reference materials?

As with other parts of the library collections and services, R&I is based on community needs; the library acts as a bridge between people and information. Public relations (PR) is the relationship between the library and its community, which helps to maintain the library's reputation. PR is more than a handshake and a flyer. It represents long-term interaction and strategic communication. Some of the aspects of PR include the following:

- Promotion: communicating the library's value to the community.
- Marketing: matching the community's needs and interests with the library's resources and services.
- Advocacy: developing understanding and support from decision-makers for improvement.

Communication

Effective oral and written communication is a core skill for librarians as with other professionals. Libraries may have excellent resources and services, but if they are not well communicated, those resources and services will not be used much.

Let's look at how communication works. Communication is basically a relationship between two parties: one sending a message via a communications channel and the other receiving it. Here is how that cycle might occur in a library setting:

- Sender: Librarian
- Message: The library has new reference math books
- Coding: Book display with sign that says "Count on these new math reference books"
- Decoding: Library user sees the book display

- Noise (possible): Person doesn't go to the library; the library is closed; person can't or doesn't see the display; person ignores the display; person can't read the sign; person misunderstands the sign
- Feedback: Person uses one of the new reference books in the library; person points out display to others; others do not react to display (this example demonstrates missing the feedback loop, which is required for the sender to know if the message got through)

When developing a communications plan for children and teens, librarians should consider both the young people and their adult supporters, such as families, caregivers, educators, and other youth-serving agencies because adults can help connect the message to the young people, mitigating possible "noise." What means of communication are most used and valued by each set of stakeholders? Even a basic message about R&I probably needs to be customized to each population. For instance, when communicating directly with children and teens, librarians may need to modify the message content and channel by simplifying language, being more concrete, and changing the format, such as using more video or social media. These modifications may also apply to English learners and people with disabilities.

While communication occurs continuously, librarians should also develop a strategic and systematic plan for communicating in order to allocate staff and resources predictably and optimize library usage. For instance, many schools have seasonal research assignments, which can be leveraged by librarians in order to "advertise" associated reference materials for maximum, predictable participation. Starting new services, such as tutoring programs, need special attention to communications planning to help make the community aware of this new offering. Communications as a management function may be considered in light of a communications planning model:

- Determine the purpose, such as fostering news literacy through using news databases.
- Identify the target audience, such as high schoolers.
- Plan and design the message, such as techniques for comparing news source communicated through a workshop or online tutorial.
- Consider available library resources, such as knowledgeable and available staff, news articles within databases, computers, and handouts (to make using printer and paper).
- Consider available communications channels and match them with the message and the audience: library portal, library social media, flyers, newsletters, newspaper articles, radio announcements, television interviews, and school public service announcements.
- Plan for obstacles and emergencies, such as no Internet so printing out some articles.
- Strategize how to connect with others to spread the message, such as teachers and youth-serving agencies.
- Create an action plan, such as co-planning and coteaching a learning activity with a social studies teacher.
- Evaluate the degree and quality of student participation, effectiveness of planning and teaching, follow-up choice, and use of news sources from aggregator databases.

Marketing

Marketing is a structured process of communicating and exchanging valued offerings with the community. As with other aspects of library operations, librarians use marketing to match and optimize their reference resources and services with community needs and interests.

In order for youth-serving libraries to add value to their stakeholders (their market), librarians need to know what their libraries can offer in terms of products and services: its internal environment. Librarians also have to analyze the external environment to understand the issues that impact the library and its stakeholders: community socioeconomics, legal and political entities, and natural contexts.

The foundation for market and community analysis is a SWOT analysis (strength, weakness, opportunity, threat). In libraries, in-house S/W may arise from personnel, boards, support groups, facilities, money, collections, services, technology, user database, open hours, and so on. External issues (O/T) might be changing population demographics, competition by other youth programs, emerging technologies, political issues, government and agency situations, changing economic environment, new legal requirements, natural disasters, and so on.

Here is an example SWOT analysis for a public library.

- Strengths: experienced children's librarian, strong print reference collection, welcoming facility that can hold fifty people.
- Weaknesses: limited operating hours (10 a.m.–noon, 1–3 p.m.), no computers for children, collection is only in English.
- Opportunities: new group of library volunteers, schools are dealing with immigrant population, and library technology grant.
- Threats (challenges): rise in the number of non-English-speaking immigrants, immigrants' misperceptions about libraries, and lack of households with Internet connectivity.

Once the library staff know what they can offer, they can determine which market to target. If the library staff try to reach everyone, that approach is called mass marketing, and they try to find an issue or value that is the common denominator for everyone, such as R&I databases. Alternatively, the library staff can focus on a few key market segments (i.e., subgroups) to provide more specific services and resources. Librarians tend to segment markets by age or type of use such as preteens who want to volunteer in the library, art teachers, science-fiction fans. Typically, a library has reference resources or services that are underused or undervalued that they want to push. Perhaps they see a target user market potential that has ignored the library, such as homeschoolers. In general, libraries try to go for the best return on their investment of time, resources, and money.

Using the SWOT analysis above, the librarian might target the new immigrant population. Perhaps a couple of volunteers can serve as translators and can help in collection development. The new technology money can be used to buy computers, and the librarian can locate non-English and bilingual online resources to help the immigrant youth and families. The librarian will need to work with immigrant leaders and local schools to explain about public libraries.

Relationships

Librarians should strive for long-term relationships with their community. For youth-serving librarians, that includes not only direct relationships with children or teens but also adult stakeholders who interact with and impact young people. By establishing and nurturing meaningful professional relationships, librarians build a stronger and broader support base and can provide more relevant collections and services for the community.

Building such relationships takes time and effort. As a youth-serving librarian, you first need to do your own job well, trying to provide high-quality library reference resources and services based on community interests and needs. The latter point underscores the need to learn about your community and interact with them. As mutual comfort grows, you can do activities together that have a common goal, such as promoting reading. Successful efforts can lead to longer-term complex collaborative projects. You should also remember that relations may change because of situational changes in personal and professional lives. In general, though, the more compatible the users and the more significant the task and needs for diverse resources and skills, the more meaningful the relationship.

When building relationships with children and teens, librarians should remember developmental issues. Young people need to be respected and not talked down to. However, young people have less experience and less nuanced understanding. They are more likely to be more successful with short-term projects and clear concrete outcomes than with more abstract long-term initiatives.

More details about interactions and engagement are discussed later in the book.

Food for Thought: The Merits of Browsing

How browsable is your reference collection?

Fortunately, most youth-serving libraries are open access. Even then the reference section often gets lost in the shuffle. This phenomenon happens for several reasons: poor signage, location (such as trapped between other sections or tucked behind the circulation desk), physical appearance (e.g., overwhelming tomes, drab covers, and older copyright), and lack of explicit publicity about them.

When reference collections include a wide spectrum of titles, they might be used more, but the impact of the titles themselves might get diffused—or seem confusing. Especially if the reference collection does not circulate, young people may end up having less access to materials in the long run. On the other hand, a streamlined reference collection might lend itself to a greater number of quick queries but might also suffer from being overlooked if other reference-like materials are in the general collection; students tend to like one-stop searching.

Once the reference collection is visible and known, it is more likely to be browsed. Indeed, browsing is a good habit to reinforce because it helps users broaden their perspectives and link concepts together. In that respect, both arrangements of reference materials—inclusive and narrowly defined sections—have advantages: smaller references can lead to more cross-disciplinary browsing and greater cross-over between reference materials and other titles in the general part of the collection, while big reference collection highlights the range of reference materials and optimizes the availability of reference titles in any given subject. Fortunately, the Dewey Decimal Classification system, which public and school libraries employ, also reinforces browsing habits because similar topics are likely to be close to each other. Shelf-specific labels, such as "science" or "biographies" can also facilitate quick perusal when browsing.

Rice, McCreadie, and Chang (2001) developed a framework for library-browsing habits. They identified four influences: physical movement, motivational purpose, cognitive knowledge, and resource focus. Individuals might be in the library and just start looking around. Sometimes they have a specific information need, other times they want to keep current on a topic (such as sports), and still other times they are responding to an invitation to browse. As a result of browsing, these individuals may accidentally or purposefully find an interesting resource, they satisfy their curiosity, they learn something, they get updated, and they may feel more relaxed.

In any case, browsing the reference shelves alerts young users to materials that they might have never considered before. Particularly since bookstores tend to sell just the most popular ready reference titles such as dictionaries and almanacs, youth might not know about standard titles found in libraries, which constitute the main market for reference publishers. Multivolume sets, such as *The McGraw-Hill Encyclopedia of World Biography* or *American Decades* are especially rare outside of libraries. While many youngsters cut their reference teeth on the *Guinness Book of World Records*, few of them discover treasures such as moon atlases or picture chronologies if they are not encouraged to browse reference shelves. From upper elementary grades on up, reference browsing can be a fun and fruitful adventure.

It should also be noted that online reference browsing can also be an addictive activity. For that reason, digital reference titles should be cataloged or somehow featured so that users will be able to browse through them easily. Databases constitute an often overlooked aspect of library portals when it comes to browsing, which is a shame since several products are very compelling such as CultureGrams, Discover streaming, and PressReader. Even highlighting one online reference source per week in the library portal can lead to repeat online browsing reference business.

REFERENCE

Rice, R., McCreadie, M., & Chang, S. (2001). *Accessing and browsing: Information and communication.* Cambridge: MIT Press.

FURTHER READING

Getts, E., & Stewart, K. (2018). Accessibility of distance library services for deaf and hard of hearing users. *Reference Services Review, 46*(3), 439–448.

Hoffman, G., & Snow, K. (2021). *Cataloging and classification: Back to basics.* Routledge.

King, D. (2021). *Mobile technology in libraries.* American Library Association.

Lee, T. H., & Choi, I. (2019). Multilingual access support evaluation guideline in the website of public library. *iConference 2019 Proceedings.* https://www.ideals.illinois.edu/bitstream/handle/2142/103329/Lee_Choi_Poster.docx?sequence=1

Mandal, S. (2018). Development of multilingual resource management mechanisms for libraries. *Library Philosophy and Practice, 1768.* https://digitalcommons.unl.edu/libphilprac/1768

Posner, B. (2016). *Library information and resource sharing: Transforming services and collections.* Libraries Unlimited.

Reference and User Services Association. (2021). *Virtual accessibility.* American Library Association. https://www.ala.org/ursa/virtual-accessibility

Reference and User Services Association. (2019). *Assistive technology.* American Library Association. https://www.asgcladirect.org/wpcontent/uploads/2017/06/

Rendina, D. (2017). *Reimagining library spaces: Transform your space on any budget.* International Society for Technology in Education.

Wisconsin Department of Public Instruction Public Library Development Team. (2019). *The inclusive services assessment and guide for Wisconsin public libraries.* Wisconsin Department of Public Instruction.

Zwierski, J., McCroskey, M., & Fountain, J. (Eds.). (2021). *Cataloging correctly for kids: An introduction to the tools and practices* (6th ed.). American Library Association.

6

Information Behaviors

Librarians empower people by meeting their information needs to become effective users of information and ideas. However, to be effective, librarians first should be aware of information-seeking behaviors of children and youth, which typically reflect developmental factors. Librarians can also look at Internet search histories and review reference desk notes to determine how their community's youth seek information help. Information behavior theories can also inform librarians about predictable practices.

With that background of young people's information behaviors, librarians can then build a wide repertoire of techniques for effectively researching and retrieving reference information from different types of print, nonprint, and digital resources, based on young people's actions, and leading them to the next level of competence.

In short, a strong theoretical and practical grounding centered on youth can build librarians' competence and confidence in providing R&I services for these populations.

BACKGROUND

How people look for information and interact with it is called information behavior. The term "information behavior" was coined in the 1990s, but librarians have addressed information needs and uses since the 1960s. Basically, with expanded technologies and a deeper understanding of the social contexts in which individuals engage with information, librarians realized that the term "information behavior" expressed the complexity of these actions than earlier, and narrower, terms such as "use studies" and "information seeking."

As a sub-discipline of library science, information behavior describes how people need, seek, and use information in different contexts, and it attempts to understand the human relationship to information. Information behavior is usually in response to a person's need—they are seeking information for a particular purpose or goal. For instance, when young people

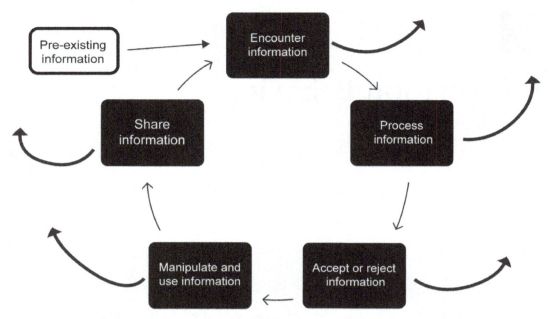

FIGURE 6.1
Information Communication Cycle. SOURCE: CREATED BY THE AUTHOR

enter a library, they do so because they are seeking information for a particular outcome. They wish to find information about something that is of relevance to them. Even if that outcome is a quiet place to think, that space can provide desired understanding through reflection. By understanding that there are different information behaviors and having the skills to be able to analyze them to identify patterns, librarians can develop interventions to help young people be more effective at meeting their own information needs.

Information behavior can be considered from the viewpoint of an information communication cycle, as presented in figure 6.1.

Figure 6.1 outlines how information can have a cyclic flow. At any point, individuals may disengage from the information which is represented by the thicker arrows.

The main factors of the information communications cycle are that

1. information preexists before individuals become aware of it;
2a. individuals quickly decide whether to ignore or engage with the information;
2b. in other cases, individuals may need information and actively look for it;
3. in either case, individuals try to process the information: comprehend it, evaluate its value (quality and relevance), and then decide whether to accept it or not;
4. they might then manipulate and use the information; and
5. individuals might communicate that information, or its use, to others—or not.

There are different reasons why people may disengage with information. For example, when seeing a website, youth may log on because the pictures are interesting, or they may ignore it completely because they don't subscribe to that website. They may be looking for a specific activity, so they look in one section only, then disengage when they don't find anything interesting. They may find an activity that looks interesting, then disengage when they realize that they can't attend. It could look something like this:

1. The Instagram page is open on the computer.
2a. Youth engage because they want something to do; ignore because they don't have an Instagram account.
2b. Youth look for music events, so they search by that term; they disengage if nothing sounds interesting.
3. Youth engage because the event looks interesting; they disengage if the event already passed.
4. Youth engage by checking their calendar to see if they are available; they disengage because it costs too much.
5. Youth engage by registering for the information; they disengage because they are too young to attend.

Information-seeking behaviors is a subset of information behavior, which Wilson (2000) defined as a "range of ways employed in discovering and accessing information resources in response to goals and interventions" (p. 49). The actual process of locating the information typically involves the following steps:

1. Identifying the domain or "universe" in which information may be located (e.g., family members, the local community's members and agencies, the "free" Internet, and subscription databases).
2. Determining possible-seeking constraints (e.g., time frame, reading ability, language barriers, transportation, technology and Internet access limitations, and money).
3. Planning a searching strategy (e.g., types of materials, locational tools such as indexes and catalogues, key terms and questions, and sequence of action).
4. Implementing the plan. Even when a likely resource is found and evaluated (i.e., engaging with the information), the person still has to locate the needed information within the selected source, which involves using key terms and locational tools such as tables of contents, indexes, and visual cues (e.g., headings, tables, and illustrations).

This process is not necessarily linear. Each step may change in light of the locational experience. For instance, the library might be closed or electric power might be out, so work might be delayed. Likewise, in implementing the plan, a material source—or a person—might lead to redefining the possible universe where information might be located. Once the information is located and retrieved, then the engagement process comes into play. As such, the seeker evaluates the information and determines whether other information is needed.

The typical goal of information seeking is successfully finding the information. Borgman et al. (1996) identified three skills needed for such success: knowledge of information organization and retrieval process to translate an information need into a search query, semantic knowledge to identify appropriate key words, and mechanical knowledge to navigate digital environments to enter and pursue queries.

It should also be noted that many information needs are what is called "imposed," meaning that another person such as a parent or teacher is requiring (imposing on) another person to find the information for an assignment or to solve a problem; imposed queries might not be motivating for young people, and they might not have enough background knowledge to search effectively.

Additionally, each person displays a unique set of information behaviors. Differences in information behaviors arise from internal factors of maturation and data processing, interaction with external factors such as people and environment, and situational differences in time and space. For example, while all people "take in" information with their senses, but which sense they use and how they process that information varies; the information might be a radio show that one listens to, or a vision-impaired person might "read" by touch. In terms of processing information, some people have dyslexia, or a person might mentally translate text into his or her first language. Likewise, external factors vary greatly; a person's culture may value certain experts, and the library's collection may constrain what relevant information that youth may find, especially if one does not have the equipment to access the library's ebooks. Situationally, the amount of time one has to engage with information influences that interaction, such as a research paper due in ten minutes as opposed to a due date of ten days. Similarly, space can be a factor situationally; for instance, if the library is closed for renovation, then people can't visit it.

In short, information behaviors vary widely and many factors are involved.

STARTING WITH USERS

Because there are different perspectives that can be taken to examine such behaviors which can impact on the analysis, youth-serving librarians are encouraged to start with the users since youth are the basis for information as their interaction with their environment can add or change their knowledge base. While information professionals are experts in their resources and information structures, users are experts in themselves, their experiences, and their situations. When user information behavior involves information professionals, then the situation calls for a trust-based interdependent relationship.

What, then, are young people's information behaviors? How do they access and engage with information in their daily lives? How can librarians identify youth's information needs? While each person is unique, user patterns do emerge by population, environment, information need, and so on. Therefore, information professionals should conduct user research (i.e., research about the user) so that decisions are based on evidence of actual user behavior rather than library worker opinion.

Etches (2013) discussed several methods of learning about users' information behavior.

- Attitudinal research about user's attitudes toward things: via surveys, user interviews, and focus groups.
- Behavioral research that reveals how users behave in a specific context: via
  - usability testing (i.e., giving a user a task to do and watching/noting him/her complete the task)
  - contextual inquiry (i.e., unobtrusively observing users in their natural environment or context)
  - walk-throughs (i.e., ask a user to "walk-through" or verbalize an information task)
  - journey maps (i.e., what physical path a user takes to do an information task)
  - cultural probes (i.e., user journals or other recording tools)
- Participatory design in which you engage the user to help you design an information-based space, service, and so on via
  - cognitive or concept map, rapid prototype (test design concepts or models)
  - reverse guided tours where users give tours of the information space

One of the most obvious and useful ways to learn about young people and their information behaviors is to observe them. Naturalistic observation helps librarians see individuals' information behaviors in situ.

- In what setting are they looking: in book stacks, online, or at a magazine stand?
- What is the time frame: day of the week, time of day, and for how long?
- Are they looking independently, with others, with information professionals?
- What kinds of resources are they using?
- Are they recording their search by taking notes, printing out results, and capturing it on a phone?
- What expressions do you see, and what words do you hear?

Obviously, there is much to observe and note.

As a librarian, your role as an insider or outsider impacts your observation. You are an insider if you work in the setting and live in the community. That insider role gives you insights into community needs (e.g., you might know about the local economic situation) and about local information resources (e.g., schools, hospitals, and government offices). On the other hand, as an insider, you might be less objective about what you see and how you interpret that evidence. The flip side, being an outsider, has the opposite consequences: less knowledge about the community and its resources, but possibly less subjectivity or "skin in the game."

Interviews are good for dealing with sensitive topics such as divorce, or when librarians need specific perspectives about a certain information behavior that might be found through a survey (e.g., that few young people know about local primary documents in the library). Similarly, a focus group is a long-standing technique for gathering information from a group of people, usually in one setting at one time. The group's dynamics foster brainstorming and generate issues from different perspectives. A group usually consists of four to ten persons representing varied profiles within a larger population (e.g., different educational grades and different neighborhoods). Usually, these methods are more useful with teenagers and adults who work with young people; youngsters often cannot articulate their feelings, especially in generalizable patterns.

It is relatively easy to discover users' information needs that are met by using material resources; at the least, librarians can observe in-house use and count circulation use. Analyzing digital information needs can be trickier. As a start, librarians can track the online use of their web portals, databases, and reference/information services (both face-to-face and online). They can also track a user's physical engagement with technology within a building.

By analyzing users' general and information behaviors and identifying patterns, librarians can develop effective mediation techniques to assist with finding information relevant to their young users. For instance, if youngsters never "hit" one of the library web pages, then a technician should check the hyperlink or make that web page more visible—or useful. Sometimes analyzing the evidence and finding the patterns can be illusive. Even when the evidence is clear, working with librarian colleagues and with the community can help shed light on findings and determine what is an appropriate and doable action to improve information services.

DEVELOPMENTAL CHARACTERISTICS

In order to provide effective R&I service, librarians need to know the young people they serve, even beyond information behaviors because youth live rich internal and external lives. Furthermore, young people experience developmental milestones. These markers help guide librarians in supporting and guiding youth's information behaviors appropriately. Because young people's development constitutes a major factor in their information behaviors, librarians should become familiar with these markers typical for each age range.

Primary Grades: Typically Ages 5–7

- Physical: has some trouble with fine motor and eye-hand coordination, learns kinesthetically, is extremely active for short spurts of time, and his bone growth not complete;
- Intellectual: thinks concretely and literally, learns through repetition, may overgeneralize language rules (e.g., all plurals add an "s"), is learning how to sequence, may confuse fantasy and reality, may have difficulty with concepts of time, and is learning that their thoughts differ from others;
- Emotional: wants individual attention and praise, is sensitive about criticism, is curious, expresses emotions freely, and realizes their action impact others;
- Social: likes social play, is learning to cooperate, needs support and guidance, depends on family, helps others, and has a couple of short-term best friends; and
- Implications for R&I services: focus on effort more than results, teach skills that include 1–2 steps, introduce library and literacy vocabulary, use picture books and stories as ways to learn how to sequence, have students act out directions, and teach through simple games, provide multiple opportunities to practice skills (in short spurts).

Upper Elementary Grades: Typically Ages 8–10

- Physical: has high level of energy, has longer mental attention span, and has gender differences in motor skills;
- Intellectual: is gaining technology skills, learns from observation, enjoys reading, is skills-oriented, can solve problems, can be persistent, performs well on simple memory tasks, and can think logically but may be inconsistent;
- Emotional: is self-confident and self-aware, is learning to judge situations and consequences, and is learning empathy and fairness;
- Social: needs supportive reinforcement from family and friends, develops close friendships, belongs to peer groups, makes choices independently of adults, differentiates between sexes, and friends are often same-sex; and
- Implications for R&I services: teach library vocabulary, build on interest in facts, teach skills such as reference tool use, teach research skills structure, incorporate single-sex pairing in activities, incorporate collaboration and competition, teach for mastery, and use multimedia resources and information that provides visual cues to text.

Middle School: Typically Ages 11–13

- Physical: has rapid physical changes (girls develop earlier than boys generally), may feel awkward, and needs physical activity;
- Intellectual: benefits from journaling and metacognitive activities, is learning to think abstractly, enjoys wordplay, likes to develop talents and creativity, is curious about the world, and may have difficulty with why questions need a supportive and intellectually stimulating learning environment;
- Emotional: experiences emotional changes and mood swings, is self-conscious and self-centered, starts to challenge authority, enjoys competition, feels a need for fairness and justice, may see the world as black-and-white, idealistic, and needs privacy;
- Social: feels need to conform, peer approval is more important than adult approval, enjoys social media, curious about sex, and like fads; and
- Implications for R&I services: focus on project-based learning, teach research processes, explicitly teach organization and metacognitive skills, encourage self-initiated questions and queries, use technology to reduce egocentrism (e.g., wikis, epals, webinars, and virtual field trips), teach point-of-view and incorporate primary sources, and teach digital citizenship—and have students create products for peers and children.

Mid Adolescence: Typically Ages 14–16

- Physical: may be physically and sexually mature and swings between great physical activity and lethargy;
- Intellectual: is developing formal logic and moral system and tests new ideas and adult values;

- Emotional: needs to experiment and take risks, may be hyper-critical and moody, is starting to explore career goals, has a growing sense of responsibility and independence;
- Social: parents have long-term influence, peers have short-term influence, girls may have anxiety about friendship, may be sexually active, and wants to make a difference but may have short-term commitment; and
- Implications for R&I services: incorporate affective domain in learning activities, incorporate dialogue, provide opportunities for short-term civic activities and research, and incorporate career exploration activities.

Late Adolescence: Typically Ages 17–19

- Physical: physically and sexually mature;
- Intellectual: prepares for the future and thinks abstractly;
- Emotional: develops personal identity, integrates moral development and personal moral system, may have emotional disorders (e.g., depression), and increased responsibility and independence but still needs adult reinforcement;
- Social: has mature interpersonal and likely sexual relationships; and
- Implications for R&I services: provide post-secondary reference resources, incorporate life skills in information-seeking processes, provide local referral sources, teach how to use specialized reference tools, collaborate with teachers to help students conduct domain-specific research (e.g., think like a scientist), provide opportunities for civic understanding and participation, encourage building positive digital reputations, and offer library aide training and projects.

UNIQUE POPULATIONS

Even within each population clustered by function or age, several subgroups have unique needs that deserve specific consideration.

Immigrants constitute about one-seventh of the U.S. population. Even with globalization, these newcomers may be unaware of educational and social practices, and they may face prejudice as well as language barriers. Newcomers are more likely to be poorer than the average U.S. citizen and may feel isolated as they experience culture shock. Library services in their original country probably differ significantly from U.S. services, particularly for school libraries. Furthermore, materials are usually available in several formats, and the technology that youth may access is usually more extensive in the United States. In many countries, the library stacks are closed, and users might have to rent materials rather than borrow them freely. U.S. library services are also likely to be more extensive, especially in terms of R&I. Youth-serving librarians should make a special effort to identify recent immigrants and give them a customized orientation. In the process, youth can share their prior library experiences, which can inform library staff about differences in resources and services.

Both immigrants and U.S. residents might be non-English speakers. In addition, English language learners (ELLs) may constitute a significant percentage of the school population.

Most U.S. libraries tend to focus on English reference sources, although they may include materials used for world language courses. Youth who read in non-Roman language systems face additional barriers in using keyboards, and even other Roman-alphabet languages may have a slightly different keyboard arrangement. Fortunately, digital reference sources are increasingly available in non-English, particularly Spanish, and formats often enable one to copy-paste into online translation tools such as Google's product or those listed at https://libguides.utoledo.edu/c.php?g=465400. Over the years, these translation applications have improved because users have provided recommended translation specifics, and the number of languages supported by translation programs has also increased. For short passages, youth might also consider using the free app Word Lens, which visually scans a page and translates it on the fly. They can also pick up visual cues. In some cases, youth can understand spoken English better than written language, so they can use text-to-speech features, which are available on PC and Mac operating systems, as well as more sophisticated software programs such as JAWS, which was originally developed for people with visual impairments. In addition, librarians can provide an international (or at least non-English) webpage on their library portal that links to educational non-English database directories (e.g., https://libguides.library.kent.edu/Non-English_Language_Databases/) and search engines (e.g., http://www.searchenginesindex.com/ and http://www.searchenginecolossus.com/). Even Wikipedia in non-English languages can serve as a starting point, and Wikipedia is also available in simple English (http://simple.wikipedia.org/). Similar to ELLs, illiterate and aliterate young people can use technology to read text aloud, depend on visual cues, and use video reference sources.

Young people with disabilities, be they chronic or temporary, constitute about 10 percent of the population. The Individuals with Disabilities Education Act identifies fourteen types of disabilities, which include different sensate and physical impairments, learning disabilities, emotional disturbances, communication disorders, and other health issues. These youth face a variety of access and processing issues as they seek information. They may have physical limitations that make it harder to engage with the material, or they may have internal processing differences, such as dyslexia or neural disorders, that cause difficulties in comprehending the information. Some may have problems asking for help because of language or social interaction challenges. At the same time, they may feel isolated or need to depend on others in order to achieve. Their information needs echo the needs of their typical peers—academics, personal interests, and issues, and they also want specific information that addresses their unique disabilities, showing them ways to succeed. Librarians need to match resources and services to specific needs while aiming for inclusivity. For instance, instruction should provide clear simple step-by-step directions and routines, combined with visual scaffolding. The library itself needs to optimize physical access through reachable shelving, adaptable computers, appropriate assistive technology, and open traffic areas.

CHILDREN'S SPECIFIC INFORMATION BEHAVIORS

Developmental Theoretical Bases

Piaget's theory of cognitive development can be applied to young people's information behavior. The preoperational stage exemplifies preschool and primary school children's information behavior. They need concrete resources and hands-on practice. Grade school children can think logically and organize objects, so they can understand classification systems. Preteens can search via key words, although they are still developing vocabulary. Teens can think abstractly so they can learn different research strategies.

Erikson's 1968 theory of socio-emotional child development identifies age-related stages that apply to information behavior. For instance, preschool youngsters are developing their personality, so R&I services should relate to children's interests and enable them to make choices. Elementary school children need to explore and use their imagination, so librarians should encourage children's initiation and goal orientation. Older elementary children like to work with others and develop their skills, so librarians should leverage collaborative projects and show how information is structured. Teens develop a sense of identity, so librarians should support their growing autonomous competence.

Vygotsky's theory of developmental psychology focuses on the impact of social interactions on information behavior. For instance, preschoolers are more likely to memorize while grade schools use socially devised mnemonics, which can be leveraged to understand constructively. Even youngsters should have opportunities to learn through social interactions, especially if they cannot accomplish tasks alone.

Focusing specifically on information-seeking behavior, Dresang (2005) developed her Radical Change Theory to explain the social nature of developmental aspects of access, connectivity, and interactivity. She asserted that children miss out on information-rich environments because they have not developed their information-seeking skills—or they choose to take the easiest searching path (e.g., use only Wikipedia). Dresang specifically addressed the interactivity aspect of information seeking: user-controlled nonlinear and dynamic processes. In that respect, digital resources align well with children's nonlinear and serendipitous approach. She also found that children prefer websites, including catalogues, with high visual content, animation, short amounts of text, and interactivity.

Youth's Information-Seeking Behaviors

Overall, youth's information-seeking behaviors differ from adults' for several reasons: smaller knowledge base and vocabulary, less experience, less abstract reasoning ability, and less education. As a result, young people plan less and wander more, browse and search equally often, scroll pages less, and take more time to complete tasks successfully (unless they are lucky) (Bilal, 2007). As noted earlier, their behaviors vary by age and maturity, cognitive and physical ability, linguistics, experience, and type of source. The information need itself impacts success in that open-ended tasks are usually more successful as they lead to more options for relevant answers as opposed to factoid information. The environment and its resources obviously impact their behaviors, which is where the library comes into play.

Starting with framing the information task, youngsters usually think and verbalize concretely, such as "Why are dandelions yellow?" instead of "Why do flowers have different colors?" Sometimes the very act of articulating their information need can be challenging, especially if they have a hard time stating what they know and what they need to know in order to define the knowledge gap. For that reason, librarians and teachers may have youngsters develop a K/W/L chart: what they know, what they do not know, and what they learn. Furthermore, in school, teachers may structure the information task for their students, even to the point of stating what information is needed and possible sources to consult.

To construct a search query, young people need to identify the main aspects of the desired information and the associated key words, both of which require some base knowledge and associated vocabulary. Even the idea of related terms (broader, narrower, synonyms) may be a new process for them to learn. This latter process is especially vital when using library catalogues and indexes. More fundamentally, young people often have difficulty in determining the scope of the information task. Remember those class assignment letters to the state government asking for "everything about the state"? On the other hand, it can be difficult to find the history of a street name of a city in another country.

Having been exposed to fewer informative environments, young people identify fewer resources and are most likely to ask their families and look around their immediate home surroundings for the information they need. Their typical second "ring of knowledge" consists of school personnel and friends, with libraries and librarians then next in line (Agosto & Hughes-Hassell, 2005).

Even if the full text is available, the process of wording a search query to find a source online can daunt young people. Most children tend to use natural language queries rather than key words and Boolean logic; they may use a single time, a topic/focus combination (e.g., Chris + actor) or repeated concepts (e.g., Chris Evans + Chris actor) (Guinee, Eagleton, & Hall, 2003). Especially as search engines increasingly include algorithms to "translate" natural language queries into combinations of key words, youth expect that the library's online public access catalogue (OPAC) will do the same thing—which it is unlike to do. Fortunately, most OPACs access methods use both the controlled vocabulary of subject headings and key words. However, when librarians tell young users that different databases have different subject headings or controlled vocabularies, those same users may well question the library's stance about standardization and consistency. It is no wonder that some users dismiss library catalogues as artificial and user-UNfriendly access tools (which in itself is another "librarianese" term). More fundamentally, youngsters may misspell words, and OPACs are usually incapable of supplying probably near spellings. Especially for imposed questions that are only orally transmitted, inaccurate words may be inputted: Beethoven may be misheard as "baked oven," for instance.

Young people often use a trial-and-error approach until they are successful, give up, or choose a different topic. They may have difficulty navigating the site; even icons can be difficult to comprehend. Yet youngsters seldom use the "help" feature or even ask the librarian. Even when they get some results, young people might not know what they mean. For instance, in using an OPAC, young people might not understand a call number or take advantage of subject headings to find similar materials. If the OPAC includes databases and articles within, many youth are not able to distinguish between the types of resources. Furthermore, youngsters tend not to use filtering features such as data range or resource type to refine their search (Nesset, 2016).

Evaluating the information found also challenges young people. As with other aspects of information behavior processes, evaluating information depends on a person's knowledge base, cognitive skills, and personal characteristics. For instance, when children access a book, they tend to flip through the volume and look at the table of contents, if it exists, because it is at the beginning of the book. Unfortunately, the headings are usually too broad to be useful; on the other hand, a long list of headings in the index can overwhelm youngsters (Nesset, 2016). Subramaniam et al. (2015) found that preteens may sacrifice credibility for speed and convenience. They are also more likely to judge websites by their site design and embedded multimedia features. Young people also base their judgment on their own vocabulary and language; when those match, they are more likely to believe those sites. Teacher and celebrity endorsements also increase the resource's reputation. Abdullah and Basar (2019) discovered that children do not consider source reputation or currency as an important criterion when seeking information. In studying high schoolers' information evaluation practices, Shenton and Pickard (2014) found that participants felt that information on the web should be current and topical, free from spelling and grammatical errors, and easily verifiable elsewhere but authorship was much less of a priority to them. Furthermore, teens are unlikely to compare the information they have found on one website with that on another website covering the same topic to determine the relative authority of the different sites (Eysenbach, 2008).

While each aspect of information behavior has its own challenges, social media technology has significantly influenced youth's information behavior overall (Newsum, 2016). At the connectivity level, today's youth have more access to Internet-connected technology, particularly via portable devices, resulting in more opportunities to practice navigating online information systems. Especially with wider bandwidth and greater device speed, young people also expect convenient, instant results. In libraries that have slower hardware and Internet connectivity, or where users have to schedule or line up for station time, youth may lose patience and decide that the library is not an efficient place to find information.

Youth's Individual Information Spaces

One characteristic of information literacy is managing information. How do youth save and organize the information they find for its later retrieval? What comes to mind can vary from scraps of paper stuffed into a locker or backpack to planner binders with course tabs, from cell phone screens of apps icons to desktop screens filled with an assortment of files, from documents spread across devices to an orderly central storage space with a system of folders, from thousands of text messages or emails to folders and subfolders of active online messages. Each of these configurations reflects individual information spaces.

The practices also reflect the learning process whereby youth integrate new information into previous knowledge, thereby creating a mental schema (Hardof-Jaffe et al., 2009). Individuals have to name, sort, and categorize the new information; these processes depend on a person's ability to recall the main idea of a resource in order to name it in a way that is easy to search for, to analyze the information in terms of its connections to preexisting information, to sort the information document into preexisting related folders or other "containers," and then to synthesize all the information into some kind of structure.

For small collections, youth might just pile the information in reverse chronological order, but larger collections usually entail some kind of folder arrangement (e.g., alphabetically) or even a hierarchy of folders (e.g., folders within folders or separate areas/drawers for different kinds of information). Some youth might develop such organizational structures after they have collected enough information of different sorts that they have to categorize and label them; other youth might start with categories and then collect information to go into those categories. As more information is gathered, each folder or category may become larger; some youth might add categories or they might shift the information from one category to another.

Youth are likely to have both physical and virtual information spaces. Either space could be dedicated to personal or academic information, depending on how they collect that information. Physically, for instance, a young person might have a desk, shelf, or backpack for schoolwork and a separate box or purse for personal information. Likewise, in virtual spaces, personal information might be kept on a cell phone and academic information be kept on a laptop (especially if the computer belongs to the school). In some cases, youth might keep all types of information in one area or virtual space. On the other extreme, youth might have scattered information in various physical and virtual spaces. Whatever the strategy—or lack thereof—reflects how the young person views and values information.

Food for Thought: Information Behavior Models and Theories

Examining information behavior models and theories can inform librarians' work with youth because these codifications help predict youth's R&I-related motivations, incentives, and practices so librarians can scaffold learning or provide interventions to optimize information results. As you read each of the following theories, think how they are played out with the young people you serve.

Probably the most popular information behavior theory that was first grounded in adolescents' research processes is Kuhlthau's (1985) information search process model. Through observation and gathering students' perceptions, Kuhlthau tracked students' thoughts, feelings, and actions throughout their research processes. She identified the stages as initiation, selection, exploration, formulation, collection, presentation, and assessment. At each stage, different issues and librarian interventions exist. For instance, at both the initiation and exploration stages, librarians can encourage youth to ask questions and connect ideas with their own lives. In context, at the selection and formulation stages, librarians can help youth focus more. Furthermore, at the exploration and collection stages, librarians can bring their resource expertise to the fore.

Zipf's (1949) principle of least effort asserts that individuals aim for getting the information needed with the least amount of effort. The underlying idea is "good enough" information.

Youth who use this approach are likely to search the most convenient sources, such as friends, Wikipedia, or Google's first page; they may also have waited until the last minute to conduct their research. Librarians can show youth ways to "work smarter, not harder" to find high-quality information rather than settling for "easy pickings" that ultimately will not be satisfying. Librarians can also work with teachers to benchmark research processes and provide timely feedback to avoid last-minute efforts.

In contrast, Bates's (1989) berry-picking model of information-seeking asserts that youth's needs and queries shift as they encounter information, which can lead them to a different direction and adjusted goal. The process is usually not met by finding one particular set of documents but rather youth gather bits of information from different sources along the way. Thus, the value of the process lies in the accumulated learning and gaining of information more than the result. This model resembles Kuhlthau's model in its emphasis on process.

Ellis's (1989) research-based information-seeking behavior resembles Kuhlthau's model but focuses on the cognitive aspects of searching and evaluation. At the start, searchers tend to consult knowledgeable experts. In chaining, searchers track citations. They also practice browsing. They extract relevant information from resources, verify the accuracy of the information, and differentiate among sources to filter the information. They also monitor current updates of information. Their ending process ties up loose ends. Librarians can help teach these processes as needed.

Byström's (1999) task-based information-seeking model starts with the task, which is subjectively perceived by the searcher as to its category (e.g., fact-oriented, problem-oriented, or general purpose) and its complexity. The task identification determines the type of information needed and the information sources used, including the content within each resource and the number of resources needed. The searcher's own experience and ambition and situational factors impact the information channels and sources considered and evaluated.

Ingwersen's (1996) information retrieval model proposes a systems approach. The model addresses the individuals' cognitive space, their social and organizational environment, and interfaces or intermediaries such as librarians as they intersect with information resources and their systems. The cognitive space includes the individual's information needs and tasks, interests, and feelings such as uncertainty. Knowing the person's environment, his or her situation informs librarians as they support that person's efforts.

Dervin's (1992) sense-making theory accentuates context, which influenced Ingwersen's model. Basically, individuals find themselves in a situation, need to make sense of some gap (e.g., problem, lack of knowledge, or understanding), and seek help, such as information. This theory aligns with just-in-time R&I service, which is often the basis for interaction: seeking help.

Wilson's (1997) model includes components of Kuhlthau in terms of acknowledging individuals' varied drives to seek information: cognitive, emotional, and physiological. These needs are affected by the person's environment, situation, and role, such as a student or a translator for their immigrant parents, which aligns with Ingwersen's model. Wilson's model also identifies activating mechanisms that affect information-seeking: stress, balance of risk and reward, and self-efficacy. Other intervening factors that impact information-seeking include cognitive dissonance (e.g., information that contradicts their prior views and values) and source accessibility and credibility. Wilson asserts that information-seeking may consist of passive attention, passive searching when information is found coincidentally, active searching, and ongoing searching. Knowing what drives youth to seek information, their approach, and possible factors impacting their search can help librarians figure out how to align their guidance with youth's approach.

Chatman's (1966) theory of information poverty brings forth another aspect of the environment: social barriers. She used the perspective of a "small world": a social group that acts based on their mutual norms. Those norms inhibit their members from taking risks to seek information outside of their small world because they distrust the ability or interest of outsiders to provide useful information, especially if it conflicts with the inner group's sense of reality. This practice results in secrecy, deception, and information poverty. Youth who live in this kind of environment might well distrust libraries, so neighborhood or school libraries headed by local librarians can be a positive pivotal point in these young people's lives.

The ultimate R&I service goal is to empower young people. The next chapter discusses how young people learn and how to design instruction in response to their information needs. There are strategies that will help librarians instruct *for* and *with* their youth community. Through this facilitating process, young people become not only better consumers of information but also better producers of information.

REFERENCES

Abdullah, N., & Basar, S. K. R. (2019). How children gauge information trustworthiness in online search: Credible or convenience searcher? *Pakistan Journal of Information Management & Libraries, 21*, 1–19.

Agosto, D., & Hughes-Hassell, S. (2005). People, places, and questions: An investigation of the everyday life information-seeking behaviors of urban young adults. *Library & Information Science Research, 27*(2), 141–163.

Bates, M. (1989). The design of browsing and berrypicking techniques for the on-line search interface. *Online Review, 13*(5), 407–431.

Bilal, D. (2007). Grounding children's information behavior and system design in child development theories. In D. Nahl & D. Bilal (Eds.), *Information and emotion: The emergent affective paradigm in information behavior research and theory* (pp. 39–50). Information Today.

Borgman, C. (1996). Why are catalogs still hard to use? *Journal of the American Society for Information Science, 47*(7), 493–503.

Byström, K. (1999). Task complexity, information types and information sources. Doctoral Dissertation. Tampere: University of Tampere.

Chatman, E. (1996). The impoverished life-world of outsiders. *Journal of the American Society for Information Science, 47*(3), 193–206.

Dervin, B. (1992). From the mind's eye of the user: The sense-making qualitative quantitative methodology. In J. Glazier & R. Powell (Eds.), *Qualitative research in information management* (pp. 61–84). Libraries Unlimited.

Dresang, E. T. (2005). Access: The information-seeking behavior of youth in the digital environment. *Library Trends, 54*(2), 178–196.

Ellis, D. (1989). A behavioural approach to information retrieval system design. *Journal of Documentation, 45*(3), 171-212.

Erikson, E. (1968). *Identity: Youth and crisis* (No. 7). WW Norton & Company.

Etches, A. (2013). Know thy users: User research techniques to build empathy and improve decision-making. *Reference & User Services Quarterly, 53*(1), 13–17.

Guinee, K., Eagleton, M. B., & Hall, T. E. (2003). Adolescents' Internet search strategies: Drawing upon familiar cognitive paradigms when accessing electronic information sources. *Journal of Educational Computing Research, 29*(3), 363–374.

Hardof-Jaffe, S., Hershkovitz, A., Abu-Kishk, H., Bergman, O., & Nachmias, R. (2009). How do students organize personal information spaces? *International Working Group on Educational Data Mining.* https://files.eric.ed.gov/fulltext/ED539080.pdf

Ingwersen, P. (1996). Cognitive perspectives of information retrieval interaction. *Journal of Documentation, 52*(1), 3–50.Kuhlthau, C. (1985). A process approach to library skills instruction. *School Library Media Quarterly, 13*(1), 35–40.

Nesset, V. (2016). A look at classification and indexing practices for elementary school children: Who are we really serving? *Indexer, 34*(3), 63–65.

Newsum, J. M. (2016). School collection development and resource management in digitally rich environments: An initial literature review. *School Libraries Worldwide, 22*(1), 97–109.

Shenton, A. K., & Pickard, A. J. (2014). Facilitating pupil thinking about information literacy. *New Review of Children's Literature and Librarianship, 20*(1), 64–79.

Subramaniam, M., Taylor, N. G., Jean, B. S., Follman, R., Kodama, C., & Casciotti, D. (2015). As simple as that?: Tween credibility assessment in a complex online world. *Journal of Documentation, 71*(3), 550–571.

Wilson, T. (1997). Information behaviour: An interdisciplinary perspective. *Information Processing & Management, 33*(4), 551–572.

Zipf, G. K. (1949). *Human behavior and the principle of least effort: An introduction to human ecology.* Addison-Wesley Press.

FURTHER READING

Bates, M. J. (2002). Toward an integrated model of information seeking and searching. *The New Review of Information Behaviour Research, 3*, 1–15.

Beak, J. (2014). A child-driven metadata schema: A holistic analysis of children's cognitive processes during book selection. Doctoral dissertation. University of Wisconsin-Milwaukee.

Bilal, D., & Beheshti, J. (Eds.). (2014). *New directions in children's and adolescents' information behavior research: Volume 10.* Emerald.

Buchanan, S., & Tuckerman, L. (2016). The information behaviours of disadvantaged and disengaged adolescents. *Journal of Documentation, 72*(3), 527–548.

Case, D. (2016). *Looking for information: A survey of research on information seeking, needs, and behavior* (4th ed.). Emerald Publishing Limited.

Evans, A. (2014). How understanding teen brain development can help improve YA reference services. *Young Adult Library Services, 12*(3), 12–14.

Harisanty, D. (2018). Personal information management of urban youth. *Library Philosophy and Practice, 1944,* 1–9.

Moore, C. L. (2016). A study of social media and its influence on teen information seeking behaviors. *The Serials Librarian, 71*(2), 138–145.

St. Jean, B., Gorham, U., & Bonsignore, E. (2021). *Understanding human information behavior.* Rowman & Littlefield.

Upson, M., Reiter, H., Hall, C., & Cannon, K. (2021). *Information now: A graphic guide to student research and web literacy* (2nd ed.). University of Chicago Press.

7

Reference Interaction

An important R&I function involves informed and caring interaction. The traditional core of reference service is the reference interview. Other terms are replacing that concept, such as conversation and interaction, in order to emphasize the process as a negotiated and partnership model. In some cases, the reference librarian and young person together have to interpret imposed questions of educators or other adults.

Standards apply to reference interactions, both in face-to-face and virtual settings. Different strategies in reference work are discussed, depending on the stage of inquiry. Additionally, reference interactions have to consider developmental issues of vocabulary, cognitive maturation, and prior experience. Synchronous and asynchronous options are addressed, such as instant messaging and web conferencing to remote individuals, classrooms, and other settings. Timing is another aspect of reference interaction: both just-in-time and point-of-need help need to be considered; on the other hand, the use of consultation appointments has gained ground for youth. Attention is drawn to outsourced reference interactions as well as collaborative efforts. All of these factors demonstrate the complexity and value of professional and career reference interactions.

THE BASIS FOR INTERACTION

A core value of librarianship is providing the right book or information to the right person at the right time. Human interaction is the core means to provide that connection. The first way for youth to get information is by asking their family: people whom they know and trust—and consider as experts. That spirit extends to librarians as collectors of recorded information. Therefore, to find that information in libraries, youth typically start by asking the first person they see who looks like a library worker: usually at the circulation desk. The reference or information or help desk is usually visible from the entrance, but increasingly, it is located further back by the reference collection. Usually, in public libraries the children's area has its own help desk; YA areas tend to be smaller and may be served by the children's librarian but more generally the general librarian as the information needs may be wide ranging and teens want to feel more grown-up. Nevertheless, libraries are encouraged to hire a teen specialist and have them provide R&I service after school when youth attendance is the highest.

Again, access to (or knowledge of where to access) information is necessary but not sufficient. Effective communication skills are vital: not only the ability to show interest and care and satisfy the information need but also to conduct the transaction in a professional and expedient way. No one likes to be rushed, but neither do youth want to wait in line for a long time.

STANDARDS FOR INTERACTION

Over time, librarians have examined effective R&I interactions with youth and have codified those best practices into competencies, standards, and guidelines. The overriding guide to interaction with youth is American Library Association (ALA)'s 2021 revised code of ethics, which stipulates the need for the highest level of service through a free flow of information through accurate, courteous interaction that affirms everyone's rights and dignity. In reviewing the literature on R&I competencies, Hicks and VanScoy (2019) identified three categories of expertise: domain knowledge, technical knowledge, and client interactions.

ALA's Reference and User Services Association (RUSA) (2017a) provides the most relevant list of professional competencies for reference interactions. Librarians should offer and design R&I processes that demonstrate interest and respond to the youth's expressed needs, which includes respecting youth and their contexts. Librarians should identify opportunities to empower youth to improve their own information behaviors, which entails communicating to foster youth-centered engagement and learning. Librarians should also collaborate with other information providers to support youth's information needs. A lifelong learning mentality undergirds these competencies.

RUSA (2013) further provides guidelines for behaviors throughout the reference interaction. Librarians need to be approachable, setting the tone so that the user feels comfortable. A librarian should exhibit genuine, objective, nonjudgmental interest in the user and the inquiry through voice, language, paralanguage (e.g., posture, eye contact, and being at the same level as the user), and timeliness. Librarians also need to employ effective listening and questioning skills to order to clearly and respectfully identify the user's information needs. While searching for the desired information, librarians should also engage the user, explaining the search strategy and collaborating with the user to achieve optimum results in a timely manner. Even after supplying the information or the referral, librarians should engage with the user for possible follow-up actions.

For instance, youth-serving librarians should exhibit certain traits that will resonate with youth and facilitate effective relationships with them to support R&I interactions. The document *Competencies for Librarians Serving Children in Libraries* was most recently revised and approved by the Association of Library Services for Children (ALSC) in 2020. To lay the groundwork for R&I interaction, librarians need to be committed to children: respecting their diversity and needs, understanding their development and implications for educational and library services, and cultivating an inclusive environment. In R&I interactions, librarians need to model good customer service for both children and their caregivers that is culturally respectful, developmentally appropriate, and seeks social justice. They also need to preserve patron confidentiality.

Likewise, in 2017, the Young Adults Library Services Association (YALSA) developed disposition competencies for librarians working with teenagers: caring warmth for all teenagers and their families, understanding of teen demographics and development, respectful and effective communication and collaboration, responsiveness to all teenagers' interests and needs, creativity and curiosity, flexibility and perseverance, maintenance of an environment that respects teen privacy and confidentiality.

Focusing on school settings, the American Association of School Librarians' 2018 standards describe competencies to support an engaging, collaborative, inclusive, and comprehensive learning environment where school librarians model progressive pedagogy. School librarians should also model safe, legal, and ethical behaviors when engaging with information.

Other research has been conducted on personal competencies for R&I interaction, which Summey (2017) drew upon to study award-winning reference librarians' significant factors in order to create an emotional-social intelligence framework for such behavior. The ability to make good decisions and perceive oneself insightfully were the most salient factors. Other traits of impulse control, self-actualization, problem-solving, reality tests, and social responsibility constituted the remaining significant factors for effective R&I interaction.

VIRTUAL INTERACTION

Even though telephone calls constitute one alternative to face-to-face reference interaction, emphasis is placed on virtual platforms such as Voice over IP, email, instant messaging and texting, online chat, and web-based conferencing. While most youth prefer face-to-face R&I interactions, virtual interactions also serve as an important way to provide R&I service for several reasons: convenience, timing (as when the library is closed), accessibility, and the possible provision of session transcripts for future use. The recent pandemic and the pivoting to remote education and library services make virtual interaction a necessity.

As with generic reference interactions, guidelines exist for virtual services. RUSA's 2017(a) guidelines point out reference interaction aspects that are unique to virtual means. The most noticeable ones are the option for both synchronous and asynchronous communication and the possibility of electronically recording or transcribing the interaction. Most virtual communication channels lose some degree of sensory cues so seem less personal, although videoconferencing closely resembles face-to-face interaction and can provide the added benefit of screen-sharing. On the other hand, some users like the sense of anonymity or think that virtual R&I interactions may be more ethnicity neutral (Powers & Costello, 2019). In any case, virtual features impact access to the electronic tools and the ability to use those tools effectively, unlike face-to-face interaction. Additionally, the benefit of recording has the negative side of possible loss of privacy, including broadcasting and third-party data collection and use. In any case, librarians should explain about possible options for communication, such as chat, video, closed-captioning, alt-text, and so on, in case accommodations are preferred.

RUSA's guidelines also detail the preconditions for effective virtual R&I interaction: administrative support, including allocation of funds and material resources to support the service; technical access, authentication, privacy, and support; clarity about the legal and fiscal implications of using licensed electronic resources, especially when sharing screens; stipulation as to the scope of service, such as operating hours, workload, turnaround time, and prioritization of face-to-face R&I interaction; and qualified, trained personnel.

As for the reference interaction itself, librarians have to be even more deliberate and clear in their introductions (including sharing names), expectations, and actions than done for face-to-face interactions (RUSA, 2013). Such actions include ensuring regular sensory contact to assure the person of continued interest and effort, which includes talking and visually showing the search strategy such that the inquirer is actively involved. Librarians also have to make sure that they provide full citation information, which may involve spelling out words in verbal-only interactions. Virtual follow-up typically includes providing contact information such as a library email address or library portal URL. It should be noted that virtual interaction accessibility may be harder to provide and maintain because of inaccessible resources and sensory limitations. Even videoconferencing needs to consider several factors (RUSA, 2021): using clear backgrounds, keeping the face visible, large print and high contrast between text and background, speaking clearly and slowly, using providing captions and recordings, describing any visuals, focusing on one action or visual at a time, and providing some pauses to re-focus.

In their research about millennials' use of virtual reference service (VRS), Connaway and Radford (2007) noted several user issues: preference for independent information-seeking; lack of awareness of library VRS; negative experiences with—and stereotypes about—librarians; reluctance to talk with strangers, especially if the librarian is anonymous; limited sensory cues to determine if the librarian really understands—or is interested in—the reference question; and fear that their interaction will not be kept private and confidential, especially if the interaction is recorded or otherwise transcribed. The researchers recommended a blend of face-to-face VRS in which youth have established a trusting relationship with the librarian face to face and can count on connecting with that some librarian virtually. They also suggested that youth collaborate with librarians to plan and deliver VRS so that there is a greater sense of agency and commitment.

Providing VRS to youngsters can be even more problematic because they are likely to think that the online librarian is a local person who knows their school and staff as well as their curriculum and assignments. Especially when public libraries use remotely based VRS vendors, children can get very confused and frustrated as well as generalize that experience to their own local libraries. Even with local public library VRS, online librarians immediately must determine the relative maturity of the virtual questioner in order to use developmentally appropriate vocabulary and questioning methods; in that respect, videoconferencing is more effective than text-only or voice-only interactions.

INCLUSIVE INTERACTION

Because library practices should be as inclusive as possible, interactions should exhibit behaviors that can be understood by the broadest audience possible; this approach is especially applicable for group presentations. Here are some general tips.

- Create a positive climate. Make learning safe and comfortable.
- Try to use the format or communications channel preferred by the person.
- Provide clear information and expectations.
- Help youth to connect R&I to their own environments.
- Offer instruction or other kinds of support if youth are not used to locating or using resources independently.
- Provide support and scaffolding for youth as needed: demonstrations, online tutorials, local expertise, peer assistants, translation tools, and technical help.
- Give youth time to process and evaluate information. Foster critical thinking by modeling analytical information processing.
- Help youth clarify and explain their understanding.
- Build fluency through practice.

The principles of universal design for learning apply well here: providing users with choices in how information is represented (e.g., format, language, and reading level), how they engage and interact with information (e.g., level of interest, amount of time, and depth of information), and how they demonstrate competence.

Cultural Competence

In the twenty-first century, society in the United States has become more diverse and more culturally aware, to an extent because of more movement of populations and because of the Internet's international communication potential. To attract and provide relevant R&I services to varieties of youth, librarians need to strive for cultural competence, which Overall (2009) defined as

> the ability to recognize the significance of culture in one's own life and in the lives of others; and to come to know and respect diverse cultural backgrounds and characteristics through interaction with individuals form diverse linguistic, cultural, and socioeconomic groups; and to fully integrate the culture of diverse groups into services, work, and institutions in order to enhance the lives of both these being served by the library profession and those engaged in service. (pp. 189–190)

Overall developed a cultural competence framework for librarians, which takes into account cognitive, interpersonal, and environmental domains. The cognitive domain consists of self-awareness and cultural knowledge and sensitivity. The interpersonal domain includes cultural appreciation and emotional, caring connections. The environmental domain considers settings and conditions, language and norms. Underlying these domains is a culture of communities, which have a rich knowledge and values base.

In order to gain cultural knowledge and confidence, librarians need to self-examine their own culture and beliefs and seek opportunities to share experiences with youth in their community. Such efforts start by establishing respectful, trusting relationships, which may involve learning about socializing customs, such as ways of introductions or concrete actions such as sharing food. Another key element in building cross-cultural relationships is care reciprocity, be it active listening, authentic interest, or authentic personal exchanges. Librarians also need to understand the context of young people's daily lives: their neighborhoods, their activities, and their social norms. Librarians can also gain cultural competence by participating in professional development opportunities that focus on diversity, inclusion, and social justice; these activities might be provided by educational institutions or community groups. Certainly, youth-serving librarians should try to connect with culturally diverse professional peers and engage in meaningful activities together. Cultural competence can not only lower barriers to R&I service but can also strengthen a sense of caring service. The result is likely more effective R&I service for youth—and more empowered youth.

Languages

Language can be a major stumbling block in R&I interaction. As much as possible, librarians should provide reference sources and help in a language that the young person can understand. At the least, provide a reference sheet of typical library terms in community-used languages (e.g., https://docs.google.com/document/d/1wReLay0zdemCXiI7Tw9fHUTkJGjat9iuvOeTNZ V0q5s/edit). In some cases, an individual may be able to comprehend English better orally, or better understand written forms of communication, so when one format does not work well, the librarian should try an alternative format. In that respect, asynchronous online R&I service can be a good alternative for English language learners because they can have time to translate content with less time stress. In general, providing written and oral information simultaneously, and incorporating visual cues, is the best practice. It should be noted that some images may be unrecognizable, demeaning, or have different meanings to different cultures. Sarkodie-Manash (2000) and Ferrer-Vinent (2010) offered several suggestions that apply well to English learners as well as other populations.

- In all interactions, use plain English and short sentences and avoid idioms. Rephrase and simplify statements. Use meaningful gestures.
- Speak clearly and slowly without accent.
- Use repetition, paraphrasing, and summaries.
- Focus attention on essential vocabulary needed for R&I service. Provide bilingual glossaries and visual references. Define new terms.
- Use visual aids and graphic organizers to help users understand content organization and relationships.
- Include frequent comprehension checks and clarification questions.
- If you can't understand the user, don't pretend to.

- If possible, instruct the user's primary language (unless a group of users represents several native languages).
- Pair users linguistically.
- Maintain a list of world speakers. International students usually like to do follow-up questions in their primary language.
- Employ hands-on learning.

Immigrant Youth

R&I interactions can be especially problematic for immigrant teens because of first-country differences in practices and values. Not only might immigrants lack knowledge about libraries and their benefits, but they may also harbor negative or fearful attitudes toward governments. Youth with different cultures might also use different speech patterns or approaches for help in different ways. Moreover, in some countries, reading is not considered very important. What with immigrant families focusing on survival and acculturation, education and technology may take a back seat. Schools should provide transition services for new immigrants, both students and their families, and such orientation should include the library. Ideally, public librarians and school librarians can co-present information about library services and procedures, including free library cards and borrowing privileges. As noted already, youth sometimes serve as the R&I translator for their parents who do not speak English or other dominant language. As much as possible, librarians should try to avoid putting the child in that situation, but at the least, they should look at—and answer—the parent.

Youth with Disabilities

Youth with disabilities represent a wide variety of issues: physical, cognitive, and psychological. Whenever possible, librarians should consult with the youngster's family and other resource team members about appropriate accommodations; focus more on meeting the young person's need rather than their disability. Frequently, youth with special needs have a peer buddy or adult aide to facilitate interaction. Nevertheless, the librarian should interact directly with the target youngster rather than ignoring that person. Several of the practices mentioned previously for English language learners (ELLs) and for virtual interactions also apply well to youth with disabilities. Some additional suggestions follow.

- Break down directions into smaller steps.
- Interact in a consistent manner.
- Use concrete, literal terms.
- Minimize obstacles and distractions, such as background noise.
- Build on student interests.
- Take into account the affective side of interaction so that youth remain positive and engaged.
- Learn how to use assistive technologies and computer features that increase accessibility.

- Use accessible means of communication, including augmented and alternative communication tools.
- As noted for universal design, provide options for information, comprehension, communication, and action.

Most importantly, librarians should remember that youth with special needs are growing and unique individuals first. Showing interest, respect, and care provide the foundation for successful interaction in any case.

REFERENCE AND INFORMATION INTERACTIVE STRATEGIES

Just as conversations have a typical flow from greetings to farewells, so do reference interactive sessions. Indeed, the interaction is set up even before the initial encounter. As noted before, the location of the R&I desk sends a message. Especially as some youth experience library anxiety, feeling vulnerable or frustrated, R&I presence needs to project a welcoming and nonthreatening ambiance. Is it easy to find and convenient for the user? Does large, clear signage identify the space? Help desk or "ask here" is probably more understandable than "reference desk"; youth can brainstorm good terms to use such as genius bar or Q/A desk and suggest possible icons as visual cues such as shaking hands or the letters I or ?/!, or the ALA or UNESCO information literacy logo (http://www.ifla.org/publications/integrating-the -information-literacy-logo-a-marketing-manual). Furthermore, libraries should have signage in Braille and in all the major languages used by youth in the community. How noisy is the area? Does the space seem too open to eavesdropping or is there a sense of relative privacy? What kind of barriers separates the user from the librarian, such as a high counter or wide desk? Can the user sit and see comfortably, including users in wheelchairs? Does the area look clean and organized? Can the user see the computer screen, either by sitting near the librarian or looking at a second, mirrored screen? Is the librarian at that location—or easily available by sight or signal? Does the work area include a nameplate or function, such as Mr. H, Your library guru? Sometimes, libraries use movable desks or tables for at-point-of-need information services. While mobility can be convenient, it also creates a sense of unpredictability, which can confuse youth.

As the librarian, do you look friendly and professional? Sometimes librarians multitask at their desks, be it reading or writing reports, processing materials, or preparing instruction. In any case, you should always be aware of approaching users and be ready to help. Especially since many youth do not want to bother an occupied librarian, you need to look excited to see them. You should acknowledge the user with a smile or other friendly signal, even if helping someone else for the moment. It is also a good practice to roam around the room occasionally, especially if you see someone who looks stumped, and initiate a conversation with that person. Nowadays, especially in a big public library, the librarian might be visible on the R&I desk monitor screen, identifying the user via the webcam on the monitor. In such cases, the librarian should greet the user and ask the user if a screen-based service is satisfactory—and the question should be close-captioned to accommodate users who are hearing impaired.

The easiest way to start is to simply state that you are available, and ask if the user would like you to help. Then you are set to interact: "So tell me what you are looking for," or "Give me some idea of what you want to do." Your tone should convey interest but not intrusiveness. Let the user fully state the information need before responding. It is a good idea to paraphrase the information need and ask if that statement captures the main issue. Then the two of you can clarify and refine the information need through open-ended and closed questions, including questions about what actions have already been taken, what sources have been examined, and what gaps or questions remain. Is it also a good idea to gain some understanding of the context: Is this a school assignment? Are you asking for a friend? How much information do you need? What format would you prefer? How much time do you have, or by when do you need the information? This point in the interaction is particularly tricky when dealing with children—or when the topic is sensitive, such as getting information about birth control. Youngsters may have difficulty verbalizing their need or knowing how to narrow the question. They might start out by asking for a science book when in actuality they need to know if a tomato is a fruit or a vegetable. They may ask for the causes of the Civil War, not realizing that their teacher was referring to Britain's seventeenth-century crisis. Respectful patience and clear language are critical; library jargon should be avoided. Sometimes students have an assignment that they don't understand, so asking if you can see the assignment can be informative; a school librarian might ask the classroom teacher for some clarification. It should be noted that youngsters tend to think that the public librarian knows the school's curriculum and teachers, so that issue must sometimes be clarified. If the young person is hesitant or uncomfortable answering some questions, try to find a way to get just the information needed without embarrassing the person (e.g., their parents are divorcing, they are failing in class, they can't read well, and they procrastinated until the last minute).

Once the information need is articulated, then the search strategy comes into play. This stage also requires thoughtful collaboration and offers a valuable learning opportunity. As a librarian, you should verbalize your searching process, pointing out that the nature of the information need drives the strategy. For instance, is firsthand, primary source information needed, or is secondary commentary more appropriate? How should the information be presented: as text, in tables or charts, as pictures, as sound? How current does the information need to be? If background information is needed, an encyclopedia might be a good place to start and can help to identify key words to use. Then you can discuss what are feasible repositories of information, such as subscription database aggregators, the library catalogue, or subject search engine. In some cases, such as pointed factual questions, specific kinds of ready reference materials are the quickest source of information, such as almanacs to find important events of the year.

In some cases, the user may have enough support to complete the search independently, but other users may need help choosing and navigating a database or library catalogue, or even using a book index. Again, as much as possible, allow the person to handle the search tool and guide them as needed; hands-on engagement, especially in combination with verbalizing the decision-making process, gives youth more control and ownership of the process and optimizes learning.

Before the interaction is completed, it is best to make sure that the user has found the desired information or at least one feasible source of information. At this point, evaluation comes into play. Sometimes, youth feel satisfied with the first resource they find and do not take the needed next step to determine if the source has the information needed. Is the information relevant, accurate, comprehensible? Therefore, it is important to verify with the user about the quality of the resource right then. Indeed, if it becomes apparent that the resource is not the right fit, then that gives you as a librarian a chance to figure out with the user the information gap and reframe or refine the query to get better results. Even if the information is useful, it is wise to ask if supplementary or complementary information is needed and to determine the most effective search strategy to use in order to get optimum results. In some cases, the young person may find that the information task is more complex than originally conceived, leading to the need for more resources and perspectives. In any case, the user needs closure, even if it means that the desired information cannot be found. Hopefully, a referral can be made to another place or expert that might have that information such as a subject specialist, service provider, or media outlet. In any case, encourage the user to reconnect if questions remain.

TYPES OF REFERENCE QUESTIONS

The nature of R&I interaction depends on the users' need and intent. For instance, getting a suggestion for a good anime graphic novel differs substantively from helping insert a video into a PowerPoint or developing a search strategy for a science fair project. Generally, reference questions fall into several categories. Each type of information need should be handled in specific ways.

Directional. Where is the copier? When is the library open? and so on. The library should provide highly visible signage and handouts to deal with reoccurring questions. A FAQ page can help online users with this type of question.

Material requests. Do you own a copy of *Charlotte's Web*? Is the field guide to birds on the shelf? The circulation desk usually handles these questions, and the online library catalogue should include holdings information so that users can learn how to find out this information for themselves. A reference chart can also be placed by the online public access catalogue (OPAC) stations to facilitate self-direction. While it is best for the librarian to walk with the user to the shelf to locate the desired item, distinctive signage and visual cues can help direct the user to the appropriate shelf if the librarian cannot leave the desk; "Go to the second shelf below the kangaroo picture to find books about Australia."

Ready reference. Who is Germany's president? Where is Pittsburgh? and so on. The librarian should have a handful of core reference resources: for example, an almanac, an atlas, a dictionary, an encyclopedia, a citation/stylebook, and the school handbook. Most of these ready reference resources are also available online and should be bookmarked for quick retrieval as well as featured on the library portal's reference page. Whenever possible, the librarian should verbalize the process of finding the fact so that the youngster can do it independently in the future. The librarian should also remind the youngster to note at least the source title, date, and page for the information found; these days, youth might use a cell phone to take a picture of the item.

Procedural-based. How do I find an article in a database? How do I find statistical information? and so on. These requests can be dealt with at point-of-need, giving just enough information to accomplish that particular task. That approach may be all the directions that the user can handle at the moment. Even then, it's a good idea for the librarian to find out the context of the request, such as the student needing a primary source from the Vietnam War era—or a dataset in order to make numerical predictions; such situational details help the librarian determine what process the student needs to learn.

Technology instruction. How do I double space? How do I download an article? and so on. Users assume that library staff know every piece of software and application on the library computers. As much as possible, library workers should become familiar with the main features of each program and practice using it. To cut down on time, one person can take the lead in knowing the program and then coach the other library workers. Workers, by the way, can include adult and student volunteers. At the least, a reference page should be available in print and online format as a "cheat sheet" to guide the novice user. If the query seems to involve a long detailed training, then the librarian should probably refer the user to an expert such as the site's technology specialist. Again, it is a good practice for the site, perhaps under the guidance of the librarian, to have a teen tech squad who can serve as peer coaches in this capacity.

Standard and in-depth reference. How do I find information on the impact of slavery on the British Empire? What research has been done on water pollution in the local river? and so on. For those librarians who like research, these kinds of questions affirm the importance of library science academic preparation and help youth become college-ready. These one-on-one or small group sessions involve an iterative series of queries about the topic and context, the user's current knowledge and skills, as well as instruction on search strategies, the use of specific resources, and processes in interpreting and manipulating information. Youth can concretely see how research truly involves re-searching. These in-depth interactions can be difficult to do when a whole class is working in the school library; if possible, scheduling a consultation provides the optimum environment for this interactive learning. However, even a five-to-ten-minute group discussion can offer a rich learning experience. Particularly when a class is doing I-Search papers, which involves metacognitive journaling while researching a self-chosen topic, the classroom teacher can require each student to have a five-minute research consultation session with the librarian; the student can choose at what point to talk with the librarian, which puts students in control and allows them to determine the point of need individually.

Other just-in-time help. What's the email address of my teacher? I missed the bus, when is the next one coming? and so on. As noted elsewhere, the library often serves as the local information safety net, the go-to place in a crisis. The librarian needs to know the resources and services of the school and community and be ready at any point to deal calmly with a panicked user's information needs.

Librarians often encounter imposed questions: that is, questions coming from another person such as a classroom teacher that a young person is obliged to answer, be it as a class assignment or a request by a relative or friend; the question does not arise from the young person request-ing R&I assistance. It can be hard to engage the youth with imposed questions. As such, that young person might not understand the question or information task or show much interest in the question, so when such a person has a hard time articulating the question, it is a good idea to ask the basis for the question, as in: "Is this a homework assignment?" or "Does this question come from someone else?" The next step usually entails trying to clearly define and describe the question, which might entail asking for possible documentation to draw upon. Luo and Weak (2013) found that teens are likely to use text messaging reference to answer imposed informa-tion needs because they think that this model is good for quick specific questions and answers.

READERS' ADVISORY

Readers' advisory constitutes a major function for youth-serving librarians. "What's another book series like *Wimpy Kid?*" "Do you have a picture book about soccer?" "I have to read a book for class that is at least 200 pages long; do you have large type books or long com-ics?" As readers' advisors, librarians are personal advisors and social agents; they help youth understand others and broaden their intellectual horizons. Especially as librarian gets to know young persons individually and their reading habits over time, recommendations of good reads become more relevant and fruitful. Librarians often ask readers what they like to read and may get a nondescript answer, such as "Anything," or librarians may ask about the last good book a youngster read, only to get the answer, "I don't remember." The best time to ask such a question is when the reader is returning the book. It is usually beneficial to ask about a young person's interests, including favorite TV shows or movies.

Knowing the library's collection certainly helps librarians suggest appropriate titles, and librarians can show the reader how to search the library catalogue using the discussed key words to locate possible books. This practice is only as useful as the catalogue's metadata, so analytics for fiction titles is particularly important. Librarians can also consult selection tools such as Wilson's core collection volumes and other professional lists. Librarians can also create their own reader's advisory booklists and bookmarks by grade level or them, which they can share to help youth in choosing relevant books independently.

Readers' advisory can also be a comfort for youth under stress, say from a divorce or family illness. Both nonfiction and fiction resources can be useful: for factual background information and for fictionalized insights into coping techniques. It should be noted, however, that librar-ians are seldom trained psychologists, so should be careful when considering bibliotherapy; school librarians can contact school counselors about the student at risk.

Students often keep reading logs in schools, and most public libraries offer summer reading programs that entail tracking reading journeys. Young people have a greater sense of responsi-bility and ownership if they keep their own logs, and they can consult those logs when they visit various libraries or bookstores. Nowadays, students can use reading log apps, and databases such as LibraryThing and Goodreads also offer an app option. Biblionasium is an alternative for younger readers; it can be linked to the Destiny library management system, although this linkage might impact issues of privacy and confidentiality.

INSTRUCTION

Librarians help empower youth by facilitating their gaining and using information competently. Not only do librarians provide *physical* access to information but also *intellectual* access—and use—or information. In a way, providing people with resources and information resembles giving a person a fish—or suggesting where to catch or buy one. Even though public librarians tend to focus on answering a user's information question by locating the resource or specific fact, they can leverage a reference interaction as a learning opportunity to instruct users, which is a central function of school librarians. Librarians share how to become effective users and producers of information; this approach resembles teaching people how to fish rather than giving them a fish. Reference instruction can range from a stock orientation to the library catalogue or basic database search protocols to complex individualized search strategies. In terms of information tasks, library-related curriculum may include information behavior, location skills, relevant resources, research skills, using information, and sharing it. Several associated literacies may be considered as part of information competency: digital literacy, visual literacy, media literacy, data literacy or numeracy, and aural literacy.

As librarians instruct *for* and *with* their communities, they need to understand how learning occurs as well as developmental issues of those persons. Basically, learning involves four entities: the learner, the content, the instructor, and the environment. To help the learner comprehend the content (gain intellectual access), librarians need to consider the nature of the concept as it is represented in a resource and its form, as well as the learner's objective, and then structure the instruction to optimize learning. For instance, if one wants to learn how to ride a bike, one needs to move. In library settings, for persons to learn how to navigate a database in order to find an article, the librarian will usually *show* how to access the database and *demonstrate* search strategies *visually* and *orally*. For persons to learn this process, they will need to *hear* and/or *see* (depending on their sensory condition) and then *physically* access and try out the process for themselves. In any case, the individual needs to engage and understand the concept and then tie it to prior learning in order to change attitudes or behavior.

Remember that instruction occurs within an environment, be it physical or virtual. Therefore, librarians need to consider space issues: location (and its impact on transportation issues for learners), availability, cost, layout, lighting and sound, furniture, equipment, physical and virtual accessibility, and services. In a virtual learning environment, be it a webinar or self-paced tutorial, librarians need to consider the online platform and its features, interactivity, accessibility, and the kind of broadband capability it needs. Increasingly, learning experiences are delivered in a blended or hybrid way, where part of the learning takes place face to face in a physical space and part is delivered online. This approach can optimize the learning experience in that it requires less transportation (usually), may increase convenience, permits more independent work, and enables the librarian to focus more on group interaction and collaborative activities when meeting in real time face to face.

Many specific factors impact learning. One factor has already been addressed: the person's developmental stage (typically associated with age, but not always). Here are some other factors.

- Internal: attention, vision, motivation, information processing, mental schema, health, personality, developmental stage, and so on.
- Experience: storytelling, shared reading, informal learning, schooling, trips, playing video games, and so on.
- Culture: family norms, neighborhood, ethnicity, religion, youth groups, professional organizations, and so on.
- Situation: deadline, grouping of people, computer crash, accident, and so on.

As for learning styles, while individuals might have preferred ways to learn, such as visually or orally, they do not impact learning significantly; the key is in the content and how best to approach it, considering the specific context. For the learner, that context includes other people. A sociocultural approach to instructional design takes this perception into consideration and factors it into the needs assessment and instructional design.

Laretive (2019) focused on factors about children that librarians should consider when helping youngsters with their information tasks. For starters, little ones may have troubles with small motor coordination and technology such as typing on standard-sized keyboard and navigating websites. They also have difficulty spelling. Cognitively, children have to use more working memory and need more time than adults because they lack internalized processes to work with information from various sources. In addition, website authority and credibility are often not important to children.

Knowing about learning processes and factors that impact learning facilitates designing learning experiences that help youth gain information competency and become more empowered. R&I instruction may consist of a just-in-time quick tip on how to use an atlas to a formal class lesson on inquiry-based research, but the same underlying principles apply. The latter involves instructional design: a systematic approach to developing learning experiences and educational programs. This reflective and iterative process generally involves aligned and congruent analysis, design, development, implementation, and evaluation. Instructional design models assume that the learner's experiences reflect a complex set of concepts, which are basically and situationally contextualized.

It is hard to take into account all the factors that can impact learning, but a good start is universal design for learning (UDL), which applies to all instruction. The idea is to provide inclusive learning experiences so that *all* individuals can have appropriate opportunities to learn. The key points include providing learners with choices in how knowledge is represented, how they engage in the learning process, and how they act and express their learning. To take a simple example, in a story hour that incorporates UDL, the storyteller tries to tell stories that would interest all children. Because some children might have difficulty with abstract ideas or images, a story that is concrete such as Numeroff's *If You Give a Mouse a Cookie* would be appropriate.

The storyteller would orally read or tell the story while showing the pictures so that children can use different senses to receive the story. Children could have the option to chime in when each new object appears, gesture, or remain still. The storyteller might lend story props for children who want to hold them and then wave them at the appropriate part of the story.

Librarians tend to give short-term targeted instruction. In a reference transaction, the librarian conducts an informal needs assessment, gets to know the person a bit, and helps to fill the person's information gap. In school settings, librarians often give a one-shot session, typically based on the classroom teacher's needs assessment of the students' information need. However, a sustained series of learning sessions facilitates deep learning that accumulates learner competence. Furthermore, the librarian is more likely to get to know a class of people when there is a series, such as a course, of learning experiences. A course may be considered as a series of lessons (teaching and learning activities) that has a beginning and an end: a curriculum, with each lesson as a step in building a knowledge and skills base. A curriculum program may be considered as a coherent series of courses that provides a "universe" of knowledge, skills, and dispositions: a systematic information instructional program. As an example, a librarian who is supervising young library volunteers could conduct a lesson/learning session on how to check out a book, provide a course on reference sources and services, or develop a curricular program on library volunteering that can encompass work habits, the various volunteer functions, and career ladder guidance.

Who says that instruction and learning cannot be fun? The concept of playful learning has gained credence, especially when authentic, situated instructional design is employed. The classic form of this approach is the library scavenger hunt, which can be tailored to reference sources. A newer variation of such hunts is an escape room activity in which learners solve a situational problem by answering questions through research skills that consult reference resources; the librarian serves as an instructional facilitator/"cluer." School librarians have often helped debate teams perform well by showing them reference strategies and resources; this activity can be updated by hosting library debates that have a student ask the opposite team for information, which is a positive spin on data gathering and lessens a combative tone. Libraries can also conduct after-hour research retreats to help students do research projects for school or other venues, such as upcoming debates. In all of these scenarios, R&I instructional interaction occurs just in time, based on users' immediate information needs, but the tone is more playful and less stressful. These activities can be planned and implemented by the library independently but are likely to be more successful if coplanned by young people or other youth-serving agencies.

COLLABORATION

Collaboration is key to providing effective R&I service. Several factors help librarians establish and maintain collaborative relationships that facilitate reference interactions, including instructional design and implementation. Potential collaborators to advance information and reference services include the school community, other librarians, youth-serving agencies, and the community at large. This section discusses how to establish and maintain collaborative partners and ideas for joint interaction.

Basics of Collaboration

The term "collaboration" appears frequently in library literature, but its meaning is sometimes misapplied. Technically, collaboration requires interdependence, and a task scope substantive enough that one person would have great difficulty accomplishing that task alone. Both parties need to interact socially and intellectually, and they need to have a shared vision, thinking, planning, creation, and evaluation.

Different levels of interaction also exist in R&I interaction, each reflecting significant aspects and scopes of action (Montiel-Overall, 2005).

- Networking involves informal social interaction that can lead to joint efforts. For instance, the librarian might talk with a teacher about information literacy during a staff picnic.
- Coordination reflects a formal relationship between equal partners. For instance, the classroom teacher might schedule the library's computer lab for word processing.
- Cooperation consists of a give-and-take working relationship where each party furthers its goals. For instance, a teacher might have students research social issues, and the librarian would provide a pathfinder of relevant reference sources.

It is possible for the school librarian to have different working relationships with the same party in different contexts or over time.

Partnerships

Youth-serving librarians often seek partnerships, which consist of working relationships of parties with common goals and roles. Partners identify their unique competencies and resources, hoping to complement and build on them to accomplish a common objective such as competent student searching skills. Successful joint planning and activities can lead to long-term sustainable partnerships.

The benefits are obvious: shared expertise, resources, planning, and assessment. However, partnerships do take time and effort, so the results need to be worth the extra work. Partnerships require sharing control, which can be uncomfortable for some. Each partner needs to learn effective modes of communication with each other, for instance; one may prefer emails and the other may like to text. Successful partnerships include the following elements, which were identified by Greene and Kochhar-Bryant (2003).

- Leadership and vision
- Clear expectations, procedures, and policies
- Defined roles and contributions
- Individual planning and monitoring
- Adequate allocation of time, funding, and resources
- Action coordination and linking
- Action monitoring and follow-through

- Professional development
- Evaluation and follow-up of efforts

Partnerships are dynamic, changing over time. At the start, each person needs to be knowledgeable and competent in his or her own domain and willing to share expertise and goals. It takes time to state expectations and clarify roles. With familiarity and some initial success, partners can feel freer to risk conflict in order to deal with differences and build a mature working relationship. Otherwise, the partnership will remain at a shallow level. In addition, the context of each person changes and can impact the partnership: marital status, family demands, professional obligations, and so forth. Because of these changes, partners need to renegotiate roles and responsibilities as needed.

For partners to become and remain effective, they need to be assessed along several dimensions.

- Assessment. Partners use a variety of strategies to assess students, resources, and services. Assessment is used to improve practice and positively impact student success.
- Planning. The librarian is a full partner throughout the curricular planning process, including instructional design and implementation. Information and digital literacies are integrated throughout the curriculum. All activities involving the library program are planned cooperatively. Partners modify plans in response to changing needs.
- Implementation. Partners team-teach and team-assess. Partners use and share a variety of resources and strategies.
- Commitment. Partners communicate regularly with each other and the school community. Partners coach each other naturally as needed. Partners depend on each other for support. Partnerships are long term and sustainable.

In the final analysis, the most salient question about partnership effectiveness is this: "Could I have attained the same results as effectively if I had done it by myself?"

Methods of Collaboration

R&I collaborative activities abound in today's digital world. The practice of collaborative intelligence, where several people contribute to the knowledge base, expands the notion of collaboration at the creation stage.

Technology has greatly expanded the options for collaborating, particularly with the expansion of social media. Types of collaboration functions include the following:

- Facilitated communication: emails, texting, instant messaging, real-time chat, threaded discussions, and tracking features of word processing software.
- Virtual meetings: for example, real-time chat and video conferencing.

- Collective information generation tools: wikis, Microsoft Teams and Google Docs, Edmodo, LibraryThing, image-sharing tools, and collaborative "walls."
- File-sharing tools: for example, DropBox, OneDrive, and SharePoint.

As with communication in general, collaboration should acknowledge and build on each stakeholders' expertise and interests. Here are group-specific collaborative activities to consider.

With students:

- Have youth brainstorm with innovative ways to incorporate technology into library R&I service.
- Have youth create a library orientation video and virtual tours on mobile devices.
- Have youth help develop the library portal.
- Have teen teams review reference resources.
- Have youth do R&I publicity: displays, eposters, podcasts, public service announcements, and so on.
- Have students "tag" reference resources on the library catalogue.

With classroom teachers:

- Be aware of the other's activities, ideas, and communication.
- Share each other's R&I products.
- Coordinate division of labor: planning, instruction, learning activity, and assessment. Typically, the classroom teacher is responsible for the content; the librarian is responsible for resources and search strategies.
- Brainstorm together; do joint needs assessment of students' information needs and abilities.
- Work together on schoolwide initiatives and committees.
- Ask teachers to recommend reference resources.

With other school specialists:

- Collaborate on developing collections and supportive bookmarks on specialized topics such as health or mental well-being.
- Create social stories for youth with an autism spectrum disorder.
- Provide adaptive computer stations for youth with disabilities.
- Collaborate on developing collections for ELLs or emerging readers.
- Create a library portal as port of the school's portal.

With administrators:

- Get a clear picture of administrators' R&I expectations and then expand on their knowledge.
- Do your homework before going to administrators.
- Volunteer to do background research for administrators.
- Develop a library R&I course for credit.

With parents and other caregivers:

- Provide parent awareness and access to reference resources.
- Maintain open communication about library R&I services: blogs, newsletters, and so on.
- Provide parent workshops showing how to use reference resources and supervise students' use.
- Ask parents to recommend reference resources.
- Recruit parent volunteers as reference tutors.
- Encourage parents to help fundraise and donate to support library R&I services.

With other librarians:

- Develop a shared R&I service vision.
- Communicate about research assignments and specific books among teaching public and school librarians.
- Conduct college library tours.
- Arrange with public librarians to visit schools during opportune times for students to get public library cards—or include public library card application with school registration packet.
- Refer to homework assistance at the public library, be it physical or virtual (e.g., http://library-tutor.org).
- Use library bookmarks and other public relations tools.
- "Like" the public library on the school library portal and vice versa.
- Collaboratively produce reference tools such as pathfinders and online tutorials.
- Collaboratively design and implement reference workshops.
- Provide regional online reference services.

With other youth-serving agencies and organizations:

- Create a list of local sites that use teen volunteers.
- Create a hotline list of local support agencies.
- Create a list of youth groups and clubs.
- Collect local history and find opportunities for youth to conduct oral history videos or podcasts.
- Facilitate storytelling opportunities for youth in children's hospitals.

With businesses:

- Co-present with youth about literacy issues at business service clubs.
- Collaborate with business service clubs to donate children's books or book cubbies.
- Create a list of local businesses that use teen interns or provide service-learning opportunities.
- Provide bookstores with summer reading lists and collaborate with them about reviewing books and cosponsoring author visits.
- Encourage business personnel to read aloud to youngsters.

Food for Thought: Mediaries

Have you considered using youth, especially teens, as R&I providers? The following practices may inspire you to consider this important source of potential expertise.

Another common information behavior is the use of mediaries: individuals who serve as a bridge between the information seeker and the desired information. With their needed expertise, mediaries can facilitate information behaviors at several stages: helping clarify the information task, recommending search strategies, providing access, and offering informational advice. In that respect, librarians may be considered professional mediators. Abrahamson et al. (2008) referred to the term "lay information mediary" as someone who seeks information on behalf or because of others, without necessarily being asked to do so or engaging in follow-up. Such mediaries tend to be informed peers or adults who serve as trusted front-line information sharers (Eysenbach, 2008). Disadvantaged youth, in particular, may seek a neighborhood friend for advice rather than an outsider or "establishment" figure in order to lower risk-taking (Buchanan & Tuckerman, 2016). Mediaries tend to be female and have more education—or more experience about the topic at hand—than the information seeker.

Youth as Mediators

Young people not only use mediaries, but they also act as one themselves for family and friends. For instance, female teens are likely to serve as mediaries to help peers in crisis, such as a health issue. Even children may find themselves in a mediary position if their parents do not speak the community's dominant English but need social services; this situation happens most frequently for new Americans whose children are in school and immersed in learning English (Fisher et al., 2014). Again, considering health issues, children may be put in an awkward position of having to translate a medical staff's diagnostic questions to their parents, oftentimes not understanding the medical terminology. Fortunately, the medical profession has vanguarded cultural competence and increasingly has training in addressing language barriers. Moreover, they also have a formal code of ethics to which they are accountable, not only in providing appropriate treatment but also in ensuring confidentiality. Young mediaries are also found in libraries getting information for their families, so librarians are also expected to be culturally competent and ethical as they strive to provide R&I that is developmentally appropriate for all parties.

Student iSquads Mediation

As youth become more information savvy, they can serve as R&I advisors. Just as with other types of service-learning or volunteering, teen iSquads can provide invaluable service to the library users. A simple model to use is internships.

As a school or library course or training, youth can learn about reference sources and research strategies—and how to coach peers in their incorporation. Even as interns, teens can pilot-test reference guides, making suggestions for improvements. They can also learn how to perform tasks that support R&I, such as downloading reference resources or software programs or creating podcasts that can focus on R&I. iSquad interns can also shadow librarians in their R&I capacity, and then debrief the interactions.

Once the iSquad members demonstrate competence in reference and research strategies and can use reference sources effectively, they can concentrate on practicing R&I coaching under the tutelage of a library worker. After an R&I interaction, the library worker should debrief with the team, pointing out good efforts and guiding them to more effective practices. When the iSquad member's coaching is consistently good, he or she can go "solo," even helping outside the library. iSquad members may develop specialties within R&I services, such as evaluating websites, navigating database aggregators, developing online tutorials, or subject-specific depth (e.g., science, history, sports, and films). Some iSquad members may like to work with peers having special needs, teach family members and other adults digital reference skills or serve as mentors for upcoming iSquad members. iSquads can also collaborate with each other to improve R&I services overall and iSquad practices in particular through face-to-face interaction and online collaborative tools. Furthermore, for large public libraries that use tiered R&I service, the iSquad can handle basic reference questions and refer more complex queries to the professional librarian specialist.

Youth-serving librarians should also address with emotional and social sides of teen service: through frequent support, recognition of effort and performance, special privileges, college and job letters of recommendation, and increased authority and responsibility. At the group level, librarians should encourage the iSquad to create a group identity through badges, mascots or avatars, taglines, or other social "markers." In addition, librarians should provide opportunities for the iSquad to socialize and celebrate benchmark accomplishments.

INTERACTION ASSESSMENT

Fortunately, librarians can easily assess interactions with youth. The most obvious evidence is the young person's successfully resolving their information task: obtaining the desired information and resource, solving the information problem, and enjoying the suggested book. When working with young people in conducting search strategies, librarians can check for youth's understanding and use this time to teach the skills necessary for youth to succeed. Another valuable indication is youth's appreciation and repeated R&I interactions—as well as referrals to their friends to use the library's R&I services.

Unfortunately, librarians tend not to see the final results of young people's research projects. Ideally, school librarians should collaborate with classroom teachers all along with students' research project efforts; this practice works particularly well for inquiry-based research whereby the librarian and teacher team up to provide feedback and guidance from beginning to end. By reviewing students' initial ideas and first resources, the team can analyze students' efforts take scaffold learning and help students gain processing skills. Even reviewing students' final projects helps librarians see what reference materials were used—or not used, thereby providing input for R&I collection development and future R&I interactions. I-search papers also provide valuable data because students write commentary on their efforts, which can inform librarians about students' information behaviors that can be optimized in future interactions.

Librarians can also use several less direct data collection methods to evaluate the effectiveness of R&I interaction: observation of youth's use of reference materials; library portal website history, especially if specific web pages focus on R&I or youth services; circulation records, especially if reference materials may be borrowed; conversations with other library personnel such as circulation workers about youth's R&I-related comments; and discussions with counterpart librarians about youth's interactions with them or youth's independent information behaviors.

Librarians can also gather young people's perceptions about R&I interactions through surveys, interviews, and focus groups. Public libraries routinely conduct sample reference service surveys, which can disaggregate the data by general age group. Wisconsin Public Libraries' 2019 assessment guide (https://dpi.wi.gov/pld/inclusive-services) provides a long list of possible questions that can be used for such data collecting; the guide also includes rubric instructions and tips for data analysis.

Another useful assessment instrument is a rubric, which can be used for self-assessment, peer review, and librarian/teacher assessment. In general, rubrics are most worthwhile when provided at the beginning of a project because they can guide the learners' efforts and serve as formative feedback so learners' can make adjustments to their work; librarians and classroom teachers can also make timely interventions or scaffold learning to optimize final work. The following two rubrics point out the need to address both process and product for research projects in particular (tables 7.1 and 7.2). The design of such rubrics is discussed in the following chapter.

Sometimes the best information mediation is between a reference resource and a young person rather than interacting directly with a person. The next chapter deals with curating and producing reference and information products.

Table 7.1. Research Process Rubric

Target Indicators	Emerging	Nearly Proficient	Accomplished	Exceptional
1. Determines information need	☐ Someone else defines the topic and what information I need.	☐ Someone else defines the topic. I can identify, with help, some of the information I need.	☐ I determine a topic and identify the information I need.	☐ I determine a manageable topic and identify the kinds of information I need to support it.
2. Develops search strategy	☐ Someone else selects the resources I need and shows me how to find the information. Someone also develops my plan and timeline. I don't know what to record.	☐ I select resources but they aren't always appropriate. I have an incomplete plan and timeline, but don't always stick to them. I return to the same source to find bibliographic details.	☐ I use a variety of information strategies and resources. I have a complete plan and stay on my timeline. I sometimes record bibliographic information.	☐ I always select appropriate strategies and resources. I have a complete plan and can adjust my timelines when needed. I always record bibliographic information for all my sources.
3. Locates and accesses sources	☐ I don't understand how to use information resources.	☐ I don't use a variety of information resources.	☐ I prefer to limit the number of information resources I use.	☐ I am comfortable using various information resources.
4. Accesses and comprehends information	☐ Someone else helps me extract details from sources. I have no way to determine what information to keep and what to discard.	☐ I can extract details and concepts from one type of information source. I sometimes apply appropriate criteria to decide which information to use.	☐ I extract details and concepts from different types of sources. I examine my information and apply criteria to decide what to use.	☐ I extract details and concepts from all types of sources. I effectively apply criteria to decide what information to use.
5. Interprets and organizes information	☐ I need help to find which sources to use. I don't know how to use facts. I have trouble processing and organizing information. I need to be reminded to credit sources.	☐ I use the minimum sources assigned. I just list the facts. I know some ways to organize information. I can use 1–2 very well. Sometimes I credit sources appropriately.	☐ I create and improve my product by using a variety of resources from school. I organize information in different ways. I usually credit sources appropriately.	☐ I compare/contrast facts from a variety of sources found both in and out of my community. I use various media for products and audiences. I organize information to best meet my information needs. I always credit sources appropriately.
6. Communicates the information	☐ I'm not sure what actions to take based on my info needs. My product is incomplete. I don't revise.	☐ I know what to do with the information I find. I complete my product, but I need help revising.	☐ I act based on the information I have processed, according to my needs. I complete, practice, and revise my product.	☐ I act independently on the relevant info I've processed, and I explain my actions clearly. I complete, practice, and revise my product several times. I ask for feedback.
7. Evaluates product and process	☐ I don't know how I did. I need someone to help me figure out how to improve.	☐ I know how well I did, and I have some idea on how to improve.	☐ I know how well I did, and I make some revisions.	☐ I evaluate the product and process throughout my work, and revise when needed.

Directions: Please check the box ☐ of the group of sentences for each indicator (such as Indicator 1). Determine information needs that most accurately represent your action when doing a research project. You should have 7 ☐ (one per indicator) when done reading the rubric.

Table 7.2. Research Product Rubric

Target indicators	Adherence to Assignment	Organization	Proof and Justification on Commentary	Use of Language and Strategies	Spelling and Grammar
6. Exceptional	☐ All aspects of assignment covered in depth. Bibliography and citations done according to the format without errors. Assignment is free of plagiarism.	☐ Well-organized structure and paragraphs that support the insightful, defined thesis.	☐ Substantial and appropriate proof with convincing justification and commentary	☐ Language is mature and clear; sentence structure is varied and well-developed.	☐ Errors are rare
5. Accomplished	☐ All aspects of assignment covered. Bibliography and citations done according to the format with few or no errors. Assignment is free of plagiarism.	☐ Organized structure and paragraphs that support clearly defined thesis.	☐ Suitable proof with convincing justification and commentary.	☐ Language is effective and clear; sentence structure is varied.	☐ Errors are infrequent.
4. Competent	☐ Most aspects of the assignment covered. Bibliography and citations done according to the format with some errors. Assignment is free of plagiarism.	☐ Organization and paragraphs that support simplistic thesis.	☐ Adequate proof with somewhat convincing justification and commentary.	☐ Language is adequate; sentence structure varies somewhat.	☐ Errors appear occasionally.
3. Emerging	☐ Some important aspects of the assignment are missing. Bibliography and citations contain frequent, distracting errors. Assignment is free of plagiarism.	☐ Unorganized structure and paragraphs with underdeveloped or vague thesis.	☐ Inadequate proof with underdeveloped or vague justification and commentary.	☐ Language is awkward; sentence structure is simplistic.	☐ Errors appear often and distract the reader.
2. Rudimentary	☐ Many important aspects of assignment are missing. Bibliography and citations incomplete. Assignment contains uncited information.	☐ Unorganized structure and paragraphs with no apparent thesis or focus.	☐ Inadequate proof with little clear or related justification or commentary.	☐ Language is unclear or repetitive; sentence structure is simplistic and lacks control.	☐ Errors appear continuously and distract the reader.
1. Unsatisfactory	☐ Most important aspects of assignment are missing. Bibliography and citations missing or incomplete. Assignment contains plagiarism.	☐ No organization is present; product lacks thesis.	☐ Clearly lacking proof with little or no justification or commentary.	☐ Language is ineffective or repetitive; sentence structure is confused.	☐ Errors make comprehension difficult.

Directions: Please check the box ☐ of the group of sentences for each indicator (such as Indicator I. Determine information needs) that most accurately represents your action when doing a research project. You should have 5 ☐ (one per indicator) when done reading the rubric.

REFERENCES

Abrahamson, J., Fisher, K., Turner, A., Durrance, J., & Turner, T. (2008). Lay information mediary behavior uncovered: Exploring how nonprofessionals seek health information for themselves and others online. *Journal of the Medical Library Association, 96*(4), 310–323.

American Association of School Librarians. (2018). *National school library standards for learners, school librarians and school libraries.* American Library Association.

American Library Association. (2021). *Code of ethics.* American Library Association.

Buchanan, S., & Tuckerman, L. (2016). The information behaviours of disadvantaged and disengaged adolescents. *Journal of Documentation, 72*(3), 527–548.

Connaway, L. S., & Radford, M. L. (2007, March). Service sea change: Clicking with screenagers through virtual reference. In *Sailing into the future: Charting our destiny; Proceedings of the Thirteenth National Conference of the Association of College and Research Libraries.*

Eysenbach, G. (2008). Credibility of health information and digital media. In M. Metzger & A. Flanagin (Eds.), *Digital media, youth, and credibility* (pp. 123–154). MIT Press.

Ferrer-Vinent, I. (2010). For English, Press 1: International students' language preference at the reference desk. *The Reference Librarian, 51,* 189–201.

Fisher, K. E., Bishop, A. P., Fawcett, P., & Magassa, L. (2014). InfoMe: A field-design methodology for research on ethnic minority youth as information mediaries. In *New directions in children's and adolescents' information behavior research* (pp. 135–156). Emerald Group Publishing Limited.

Greene, G., & Kochhar-Bryant, C. (2003). *Pathways to successful transition for youth with disabilities.* Merrill.

Hicks, D., & VanScoy, A. (2019). Discourses of expertise in professional competency documents: Reference expertise as performance. *The Library Quarterly, 89*(1), 34–52.

Laretive, J. (2019). Information literacy, young learners and the role of the teacher librarian. *Journal of the Australian Library and Information Association, 68*(3), 225–235.

Luo, L., & Weak, E. (2013). Text reference service: Teens' perception and use. *Library & Information Science Research, 35*(1), 14–23.

Montiel-Overall, P. (2005). A theoretical understanding of TLC. *School Libraries Worldwide, 11*(2), 24–48.

Overall, P. M. (2009). Cultural competence: A conceptual framework for library and information science professionals. *Library Quarterly, 79*(2), 175–204.

Powers, M., & Costello, L. (2019). *Reaching diverse audiences with virtual reference and instruction: A practical guide for libraries.* Rowman & Littlefield.

Reference and User Services Association. (2017a). *Guidelines for implementing and maintaining virtual reference services.* American Library Association.

Reference and User Services Association. (2017b). *Professional competencies for reference and user services librarians.* American Library Association.

Reference and User Services Association. (2013). *Guidelines for behavioral performance of reference and information service providers.* American Library Association.

Sarkodie-Manash, K. (Ed.). (2000). *Reference services for the adult learner.* Haworth Press.

Summey, T. (2017). Emotion in the library workplace. *Advances in Library Administration and Organization, 37,* 129–146.

Young Adults Library Services Association. (2017). *Teen services competencies for library staff.* American Library Association.

FURTHER READING

Abubakar, M. K. (2021). Implementation and use of virtual reference services in academic libraries during and post COVID-19 pandemic: A necessity for developing countries. *Library Philosophy and Practice, 4951.* https://digitalcommons.unl.edu/libphilprac/4951

American Association of School Librarians. (2018). *National school library standards for learners, school librarians, and school libraries.* American Library Association.

American Library Association. (2013). *Virtual reference: A selected annotated bibliography.* American Library Association.

Breeding, M. (2016). Refining digital strategies. *The Systems Librarian* (Jan.), 9–11.

Brown, C. (2021). *Librarian's guide to online searching; Cultivating database skills for research and instruction* (6th ed.). Libraries Unlimited.

Caputo, C. (2021). *Library services to homeschoolers: A guide.* Rowman & Littlefield.

Daul-Elhindi, C. A., & Owens, T. (2019). *Reference 360: A holistic approach to reference instruction.* University of Omaha. https://digitalcommons.unomaha.edu/crisslibfacpub/44

LaGarde, J., & Hudgins, D. (2021). *Developing digital detectives: Essential lessons for discerning fact from fiction in the 'fake news' era. International Society for Technology in Education.* International Society for Technology in Education.

Lanning, S. (2014). *Reference and instructional services for information literacy skills in school libraries.* Libraries Unlimited.

Lanning, S., & Gerrity, C. (2022). *Concise guide to information literacy* (3rd ed.). Libraries Unlimited.

Mnzava, E. (2020). Twitter library account: Highlights for the users and librarians. *Library Hi Tech News.* https://www.emerald.com/insight/content/doi/10.1108/LHTN-07-2020-0064/full/html

Nutefall, J. (2016). *Service learning, information literacy, and libraries.* Libraries Unlimited.

Orr, C. (2014). *Crash course in readers' advisory.* Libraries Unlimited.

Powers, M., & Costello, L. (2019). *Reaching diverse audiences with virtual reference and instruction: A practical guide for librarians* (Vol. 59). Rowman & Littlefield.

Radford, M. L., Costello, L., & Montague, K. (2021). Surging virtual reference services: COVID-19 a game changer. *College & Research Libraries News, 82*(3), 106–107.

Readers' advisory. (2021). *Library training and learning hub.* http://librarylearn.org/reders-advisory/

Reisig, J. (2018). *Access: Unlocking the power of research: A guide to library services and information literacy.* CreateSpace Independent Publishing Platform.

Ross., C., Nilsen, K., & Radford, M. (2018). *Conducting the reference interview* (3rd ed.). American Library Association.

Shenton, A., & Pickard, A. (2014). Facilitating pupil thinking about information literacy. *New Review of Children's Literature and Librarianship, 20*(1), 64–79.

Vadnais, A. (2019). Reaching out and giving back: Academic librarian works with grade K-12 students. *Reference & User Services Quarterly, 59*(2), 113–119.

VanScoy, A. (2019). Conceptual and procedural knowledge: A framework for analyzing point-of-need information literacy instruction. *Communications in Information Literacy, 13*(2), 3. https://pdxscholar.library.pdx.edu/cgi/viewcontent.cgi?article=1348&context=comminfolit

Walz, J., Jones, A., McCoy, E., & Rice, A. C. (2018). Annotated bibliography: The reference desk: grand idea or gone down the river?. *The Christian Librarian, 61*(2), 8. https://digitalcommons.georgefox.edu/cgi/viewcontent.cgi?article=2024&context=tcl

8

Curating Reference and Information Products

Sometimes the best information mediator is a reference source rather than a person, and librarians can show youth how to use these access tools. This chapter discusses the process of curating and designing information packages, addressing content, and formatting issues. Librarians have curated and packaged information for years: bibliographies, pathfinders, webliographies, themed bookmarks, and displays. Nevertheless, curating, selecting, and organizing information has become a popular value-added information function. Another "old" related service is selective dissemination of information, which has been updated with individualized information spaces. Social media further expands the concept of curating to facilitate crowdsourced curation, be it by librarians or youth. In fact, youth-serving librarians increasingly add curation as a "cool" way for students to gain information literacy and "own" their own research. Curated materials may be organized and stored in several ways, facilitated by technology: in library portals and other one-stop reference and information centers, in in-house and federated repositories, and as entrepreneurial endeavors.

LIBRARIANS AS INFORMATION PACKAGERS AND CURATORS

Librarians have a long history of "packaging" information; that is, providing value-added service by transforming existing recorded information into a new information product or "package." This process can take several forms and use information at several levels. For instance, children's librarians routinely create engaging story hours by thoughtfully selecting a sequence of stories, music, poetry, and other media to entertain and teach concepts such as responsibility, the richness of cultures, kindness to animals, and so forth. Librarian technologists might create reference sheets or online tutorials that include "screen dumps" to demonstrate how to use e-readers. Youth-serving librarians often extract information from books to do booktalks and other reader's advisory activities for groups and on a one-to-one basis. Librarians might also create anthologies of excerpts from information sources such as quotations. As a core practice, librarians for all clientele create citation bibliographies and variations thereof of relevant topics. One could even make a case that displays constitute a form of information packaging.

More recently, the term "curation" has been applied to such information packaging, with the librarian designated as a curator. In its original meaning (International Council of Museums, 2004), a curator is defined as a content specialist responsible for a collection, including its physical condition (although curators of digital data objects are now common). A curator decides what items to collect, documents the acquisition process as well its provenance and description, and manages how the item is cared for. A museum curator conducts research based on the collection, such as its context and significance. The curator might investigate how an item was produced and preserved, a creator's influences, or the development of a school of thought. The curator shares that research with peers and the public through publications and exhibits. Increasingly, curators interpret selected items and develop supporting documentation and workshops for those exhibits, along with being in charge of displaying the chosen items, including their sequencing and layout. Besides collecting these assets and certifying them for their trustworthiness and integrity, digital curators need to develop searchable long-term repositories for them. They also need to relate these sets of digital assets semantically and ontologically, which may be done through metadata and the semantic web.

Unlike traditional curators, most librarians see the value of the library collection, including R&I materials, in its hands-on use rather than its provenance or its intrinsic value even if never used. Nevertheless, youth-serving librarians do much work that is curator-related: selecting materials to add to the collection, organizing them, and maintaining them. Librarians may also interpret and provide context for source material and help youth gain those skills. Thus, information packaging can be construed as a curatorial function.

The process of curating and developing information products can apply to R&I services as they inform and guide users. For instance, such products can supplement and complement physical and virtual reference interactions. They can also serve as "passive" instruction and reader's advisory service, available when librarians are busy with other people—and 24/7 if posted on the library's web portal. Furthermore, some youth prefer accessing information directly rather than asking librarians. In particular, library guides, videos, and online tutorials provide anytime/anywhere instruction. More generally, librarian-generated R&I products also contribute to library public relations because they demonstrate professional expertise and interest in youth's information needs.

A REVIEW ABOUT PLANNED COMMUNICATION

Effective oral and recorded (i.e., preserved) communication is a core skill for librarians. Libraries may have excellent resources and services, but if they are not well communicated, those resources and services will not be used much. Therefore, curating information requires careful design and development.

As librarians are curating and packaging information for children and teens, they usually have to begin by considering their audiences: both the young people and their adult supporters, such as families, caregivers, educators, and other youth-serving agencies because adults can help connect the message to the young people, mitigating possible "noise." When communicating directly with children and teens, librarians may need to modify their message content and channel by simplifying language, being more concrete, using a more casual tone, or changing the format such as using more video or social media. These modifications may also apply to second language learners. Indeed, the same general message, such as suggesting good magazine to read, would have different text and format for youngsters (e.g., a colorful bookmark) and for teachers (e.g., a lesson plan for integrating media literacy into a social studies class) and for parents (e.g., a school newsletter article about accessing and subscribing to children's magazines).

While communication occurs continuously, librarians should also develop a strategic and systematic plan for packaging information in order to allocate staff and resources predictably and to optimize library usage. For instance, many libraries have R&I workshop series and summer reading programs, which can be planned and scheduled in order to "advertise" them for maximum, predictable participation. Starting new services, such as family literacy programs, needs special attention to communications planning to help make the community aware of this new offering.

Curating and packaging information as a management function may be considered in light of a communications planning model:

- Determine the purpose, such as fostering news literacy.
- Identify the target audience, such as middle schoolers.
- Plan and design the message, such as techniques for evaluating a news source communicated through a poster, screencast, or online tutorial.
- Consider the library's resources, such as knowledgeable and available staff, news articles, computers, information kiosks, and handouts (to make using printer and paper).
- Plan for obstacles and emergencies, such as no Internet so the need to printout handouts.
- Strategize how to connect with others to spread the message, such as teachers and youth-serving agencies.
- Create an action plan, such as co-planning and coteaching a learning activity with a social studies teacher.
- Evaluate, such as degree and quality of student participation, effectiveness of planning and teaching, follow-up choice, and use of print and online news sources.

The University of Kansas Center for Community Health and Development Community Tool Box has good details about developing a communications plan (https://ctb.ku.edu/en/table-of-contents/sustain/social-marketing/awareness-through-communication/main/)

A communication plan can work on an individual event or product level, on a web page or website level, within a time frame such as a semester or yea, or as a comprehensive long-range plan. Thinking systematically, a communication plan for curating and producing R&I

products should aim for consistent branding in terms of a unifying logo or icon, font style, color palette, and overall appearance. At the international level, for instance, a symbol for information literacy was developed by IFLA (https://www.ifla.org/publications/integrating-the-information-literacy-logo-a-marketing-manual/). Branding distinguishes a line of products and builds connotations that lead to valuing and loyalty; library users should be able to identify the product as one provided by the library. More substantially, the plan should include curation criteria, which align with the library's R&I selection policy but might be more specific, depending on the scope of the project; for instance, creating a library guide for a class assignment on COVID-19 vaccinations will differ significantly from a library guide on science fair projects.

CURATING LIBRARY PORTALS

The library's web portal serves as a good starting point when thinking about curating R&I information. The portal may be considered the library's virtual door, providing an idea of the library's program of resources and services. Increasingly, especially with the arrival of the COVID-19 pandemic, the library's web portal has been the sole way to use the library's assets. That user may well continue for years as people enjoy its convenience—and the library staff has provided online programing, other R&I services, and access to digital resources. Examining the library's web portal relative to R&I services from the perspective of youth can be eye opening and can set the stage for curating and creating R&I products for that population.

Library Catalogues

One of the original reasons for a library web portal was to provide access to the library's catalogue of the collection, particularly when users could access it remotely. However, to this day, most library catalogues are not youth oriented. Public libraries serve all ages, and smaller libraries are unlikely to have a separate interface for children's collections, although they may have a searching feature that can limit the user to searching just the children's materials. School libraries are more likely to have a choice in their interface that is more targeted to different age groups. For instance, an elementary school library's catalogue might use more icons and broad topics for children to browse. Similarly, vocabulary might be simpler for children's version of the catalogue. Fortunately, most library catalogues have also simplified the citation layout, labeling each access point on a separate line. Today's catalogues also leverage users' key words, which were not available access points within print catalogues. Nevertheless, youngsters still need to learn how to comprehend and use call numbers. It should also be noted that, even today, few library catalogues include non-English interfaces, especially for catalogue programs targeted to school libraries. On a positive note, Queens Public Library uses Google's translate tool to help users find materials using their primary language, and New York Public Library's catalogue interface is available in several world languages and has separate sections for resources in specific languages (https://www.nypl.org/spotlight/multilingual).

As noted in prior chapters about youth's information behavior, children sometimes have difficulty navigating a website. Fortunately, most library catalogues now start with a simple "discovery" bar, which is customary in search engines; the advanced search option continues to solicit key words for various access points. As more libraries subscribe to ebooks, cataloguing programs can link to the full text, which is handy. On the other hand, the process of opening the full text online or downloading it can frustrate individuals of any age, especially if their only Internet access device is a cell phone. In addition, children (and some adults) may get the idea that the *entire* library's collection is available as digital full text, and they may be disappointed with the reality of different formats for different materials. On the other hand, children in especial often do not understand why they have to access articles through a different database. In some libraries, especially academic or large public libraries, the library catalogue does link those databases so that one simple search phrase can result in citations and sometimes full texts to books, magazines, and their articles, as well as audiovisual resources and excerpts within. While that one-stop searching sounds great, the results can be overwhelming, especially if users do not know how to use faceted searching delimiters; in that respect, providing a subset of the general public library catalogue for children is a smart practice. Teens, however, may well need various types of information, although it is probably easier for school libraries and smaller public libraries to use a basic library catalogue and link to database searches alongside the library catalogue link on the portal's home page. In either case, libraries should provide links on that home page to a help site and a short screencast to show people how to use these access tools. Reference information sheets showing screen dumps and simple directions in major community languages should be placed alongside each catalogue-only computer station.

Librarians usually have few options in customizing or "curating" the library catalogue. The main option besides a kid-friendlier interface is "branding," which is more of a visual surface effort than a substantive improvement. Customization is more likely to occur in adapting the catalogue computer station itself to optimize its accessibility. At least one catalogue-only computer should be conveniently located; it should have a large monitor, accessible input device (e.g., trackball mouse), and accessible navigation options (e.g., larger and slower cursor, high-contrast screen, larger font, and text reader). Similar set-ups should also be available in the reference area. While this process stretches the definition of curating, it does support the idea of packaging information to benefit the user.

Web Portal Packaging Features

Each aspect of the portal informs the user, so in a broad sense, the entire library portal may be considered an R&I function. However, this platform can serve to explicitly support R&I services such as readers' advisory, library guides, and specific instruction. In taking a quick scan of a library's web portal, is R&I content highly visible? More specifically, is R&I content for youth apparent and easily found by youth?

Most libraries have a tab or "tile" for research, reference, or databases, especially as reference resources are increasingly online. Some public library portals have a filter option so reference materials and databases can be searched by age group. Increasingly, database aggregators include tutorials on their linked page, which explains that database and how to use it; because the vendor produces these tutorials, they are useful and professional looking. It is usually smart to cross-list relevant web pages under both the age-group section and the reference section to optimize access, just as library catalogues provide several access points for each work.

Public library web portals often have a tab, sometimes with its own dropdown menu, for children and for teens—together or separately. Within this section, youth may find a webliography of developmentally appropriate digital reference resources, including websites; topical library guides or pathfinders; readers' advisory websites or lists; homework help or Ask-a-Librarian links; links to other libraries or R&I repositories; and upcoming activities or events that could be R&I-related such as money management workshops. Large public libraries or their systems may develop topical web portals as subsets of their umbrella web portal; for example, https://sfpl.org/locations/main-library/james-c-hormel-lgbtqia-center-3rd-floor and https://www.lapl.org/about-lapl/ada.

School libraries support the curriculum and have an explicit instructional mission, so their web portals are more likely than their counterpart public library websites. Valenza (2007) identified the following elements of outstanding school library websites: online public access catalogue (OPAC) presence and links to other libraries' OPACs, aggregator database access, ebooks, news, pathfinders, web search tools, online reference resources, homework help, college and career planning sources, and online reference service links. School library portals sometimes with help videos or guide tips; tutorials and videos on research skills, citation help, information and media literacy, and digital citizenship; reader's advisory content such as new and popular books, booklists, student suggestions culled from library surveys, and links to reader websites such as Goodreads; and R&I products for teachers. Elementary school library web portals sometimes have a parents' web page, which may include R&I-related content.

Each of these sections or features constitutes an R&I product or set of products that need to be planned and developed. With all these possible ways to feature R&I, librarians can overdo the amount of content and overwhelm their uses, especially youth. Furthermore, the more content that is posted, the more work is needed to keep content current and to check for, and update, links. In that respect, the spirit of curation is vital: librarians need to be very selective and provide a small number of tabs or sections and for each section to list only the most relevant and worthwhile R&I resources. To that end, it is usually better to list repositories and collections of useful information (e.g., http://www.refdesk.com/kids.html, http://www.sldirectory .com/virtual.html, http://usa.gov) rather than a long list of individual titles (e.g., http://www .rhymezone.com) unless the website is likely to be used frequently (e.g., http://www.infoplease .com); at the very least, resource lists should be "chunked" for easy retrieval (e.g., instead of listing thirty science websites, list a handful of sites for each branch of science: biology, chemistry, earth sciences, and physics). Fortunately, youth-serving librarians can draw upon the websites that they themselves consult when answering reference questions to form the basis of website lists. In those cases where an in-house webliography on the library portal is routinely updated, it is sometimes easier to link to an online document (e.g., Google Doc) that may be easier to change than the website itself; this decision depends on the librarian's access to portal editing and the ease of making those changes.

CURATE MORE THAN CREATE

Creating R&I products takes considerable time: in locating and selecting R&I sources; creating original content such as background information, commentary, or directions; designing and developing the product itself; and digitizing and posting it. It is better to provide a few professional-looking and highly valued products than lots of trivial, sloppy ones. One might use the analogy of a small closet of timeless, well-fitting and well-maintained, matching clothes versus a huge closet full of a hodgepodge of faddish clothes that don't fit now.

Many youth-serving libraries and agencies already have useful repositories, web portals, and other R&I products that can be linked or adapted for specific communities and stakeholders. Especially with a good communication plan and selection criteria, youth-serving librarians can leverage their professional expertise to locate and incorporate such online resources. At the least, finding high-quality R&I products can inspire librarians as they package information from their own collections.

Of course, in any adaption or dissemination, especially online, librarians need to comply with copyright law. It is always wise to obtain written copyright permission from the creators. Creative Commons (https://creativecommons.org) offers a variety of copyright licenses that can facilitate reuse, revising, remixing, and redistribution of content for educational purposes. Because public and most school libraries are nonprofit organizations, and their objective is education and research, they can generally follow fair use guidelines exemptions, which are listed in Section 107 of Title 17 U.S. Code 106:

1. the purpose of the character of the use, including whether such use is of commercial nature or is for nonprofit education;
2. the nature of the copyrighted work;
3. amount and substantiality of the portion used in relation to the copyrighted work as a whole; and
4. the effect of the use upon the potential market for or value of the copyrighted work.

As long as the information sources are credited ("anchoring" it) and copyright and other intellectual property rights are observed, youth-serving librarians are seeing the advantages of combining and synthesizing information in different content "containers" as a value-added service for their users.

PURPOSE-SPECIFIC INFORMATION PACKAGING

The most common type of information packaging is organizational: selecting and organizing resources based on the user's needs. Be it a reserve shelf or cart, a bibliography or webliography of sources, a database or repository, or a course "reader," these "packages" help youth access the information they need. Typically, the librarian collaborates with subject matter experts, be they classroom teachers or specialists such as nurses, to identify the type of materials wanted to satisfy the information need. Librarians might well consult other youth-serving professionals or existing compendia of sources, such as the LibGuide community or an existing bibliography, to choose appropriate sources. The resulting product might support individual coaching, a one-time informational workshop, or provide a canon for an educational department. In most cases, such resource lists should include full citations, brief annotations, and call numbers if the items are physically located in the library. Metadata should be included in any digital products to facilitate their access and retrieval.

Information packaging may involve extracting information from various resources and synthesizing them into a coherent product such as a literature review or position paper, most likely in service of youth-serving organizations. The most obvious product would be background research for an educational or social issue such as hybrid instruction or strategies to support recent immigrants who are English language learners (ELLs). Another excellent example of information synthesis is a guideline, such as tips for copyright compliance.

At an even deeper level, librarians might interpret information from various sources. Extending the idea of copyright, developing guidelines for determining fair use of materials requires careful analysis and interpretation (and librarians should place a note on such guidelines that they are not legal experts unless they have the legal credentials to prove so). Normally, interpretation requires in-depth specialized information and probably some element of values, but where that exists, such as expertise in special education, the librarian should feel confident in sharing that knowledge. Harking back to developmentally appropriate information packaging, such guidance would differ for little children from teenagers. Furthermore, to address issues of universal design for learning (UDL), librarians would do well to provide guidance in various formats: bookmarks, screencasts, podcasts, and online tutorials. Librarians might also collaborate with youth to have them create multimedia messages about intellectual property for their peers and younger children.

User-centric information packages fulfill a need expressed by the user, such as a reading specialist or group (e.g., international students). Therefore, when packaging information sources, librarians should balance universal design with cultural responsiveness: validating and affirming different cultures by providing youth with information that engages and empowers them. That packaging process may reflect cultural bias that might disadvantage some youth; specific ideas might be supported and others omitted, thus shutting down opposing viewpoints. Even a simple factor of packaging information reflecting only urban practice might ignore the needs of rural youth. Librarians should enable students to choose from a wide spectrum of reading materials reflecting a variety of perspectives. The ALA Association of College and Research Libraries (ACRL) Racial and Ethnic Diversity Committee (2012) developed cultural competencies to help librarians provide services to increasingly diverse populations, which recognized the need to "serve and advocate for racial and ethnically diverse constituencies" (p. 1). These competencies include cultural competencies such as understanding cultural history, traditions, values, beliefs, and artistic expressions as well as appropriate delivery of information packages.

Information packaging can also be categorized in terms of its focus. For instance, library-centric information packages would share information about library resources and services. Information literacy-related packages would help youth interact with information more effectively. FAQs can also serve as a library-centric service to explain how to use databases or cite resources.

FORMAT-SPECIFIC INFORMATION PACKAGING

As librarians curate information, they need to choose the most effective format to convey the content. In that respect, format may be considered the "container" or the package for the information therein. Each format has its unique characteristics and "grammar," characteristics that express information uniquely. It is important to understand how to "read" information in light of its communication channel and to determine the most effective way to structure and communicate information.

Textual Products

Even textual reference information that is traditionally distributed in a print medium may be formatted in various ways, depending on the content. Most of these documents can also be created and communicated digitally. To jumpstart digital documents, librarians can take advantage of templates found in some publishing applications and from website collections such as https://poweredtemplate.com/graphic-templates/library/. The following types of possible text-based documents are defined, and tips for each of these formats are also noted.

Flyer: a one-page document to announce events or news. Tips and templates are available at

- Barbour, D. (2015, January 23). Catch patrons' attention with these 7 easy flyer tips. *5 min Librarian.* http://www.5minlib.com/2015/01/catch-patrons-attention-with-these-7.html
- Cheat sheet: Create an event flyer. *LibraryAware.* https://libraryaware.uservoice.com/knowledgebase/articles/1929841-cheat-sheet-create-an-event-flyer
- McGuire, S. (2021, June 17). 50+ captivating flyer examples, templates and design tips. *Venngage.* https://venngage.com/blog/flyer-examples/

Brochure/pamphlet: a one-page document to summarize information about a group, product, or service. Two-sided trifold brochures are the most common format. The cover is on the right-hand third of side one, and details are presented in short sections (often bulleted) on side two. The left-hand third of side one summarizes the key points, and the center of side one is reserved for library contact information. Graphics should complement the text. Other tips are available at:

- Mercer, J. (2022). Creating effective library brochures. *SWKLS Training.* https://training.readinks.info/creating-effective-library-brochures
- Pennisi, L. et al. (2011). How to create an effective brochure. *NebGuide.* https://extension publications.unl.edu/assets/pdf/g2028.pdf
- University of Kansas. Center for Community Health and Development. (2022). Section 13. Creating brochures. *Community Tool Box.* https://ctb.ku.edu/en/table-of-contents/participation/promoting-interest/brochures/main

Bookmark: a thin document to mark a page in a book; a bookmark can provide information and promote reading, a library, R&I services, and resources. Tips and templates are available at:

- Cahill, A. (2020, October 16). A quick guide to DIY library bookmarks. *Book Riot*. https://bookriot.com/diy-library-bookmarks/
- Cheat sheet: Create a bookmark. *LibraryAware*. https://libraryaware.uservoice.com/knowledgebase/articles/909618-cheat-sheet-create-a-bookmark

Newsletter: a news bulletin or report to inform a group periodically about activities, products, services, and people. Best practices are discussed at:

- Library newsletters: Best practices. (2021). *Novelist*. https://www.ebsco.com/sites/g/files/nabnos191/files/acquiadam-assets/Library-Newsletters-Best-Practices-White-Paper.pdf
- Morris, G. (2020, October 28). Library newsletter: Best practices with examples. *Sender*. https://www.sender.net/library-newsletter/
- University of Kansas. Center for Community Health and Development. (2022). Section 10. Creating newsletters. *Community Tool Box*. https://ctb.ku.edu/en/table-of-contents/participation/promoting-interest/newsletters/main

Press release: an official statement to media outlets giving information about a specific matter (e.g., new reference service upcoming workshop or other information event). Tips are available at:

- Association for Library Collections and Technical Services. (n.d.). *Tips for writing press releases*. American Library Association. https://www.ala.org/alcts/preservationweek/plan/pressrelease
- Hursh, A. (2019). Want more media coverage for your library? Here's how to fix your press release! *Super Library Marketing*. https://superlibrarymarketing.com/2019/04/01/librarypr/
- University of Kansas. Center for Community Health and Development. (2022). Section 3. Preparing press releases. *Community Tool Box*. https://ctb.ku.edu/en/table-of-contents/participation/promoting-interest/press-releases/main

FAQs: a document in the form of questions and answers about frequently encountered issues. How-tos are available at:

- Attias, C. (2021, March 2). How to create an effective FAQ page (with examples). *WiX Blog*. https://www.wix.com/blog/2017/12/how-to-create-faq-page/
- Biroscak, M. (2021, October 20). How to write an FAQ page—with examples. *Jimdo*. https://www.jimdo.com/blog/how-to-write-an-faq-page-with-examples/
- Sabrina. (2013, June 2). How to create a great FAQ page for your library. *Q&A*. http://www.textalibrarian.com/mobileref/creating-a-great-faq-document/

Reference "cheat sheet": a short document that gives directions on a process, such as using a library catalogue or a scanner, creating a spreadsheet, or citing an information source. How-tos are found at:

- Beaty, K. (2017, July 14). *Creating and printing quick reference materials.* Formax Printing Solutions. https://www.formaxprinting.com/blog/2017/07/creating-and-printing-quick -reference-materials
- *wikiHow* staff. (2021, June 25). How to create a "cheat sheet" (allowed reference sheet). https://www.wikihow.com/Create-a-%22Cheat-Sheet%22-(Allowed-Reference-Sheet)

Research guide/library guide/pathfinder: a bibliography of resources with optional annotations or guidance to locate information. A pathfinder tends to provide a higher level subject-specific reference strategy that may be customized to one library; a pathfinder is usually structured as follows: topical information, relevant key terms, principal reference sources, relevant periodicals, and relevant classification numbers. Tips are available at:

- Latham, B. (2021). *LibGuides: An introduction and how-to-guide.* Houston Cole Library. https://libguides.jsu.edu/c.php?g=116755&p=760942
- Nebraska Library Commission. (2016, March 9). NCompass Live: Modern pathfinders: Creating better research guides. *YouTube.* https://www.youtube.com/watch?v=RX-q3q_X6MM
- Paschke-Wood, J., Dubinsky, E., & Suit, L. (2020, October 21). Creating a student-centered alternative to research guides: Developing the infrastructure to support novice learners. *In the Library with the Lead pipe.* https://www.inthelibrarywiththeleadpipe.org/2020/student-centered-alternative-research-guides/

Rubric: a scoring guide to specify and rate elements to assess demonstrations of competence (e.g., projects and presentations). Tips are available at:

- Chaaban, M. (2019, February 8). *Best practices for designing effective rubrics.* Arizona State University. https://teachonline.asu.edu/2019/02/best-practices-for-designing-effective-rubrics/
- Schrock, K. (2021). Assessment and rubrics. *Kathy Schrock's Guide to Everything.* https://www.schrockguide.net/assessment-and-rubrics.html
- Tips to writing a strong rubric. (2022). *Quick Rubric.* https://www.quickrubric.com/about/tips-to-writing-a-strong-rubric

Surveys: a set of questions and the process of data analytics, typically to gather facts and opinions, such as perception of library users. Commercial tools are available, and library research often includes sample questions; it is usually better to adapt a proven instrument rather than starting from scratch. Examples and tips are found at:

- Library surveys for success. *WebJunction.* https://www.webjunction.org/events/webjunction/library-surveys-for-success.html
- *Library user survey templates & how-tos.* Library Research Service. https://www.lrs.org/library-user-surveys-on-the-web/
- *Measuring and assessing reference services and resources: A guide.* Reference and User Services Association. https://www.ala.org/rusa/sections/rss/rsssection/rsscomm/evaluationof ref/measrefguide

Visual Products

Packaging of reference-related information often focuses on the visual representation of that information. When curating and creating visual messages, librarians need to consider the visual elements of line, space, shape, form, value, color, and texture. These elements are combined using the visual principles of balance and symmetry, harmony and unity, rhythm and movement, proportion, and emphasis (Webb, 2020). Together, these properties evoke emotion and meaning. When used in visualizing data, visual representations can both facilitate and manipulate understanding.

Signage: a graphic object that communicates information publicly, for example, identifies, indicates location, or directs to an area or source. Tips are discussed at:

- *18 tips for effective sign design.* (2014). ReedSigns. tps://www.reedsigns.com.au/18-tips-for-effective-sign-design/
- Hursh, A. (2020, September). Five tips to create amazing library digital signate. *Novelist.* https://www.ebsco.com/blogs/novelist/five-tips-create-amazing-library-digital-signage
- *Top ten tips for signage design that grabs attention.* (2014, November 13). Las Vegas Color Graphics. https://www.lasvegascolor.com/tips-signage-design/

Poster: for attention-getting, graphical synthesis; posters are often used to explain classification systems and promote reading. In general, posters and flyers should have one message and one graphic. Tips and templates are found at:

- Cheat sheet: Create a reading map. (n.d.). *LibraryAware.* https://libraryaware.uservoice.com/knowledgebase/articles/1930174-cheat-sheet-create-a-reading-map
- *Poster design: Overview.* (2022). University of Pennsylvania Libraries. https://guides.library.upenn.edu/posters
- University of Kansas. Center for Community Health and Development. (2022). Section 11. Creating posters and flyers. *Community Tool Box.* https://ctb.ku.edu/en/table-of-contents/participation/promoting-interest/posters-flyers/main

Bulletin board: a board for displaying a variety of information attractively, such as displaying different kinds of maps. Bulletin board can be interactive, with youth engaging or modifying them. For instance, reference book covers can be displayed, with users opening the covers to read an introduction to that book. Computer monitor background screens can also be customized as bulletin boards. Ideas and tips are shared at:

- Schrock, K. (2020). Bulletin boards. *Kathy Schrock's Guide to Everything.* https://www .schrockguide.net/bulletin-boards.html
- Techman, M. (2014, December 23). DIY library bulletin boards: Tips, resources, and ideas. *School Library Journal.* https://www.slj.com/?detailStory=diy-library-bulletin-boards-tips-resources-and-ideas

Display/exhibit: a 3D space to display a variety of information, such as a display of new reference books and a thematic display of titles accompanied by props (e.g., travel books with a globe), cultural artifacts, or exhibits of a process such as calligraphy; displays can also include associated bookmarks. Tips and ideas are shared at:

- Karissa. (n.d.). Library display ideas. *Ontarian Librarian.* https://ontarianlibrarian.com/ library-display-ideas/
- LaGarde, J. (2020, May 17). Six topis for building book displays that matter. *The Adventures of Library Girl.* https://www.librarygirl.net/post/six-tips-for-building-book-displays-that -matter
- Tarbett, M. (n.d.). *Market your library like a bookstore: Tips and tricks for displays.* West Virginia Library Commission. https://librarycommission.wv.gov/Librarian/Documents/ Market%20Your%20Library%20Like%20a%20Bookstore.pdf

Slide show/photo album: a sequence of images to present a collection (e.g., artistic movement and biomes over time) or a process (e.g., life cycle of an animal and plate tectonics). Authoring tools such as Google Slides, PowerPoint, and Adobe Creative Cloud are digital ways to import and sequence images. Tips are seen at:

- *Create slideshows for free in minutes.* (2022). Adobe. https://www.adobe.com/express/create/ video/slideshow
- Technology for Teachers and Students. (2018, July 9). Easily create a photo slideshow in PowerPoint. *YouTube.* https://www.youtube.com/watch?v=87dj0tGfEaE

Online image sharing platform: an online application to store, crowdsource, store, "tag," share, and broadcast visual information. Good sharing sites and ideas are available at:

- Prospero, M. (2022). The best photo storage and sharing sites in 2022. *Tom's Guide.* https:// www.tomsguide.com/best-picks/best-photography-sites
- Williams, S. (2014, April 16). Five ways libraries are using Instagram to share collections and draw public interest. *LSE.* https://blogs.lse.ac.uk/impactofsocialsciences/2014/04/16/five -ways-libraries-are-using-instagram/

Data-Based Products

Another significant literacy needed for successful reference and information use is data literacy or numeracy. Librarians can curate and create information packages that represent reference-related information numerically, typically to teach youth how to make meaning of data. A good curated collection of websites that teach data literacy is found at https://www.merlot.org/merlot/viewPortfolio.htm?id=1188590&hitlist=userId=23711&. The following types of information packages address data literacy.

Spreadsheet: a document, often a computer application, with data arranged in rows and columns of a grid to display statistical data. How-tos and practices are available at:

- *Data management recommended practices: Spreadsheets.* (2021). University of Pennsylvania Libraries. https://guides.library.upenn.edu/datamgmt/spreadsheet
- Grubbs, M. (2016, July 13). Google sheets 101: The beginner's guide to online spreadsheets. *Zapier.* https://zapier.com/learn/google-sheets/google-sheets-tutorial/

Graph: a visual way to display data analysis. Most spreadsheets generate graphs; the most important factor is choosing the right graph type to express the data appropriately. Tips and examples are found at:

- *Communicating with charts and graphs.* (2010). NEDARC. https://www.nedarc.org/tutorials/utilizingdata/communicateNumbersEffectively/communicatingWithChartsAndGraphs.html
- Lile, S. (2020, January 10). 44 types of graphs perfect for every top industry. *Visme.* https://visme.co/blog/types-of-graphs/

Infographic: a poster-like document to visualize data and other information. Infographics are particularly useful for public relations to make your case about library R&I value. How-tos and examples are available at:

- Geuens, R. (2022, January 10). How to make an infographic in 20 minutes (2022 guide). *Piktochart.* https://piktochart.com/blog/how-to-create-an-infographic-and-other-visual-projects-in-5-minutes/
- *Infographics: Overview.* (2018). University of Pennsylvania Libraries. https://guides.library.upenn.edu/infographics/overview

Aural Products

Librarians routinely share their R&I expertise orally, such as in reference interactions and, in some cases, storytelling. Aural literacy is sometimes overlooked but is vital for youth with vision impairments and is favored by many cell phone users. Librarians can leverage that information modality by orally recording R&I concepts and practices and broadcasting them via audio files such as web-based podcasts. They can provide information, such as booktalks or fun facts, and they can instruct. Podcasts need to be scripted tightly but shouldn't sound as if they are being read. Most podcasts are less than five minutes long; some of the most effective ones are less than a minute long, serving as informational advertisements. Podcasts usually start with a strong engaging or startling message, develop the idea—including benefits for the listener—and finish with library contact information. Introductory and end theme music help provide consistent branding (see http://wiki.creativecommons.org/Content_Directories for an extensive list of Creative Commons audio sources). Tips and examples are found at:

- *Podcasting in libraries: An introduction.* (2021). South Carolina State Library. https://guides .statelibrary.sc.gov/podcasting
- Dowling, B. (2017, October 6). Engaging patrons with library podcasts. *Public Libraries Online.* http://publiclibrariesonline.org/2017/10/engaging-patrons-with-library-podcasts/
- Young Adult Library Services Association. (2008). Teens podcasting @ your library. *Tune In.* https://www.ala.org/yalsa/sites/ala.org.yalsa/files/content/teentechweek/ttw08/resourc- esabcd/techguide_podcst.pdf

Kinesthetic-Based Products

Youngsters largely learn kinesthetically: hands-on engagement. Library scavenger hunts are a traditional way to orient youngsters to the library, including reference areas. Librarians routinely have youngsters use library catalogues to physically locate times. Librarians can gamify instruction and have youngsters role play information behaviors. Indeed, these real-life practices offer opportunities for authentic formative and summative assessment, which can then be analyzed to improve R&I services and young people's information behavior.

Play/skit: acting out behaviors for kinesthetic, interactive examination of issues holistically. Story hours sometimes encourage children to act out stories. Youth can role-play serving as librarians (Rich et al., 2019) and https://playtolearnpreschool.us/library-dramatic-play-center/.

Game: physical and virtual games to engage participants in interactive learning. Youth can also create R&I games for the library. Tips and practices are shared at:

- American Library Association. Game Round Table. (2022). *Games in libraries.* American Library Association. https://games.ala.org/
- Weller L. (2018). *Gamification and library instruction.* University of New Mexico. http:// www.unm.edu/~lweller1/gamification/
- El-Tayib, B. (2020, January 24). Bring tabletop role-playing games into the library and classroom for educational opportunities across curricula. *School Library Journal.* https://www.slj .com/?detailStory=bring-tabletop-role-playing-games-into-classroom-for-cross-curricular -educational-opportunities

Social story: a social learning tool, usually depicting a social situation or process such as using the library, that uses visual cues to help youth gain interpersonal communication skills. Social studies are particularly useful for youth with autism spectrum disorders; such stories are most effective when individualized or at least created for a specific library, using a first-person point of view. The social stories may be presented in print or digital format. Examples are provided at:

- *Libraries and Autism.* http://www.librariesandautism.org/newresources.htm
- Autism Services, Education, Resources, and Training Collaborative. (2022). *At the library social story, parts 1-2. Pennsylvania* Bureau of Supports for Autism and Special Populations. https://paautism.org/resource/library-social-story/
- *Social stories about visiting the library.* (2022). Johnson County Public Library. https://www.pageafterpage.org/social-stories
- Social stories. (2022). *School Library Outreach.* https://blogs.glowscotland.org.uk/glowblogs/glasgowslo/social-stories/

Multimedia Products

To engage several senses and optimize UDL, librarians can curate and create multimedia information packages and products.

Video (including sharing videos platform, e.g., TikTok and YouTube): a digital film for permanent documentation of information processes and for recorded library orientations or tours. Several devices can now generate videos: from cell phones to professional video cameras. Likewise, video editing tools can range from computer operating system tools to high-end software applications and professional hardware. Furthermore, Beebom lists top videos that may be hosted and shared on several platforms (https://beebom.com/video-sharing-sites/). More strategies and tips are available at:

- Blechner, J. (2021, July 12). *Tips for creating and editing videos.* Harvard Law School Library. https://guides.library.harvard.edu/video-tips
- Bywatersolutoins. (2020, April 17). *How to create video content for your library!* YouTube. https://www.youtube.com/watch?v=Y7FU_DSNOcM
- King, D. (2018, November 1). Making library videos: Seven simple steps to visual marketing. *American Libraries.* https://americanlibrariesmagazine.org/2018/11/01/making-library-videos/
- Perry, A. (2011). Lights, camera, action!: How to produce a library minute. *College & Research Libraries News.* https://crln.acrl.org/index.php/crlnews/article/view/8563/8914

Screencast: a video recording (usually with audio) of the information displayed on a computer or mobile device screen to show digital processes or other content. Nowadays, most videoconferencing tools include a recording feature so that real-time sessions can be viewed at one's convenience. Techniques and tips are found at:

- Boeninger, C. (2012). How I make instructional library web videos and screencasts and how you can too. *Library Voice.* https://libraryvoice.com/technology/how-i-make-instructional-library-web-videos-and-screencasts-and-how-you-can-too

- Oldenburg, K. (2020). *Screencasting: Introduction.* Vancouver Community College Library. https://libguides.vcc.ca/screencasting

Presentation program: a software program (e.g., PowerPoint, https://visme.co/blog/powerpoint-alternatives/) for creating multimedia digital content, typically for presentations that combine formats. Techniques and tips are provided at:

- Childress, A. (2019, November 27). How to make an educational PowerPoint presentation—quickly. *Envatotuts.* https://business.tutsplus.com/tutorials/make-an-educational-powerpoint-presentation-quickly--cms-30581
- *Tips for making effective PowerPoint presentations.* (2017, August 8). National Conference of State Legislatures. https://www.ncsl.org/legislators-staff/legislative-staff/legislative-staff-coordinating-committee/tips-for-making-effective-powerpoint-presentations.aspx
- *Using PowerPoint and alternatives successfully.* (n.d.). Lumen. https://courses.lumen-learning.com/boundless-communications/chapter/using-powerpoint-and-alternatives-successfully/

Tutorial: a sequential instructional program or product for self-paced learning. While a tutorial may be in print format, such as a guidebook, tutorials are increasingly in digital form and often delivered online as web pages, library guides, videos, screencasts, and presentations. Effective tutorials usually are interactive and include checks for understanding as well as ways to scaffold learning. Tips and resources are found at:

- Dease, N. (2021). *Making video tutorials.* Pratt Institute Libraries. https://libguides.pratt.edu/making-video-tutorials
- Lieberman, A., & Santiago, A. (2019). Developing online instruction according to best practices. *Journal of Information Literacy, 13*(2), 206-221. https://doi.org/10.11645/13.2.2649

Web page: a hypertext document that combines formats displayable by an Internet browser. Librarians tend to create R&I web pages for dissemination via the library web portal or social media platforms. Tips and best practices are discussed at:

- Bertland, L. (2021). Writing school library web pages. *Resources for School Librarians.* https://www.sldirectory.com/libsf/resf/wpages.html
- Paciotti, P. (2019, December 4). 6 steps to create a great school library website. *Looking Backward.* https://lookingbackward.edublogs.org/2019/12/04/school-lib-website/
- Silkalns, A. (2022). 19 best library website design inspiration for effective learning tools 2022. *Colorlib.* https://colorlib.com/wp/library-website-design/
- Young, D. (2022, January 5). The best way to build a library website 2022 [with no tech skills]. *Website Academy.* https://websiteacademy.com/the-best-way-to-build-a-library-website-with-no-tech-skills/

Social Media Products

Social media has become the default external public relations communication channel, especially for youth. Besides its low bar for access and dissemination of information, social media provides many platforms for active involvement and community building. At one point, many librarians were very wary of Web 2.0 (the precursor for the spirit of social media), and abuses of various kinds still exist, especially cyberbullying, trolling, revenge leaks, and fake news. Nevertheless, social media continues to grow, and librarians can leverage social media to increase "brand" awareness, attract more young people to the library, and produce valuable R&I content for young people to encounter, use, and respond to. In 2018, ALA developed social media guidelines for public and academic libraries, which can provide a framework for policies and procedures (https://www.ala.org/advocacy/intfreedom/socialmediaguidelines).

Blog: a regularly updated website or web page that is typically maintained by one person or small group for informal diary-like entries (i.e., weblog) for time-sensitive information and commentary (usually displayed in reverse chronological order). Blogs typically address different aspects of a broad topic such as reading promotion or information services, and they can vary in length from a few sentences to lengthy treatments. Embedded links and media make the blog more attractive. Comments make blogs more engaging, but the librarian needs to monitor them for appropriateness and relevance. Examples and tips are found at:

- Hursh, A. (2021, April 5). Library blogs are the best? How to use your website to amplify your library marketing message on your own terms. *Super Library Marketing.* https://super librarymarketing.com/2021/04/05/libraryblog-2/
- School library blogs. (2022). *Teacher Certification Degrees.* https://www.teachercertification degrees.com/top-blogs/school-library/
- Schwarzkopf, A. (2015). *Strategies for success: Top 5 blogging tips.* Toledo Lucas County Public Library. https://www.toledolibrary.org/blog/strategies-for-success-top-5-blogging-tips

Social network: an online platform (e.g., FaceBook, Twitter) to share information and other messages. Youth-serving libraries often use social networks to advertise existing new services and resources, including R&I, and to keep users involved through interest groups, online book clubs, and crowdsourced reviews. Platforms such as Twitter can be used for on-the-fly R&I interactions. LIS BD Network provides strategies at https://www.lisbdnetwork.com/library-services-through-social-networking-sites/

Social bookmarking: a social network platform to discover, curate, store, and share content. Social bookmarking websites such as Symbaloo provide a fun visual alternative to resource lists. Social bookmarking is also a good way to crowdsource relevant sources. More social bookmarking websites and tips are offered at:

- Agarwal, A. (2021, December 28). Top 50 social bookmarking sites for 2022 with high DR to get quality links and more exposure. *Bloggers Passion.* https://bloggerspassion.com/social -bookmarking-sites/

- Alerts: Social bookmarking. (2020). University of Missouri Libraries. https://libraryguides .missouri.edu/c.php?g=28298&p=174233
- Symboloo alternatives. (2021). *Alternativeto.* https://alternativeto.net/software/symbaloo

Many of these information packages may be considered as learning objects: self-contained, modular learning aids such as simulations, presentations, and assessments. They may be repurposed for use in different contexts, and they are usually in digital format to facilitate their access and use. Learning objects work very well for librarians who can incorporate them into several R&I arenas. Learning objects need to have high-quality content, be easy to use independently, and reflect good instructional design. Illinois University has produced a press book (https:// iopn.library.illinois.edu/pressbooks/instructioninlibraries/chapter/online-learning-objects-videos-tutorials-and-library-guides/) and reference guide (https://guides.library.illinois.edu/c .php?g=347363&p=2343177) about creating and using learning objects.

CURATING R&I PACKAGES AS COLLECTIONS

Learning objects and other R&I information packages and products can be collected and curated into repositories and other types of databases that are subject-specific or cross-subject areas. The most obvious example is the library web portal itself. A low-tech collection could consist of a collection of print research guides, a display of thematic bookmarks, or even the traditional vertical file.

As an example of a digital learning object repository, MERLOT reviews and collates learning objects, peer reviews each potential learning object using tier criteria, described at http://taste .merlot.org/evaluationcriteria.html/; this database also exemplifies a federated search engine in that most of the materials therein are actually links to the learning objects, wherever they are hosted. MERLOT also serves as a one-stop source for searching other educational repositories such as Digital Public Library of America, Library of Congress's American Memory, National Science Digital Library, New York Public Library Digital Collections, and Open Knowledge Repository. Youth-serving librarians can examine these and other repositories, including those listed in chapter 3, to curate a short, searchable list that would be appropriate for young people, thereby providing a curated alternative to Google searching.

Library repositories are most often found in academic libraries, usually to support their academic community's scholarly publications. For youth-serving librarians, repositories could be used to collate information products, the target audience being youth, youth-serving groups, or librarians. As with other databases, repositories require careful planning, with input from any stakeholder group. Librarians need to determine the purpose and scope of the repository; the software to store and organize the products; how the products will be chosen, collected, and described; how and what the metatags will be determined; roles for each process; possible incentives to contribute; administrative and technical support; and implementation documentation (Callicott, Scherer, & Wesolek, 2015). ACRL developed a scholarly communication toolkit on repositories, which includes several useful resources https://acrl.libguides.com/ scholcomm/toolkit/repositories.

COLLABORATIVE PACKAGING OF INFORMATION

Group curation offers a way to generate substantial packages of information in various forms. The product can be as simple as a Google site, Pinterest board, or Digg stack. The key is developing criteria for selection and incorporation. Especially with the advent of social media, packaging information has much more appeal as a collaborative process. Information sources can be curated as part of the creation and dissemination process, and curation can be accomplished collectively.

For example, in group curation, people with similar interests and expertise collaboratively build a body of knowledge. A good case could be made that Wikipedia exemplifies this collective intelligence as people contribute articles that synthesize a specific topic through a careful selection of information sources. These days, Google Docs and Microsoft Office online are the de facto standard platforms for such group curation, largely replacing some wiki applications. Typically, groups of experts form, often based on professional networking and peer review. They identify a topic to curate and establish criteria for the selection and description of information resources. Sometimes each person in the group takes the lead in a specific facet of the topic to delegate responsibility and expertise; again, Wikipedia is a stellar example of this model.

For any kind of collaborative effort to work, several elements have to be in place. Librarians need to identify how the collaborator benefits the library's R&I services and vice versa, and how they can build and sustain a collaborative partnership. As partners, librarians and collaborators should identify mutual R&I needs and goals along with services using available material and human resources. Then they can determine their strategies, identify roles and functions, and clarify expectations. They need to make sure to document agreements and supporting information. It is usually a good idea to start with a pilot project to assess the members' performance along the way to provide possible interventions as well as the end product, which can serve as a prediction for future collaboration success. Since the focus in this book is R&I services for youth, that mindset should be the guiding principle for these collaborative efforts.

Collaboration among Librarians

Another way to think about collaboratively curating information products is knowledge management, which entails organizing and managing information and resources within an organization. Knowledge management usually entails creating a searchable database of internal documents; one could make a case that such a database exemplifies a type of repository. The same factors used in creating a repository apply to knowledge management databases. Knowledge management databases basically collate the knowledge of its group's members to centralize documents for effective storage and retrieval, cross-fertilize organizational expertise, and facilitate professional development. Typical documents included in such databases for youth-serving librarians would include not only the information products they create and use but also instructional plans, story-hour plans and products, other programming plans and products, reports, policies and procedures, meeting minutes, community contact information and associated documentation, and press releases and other public relations documentation. School librarians can spearhead knowledge management initiatives at their site, coordinating school personnel's documents associated with curriculum, co-curricular activities, administration, facilities, assessments and reports, and community relations; such efforts not only help the school as a whole coordinate effort, but they also demonstrate librarian expertise and value, as well as facilitate librarian access to documents that can inform their own work. Guidance can be found at https://limbd.org/ knowledge-management-strategy-for-a-library/.

More generally, as disseminators of information, librarians can collaborate with their peers to plan and develop collections of R&I sources. For instance, public library systems sometimes have branch libraries with specialized collections, reflecting their neighborhood communities (e.g., by culture, local industries, subject expertise, and clientele demographics). Likewise, large school districts may have specialized magnet schools with library collections that have in-depth resources in certain subject areas, specific populations, or specific grade levels. In both cases, R&I services can be two-tiered, with general questions handled at all sites and referrals made to those specialized libraries. Simultaneously, those libraries are likely to produce supporting specialized R&I products. System-level library web portals can collate and link to the specialized resources; ideally, the affiliated librarians can create a system-wide communication plan such that each librarian is responsible for packaging that library's information assets. Such collaboration can also occur on a local level that involves all types of youth-serving libraries. The result could be a robust searchable collection or repository of digital reference sources that would not unduly burden any one librarian but would rather leverage each person's expertise and scale up librarians' educational contributions. These collaborative approaches are not only cost-effective and leverage collective intelligence, but they optimize the chances that all youth can find resources and support that they want and need.

Collaborating with Other Youth-Serving Adults

Librarians are multidisciplinary information and organization experts. Youth-serving librarians usually have more knowledge of youth's interests and information needs, and school librarians, in particular, are more likely to know about educational settings and their curricula. Other youth-serving adults provide valuable complementary expertise and resources: knowledge of the community and its services, specialized subject-matter expertise, pedagogical experience, technical skill, health and well-being knowledge, mass communication expertise, artistic and performance skill, business experience and networking ability, legal and political experience, social services expertise, social issues expertise, cultural competence, and language skills. All of these experts might have worked with youth in their areas of expertise such as health-care providers, musicians, sports coaches, youth club leaders, lawyers, and social workers.

Each of these experts has a knowledge base and uses resources that could inform R&I services in general, and the more that librarians know their communities, the more effective they are in collaborating with them. In that process, each of these expert groups should be considered in light of their usefulness in curating and creating information packages for youth. They may well have relevant information packages themselves, or groups have identified the need for information packages that can help their youth clientele. Here are just a few examples.

- Classroom teachers. Librarians and teachers can collaboratively develop general subject research guides as well as assignment-level guides. Librarians can teach students how to curate and create class-specific information packages, including digital literacy and citizenship training.
- Sports coaches and recreational leaders. Librarians can collaborate with them to create sports medicine and sports career exploration guides. Library aides can videotape sports fitness practices to add to the library's collection or video channel.
- Club advisors. Librarians and clubs can exchange R&I resources and curate a joint information package. Club members could have technical or creative expertise to help librarians produce information packages.
- Counselors, psychologists, and social workers. They can suggest needs for information packages and can exchange R&I resources with librarians and then collaboratively curate and create information packages such as wellness activities and guides.
- Technical advisors. They can suggest good training resources and help librarians create information packages.
- Health care providers. They may want good preschool reading material—or may have their own curated list (e.g., https://reachoutandread.org/). Librarians can collaborate with them on family literacy activities.
- Business groups. They can provide information about possible volunteer opportunities that librarians can collate as a list for youth. Librarians can collaborate with businesses, integrating youth participants to videotape business interviews for career development.
- Fine and performing artists. Drama groups can act out library procedures. Artists can help librarians produce professional-looking information packages. Library aides can interview artists for career exploration videos. Art educators and librarians—and library clubs—can collaboratively develop career guides.
- Government officials: They can provide information packages that libraries can disseminate, in both print and digital formats. Librarians and their aides can collaborate with government officials to create youth-friendly podcasts on subjects such as children's rights and social services.

Students as Collaborators

Librarians should encourage youth to practice curation functions such as selection, annotation, interpretation, synthesis, organization, and presentation. Each of these activities can promote youth engagement and contribute to curating and creating R&I packages. Especially as young people offer an insider perspective on relevant topics and resources, their involvement can lead to more valuable information products. Furthermore, as librarians train and supervise youth curation, they offer career exploration opportunities.

When young people collaborate in information curation and packaging, they exemplify the outcomes of generative learning theory, which asserts that students are active participants in the learning process, connecting presented information with their prior knowledge, and generating a new understanding of information (Wittrock, 1974). The learner's interest and self-attribution of effort lead to motivation, which activates the learning process. The learner gives sustained attention to receive, analyze, and store information. Next, the generative process coordinates and generates information, integrating, elaborating, and reconceptualizing it. Youth use generative learning strategies when they manipulate, elaborate on, and apply R&I information products. Librarians can support these generative strategies by providing opportunities to collaborate in contributing to information packaging.

Working with Existing Information Packages
Opportunities for youth to work with existing R&I information packages, and add to them, can occur in several ways.

- Polls. Library web portals and social media sites can poll youth about their favorite social media tools such as bookmarking sites and platforms for sharing R&I content.
- Surveys. Library web portals and social media sites can solicit suggestions for topical R&I resources.
- Library youth groups. Preteen and teen library councils, steering committees, and interest clubs can review R&I information packages and suggest additional resources. They can also videotape librarian instruction or story hours.
- Library aides. Especially as they help library users, aides can report on information needs and information packages that are frequently consulted. Aides can also review the hit statistics for R&I information products as well as check for broken links.
- Reference interactions. Librarians can observe young people's reactions and use of R&I information packages, including additional information needs and suggestions for inclusion of other relevant information sources.
- Library instruction. Librarians can observe young people's reactions and use of R&I information packages, including additional information needs and suggestions for inclusion of other relevant information sources. In addition, if the instruction includes asking youth to locate additional resources, those materials that are deemed useful can be added to existing information packages.
- School classes. As students are doing research projects, they can generate a class list of useful resources that can be captured in a social bookmark or other resource sharing tool (e.g., Google Doc, Padlet, Symbaloo Wakelet) and added to the library's collection or repository of research guides.

Youth Curation and Creation of Information Packaging

As a group or individually, young people can create their own R&I information package. Of particular benefit is the creation of open educational resources (OER): resources that are usually in an electronic or digital format, and are freely available at little or no cost. Just as important, they may be used without expressly documented permission. Depending on the content creator's license, OERs may be retained, reused, redistributed, revised, and remixed (Wiley, 2021). The resource itself is attributed so as to credit the creator's recorded ideas. Not only do OERs facilitate access to information, but they are often licensed under Creative Commons agreements, which offer an alternative perceptive to copyright: a process that youth should learn about.

Youth-generated R&I OERs can be as easy as librarians asking library aides or club members to create a review of an R&I resource, which can be posted on the library web portal or social media platform. Other simple R&I products that young people can create for libraries include topical displays, instructional posters, screencast tutorials, short library tour videos, and topical bookmarks or web pages.

As R&I librarians engage with youth and other youth-serving professionals such as school teachers and club advisors, some of the research projects that young people produce can be submitted as OERs to library repositories and open access digital repositories. Typical R&I-related OERS might include study guides, topical presentations, screencast tutorials, annotated bibliographies, local oral histories, R&I websites or ebooks, digital storytelling, and informational podcasts. Encouraging such OERs can increase the chances that the librarian gets to see young people's final projects—as well as broadening authentic audiences for those projects, especially if the librarian showcases the young person's work to the library web portal or social media platform and adds it to the library's collection or in-house repository.

For youth-generated R&I packaged OERs to go beyond their immediate setting usually requires librarians to collaborate with youth-serving stakeholders, such as schools and youth group leaders. Oftentimes librarians have to explain OERs and their benefits for youth, the organization, and communities at large. Libraries may have their own in-house repository or they can suggest other relevant repositories (e.g., https://researchguides.njit.edu/oer/text-books/repositories) or venues for publishing young people's work in general (e.g., https://www.nytimes.com/2018/11/15/learning/out-of-the-classroom-and-into-the-world-70-plus-places-to-publish-teenage-writing-and-art.html).

Science publishers, in particular, are providing venues for youth to publish their science research (https://www.sciencejournalforkids.org/articles/lesson-ideas/science-journals-for-student-research/). One exemplary open access journal is the *Journal of Emerging Investigators*, which publishes biology and physical science research conducted by middle and high schoolers. This journal also mentors teens in terms of peer review and publishing. Another interesting approach is used by the open-access journal *Frontiers for Young Minds*; scientists write research articles for teens to review and give feedback on, and then the final article and review are published in the journal.

Citizen journalism is another arena where young people can create information products. Youth particularly like interactivity that is the result of co-production, where they collaboratively participate in producing and manipulating information. Furthermore, students respond well when given responsibilities to serve their communities, which leads to more positive personal development (Bennett, 2008). For instance, by collecting and disseminating news about community concerns and collaborating with media outlets, students can act as social agents and see themselves as contributors to societal development (Dahlgren, 2005).

In the case of citizen journalism, student contributions can be enhanced through professional mentoring and monitoring. To help these young people communicate effectively in this public arena, librarians can teach investigative skills, and other educators can teach students critical thinking and communication skills. Librarians can help identify potential community workplace volunteer opportunities. Youth can leverage their own interests and peer networks to provide insider information to media outlets; their unique position benefits the media as well as the public at large. By collaborating with the education community, including youth, journalists can maintain professional oversight and mentor upcoming potential employees. On their part, students gain privileged access and insights into the professional world of the media and its relationship to R&I, as well as opportunities to impact their community as informed digital citizens.

Food for Thought: Consumed by Research

The following case study models how to collaboratively integrate information literacy, focusing on research skills, across the curriculum.

A library-led needs assessment found that students needed to improve their research skills. The school librarian needed to make sure those research skills were identified and consistently presented across curricula. At a faculty meeting, these gaps were discussed, and possible interventions were brainstormed. Among the problems was the existence of an outdated and little used school research handbook. While the English department was approached to update the old guide, it was decided that the school librarian should spearhead this effort. The school librarian aligned the research steps to the school's new list of required research skills and to the AASL standards. A committee of academic department representatives and the school librarian reviewed and modified the handbook. Sample students also gave valuable feedback, including thoughts about wording, which was incorporated into the final product. A supplemental teacher's guide was also created to help faculty instruct students in research processes. The committee made sure that the handbook could be used as a "consumable" workbook, and that students and teachers could take one page/step of it as a research process focus worksheet. Committee members pilot-tested the research handbook with their classes and polished the handbook. The final version of the research handbook was given to all faculty and students, and the handbook was posted on the library's web portal for easy access at school and home. To measure the impact of the research handbook, the same assessment methods were used at the end of the semester as were used one year prior for the baseline needs assessment. Among the findings were the following:

- Great use was made of the research guides by students and teachers.
- More attention was made to the research process along with the research product.
- More students completed research assignments, and work was more solid.
- Resources were cited more often and more accurately.
- Less plagiarism was evident.
- The school librarian was more involved in the research process, including the assessment of research products.

LIBRARIANS' ROLES

At this point, it is obvious that librarians can curate and create independently or in collaboration with youth and their adult supporters in several ways and at several points to curate and create information packages. The resultant product will probably be more useful and used if curated and created collaboratively—or at least with input from youth and other relevant stakeholders.

- Need. Librarians might see a need for an information package that they either do not have the time or ability to produce the package, or they need outside information and resources to provide the information in packaged form. The need for an information package might well come from library users, the educational community, or other youth-serving groups.
- Initiation. Librarians can initiate the information packaging process with young persons directly or via their adult supporters. Alternatively, young people, their adult supporters, or the community at large might initiate the process.
- Production. Librarians can vary their contribution to the package curation from consultant to leader. They might take on specific functions such as selector, analyst, writer, organizer, technician, submitter, administrator, or publicist. Within their role or function, librarians might work independently, in tandem, or in close collaboration.
- Training. Librarians might train youth in using the targeted resources, explaining the information skill, curating an information package, or generating the information package. Training may vary in terms of depth, length, and format. Sometimes it is the librarian who needs the training, particularly in advanced packaging techniques such as video editing or coding; some youth and community adults can provide that training in different ways.
- Monitoring. Librarians may vary the amount of supervising and monitoring depending on the difficulty of the task, the knowledge and skill of the persons involved, the dependability of the participants, the timeframe of the process, the materials and fiscal resources needed, the potential impact of the product, the amount of time available, and the availability of other persons (both youth and adults) to monitor the task. Monitoring might be largely hands-off or deeply involved, and the timing of monitoring might differ: from frontloading the oversight to ongoing monitoring, or to merely approving the final product.

REFERENCES

Association of College and Research Libraries. (2012). *Diversity standards: Cultural competency for academic libraries.* American Library Association.

Bennett, W. (Ed.). (2008). *Civic life online: Learning how digital media can engage youth.* MIT Press.

Callicott, B., Scherer, D., & Wesolek, A. (2015). *Making institutional repositories work.* Purdue University Press. http://library.oapen.org/handle/20.500.12657/31579

Dahlgren, P. (2005). The Internet, public spheres, and political communication: Dispersion and deliberation. *Political Communication, 22*(2), 147–162.

International Council of Museums. (2004). *ICOM code of ethics for museums.* International Council of Museums.

Rich, S., Bradley, D., Brennan-Wydra, E., Culler, T., Hanley, E., & Kalt, M. (2019). *Librarian role-playing as a method for assessing student information literacy skills. Paper* presented at the 82nd annual meeting of the Association for Information Science & Technology, Melbourne, October 19–23. DOI: 10.1002/pra2.00018

Valenza, J. (2007). *Discovering a descriptive taxonomy of attributes of exemplary school library websites.* Doctoral dissertation, University of North Texas. http://digital.library.unt.edu/ask:/67531/metadc3911/ml/

Webb, J. (2020). *Digital principle for photography.* Bloomsbury Visual Arts.

Wiley, D. A. (2021). Open educational resources: Undertheorized research and untapped potential. *Educational Technology Research and Development, 69*(1), 411–414.

Wittrock, M. (1974). Learning as a generative process. *Educational Psychologist, 19*(2), 87–95.

FURTHER READING

Fabbi, J., Bressler, D., & Earp, V. (2007). *A guide to writing CMC collection development policies.* American Library Association.

Mehra, B., & Davis, R. (2014). A strategic diversity manifesto for public libraries in the 21st century. *New Library World, 116*(1/2), 15–36.

Nylen, B., & King, S. (2021). Video models and the transitioning of individuals with developmental disabilities: A systematic literature review. *Education and Training in Autism and Developmental Disabilities, 56*(3), 341–353.

Polger, M. (2021). *Library signage and wayfinding design: Communicating effectively with your users.* American Library Association.

Puckett, J. (2015). *Modern pathfinders: Creating better research guides.* American Library Association.

Legal and Ethical Issues

Librarians routinely have to deal with legal and ethical practices when providing R&I services to youth when developing and maintaining R&I collections and when interacting with youth. Youth-serving librarians are responsible for library collections and their use in terms of access, authentication, and security. Similarly, reference creators need to take user access needs issues into consideration as they curate and create R&I products.

Youth-serving librarians also strive for equitable access and treatment, modeling it and teaching it to youth. These interactions serve as learning opportunities for librarians to guide youth in responsible and ethical access, use, and sharing of information; indeed, each aspect of research processes involves ethical or legal considerations.

Professional position statements offer guidance in this arena, although actual incidents can be knotty; to that end, criteria for ethical decision-making are provided for this issue. The chapter ends with suggested next steps for youth-servicing librarians to review and improve their institution's legal and ethical policies and procedures, particularly in terms of equity and social justice.

THE BIG PICTURE

Librarians face legal and ethical issues daily. Is an information resource reliable? Can book selection be a form of censorship? What information is fair to copy? To what degree should library records be kept secure and confidential? Must I provide accurate answers to all queries, such as how to make a gun using a 3D printer? When is equal not equitable? Legal issues are particularly thorny when dealing with children and teens because they have slightly different rights than adults. For instance, children have somewhat limited right to free speech, particularly if it could harm other children. On the other hand, children have more laws protecting them than do adults. Employment by minors, though somewhat regulated by states, may impact library staffing.

Legislation differs from ethics in that ethics reflects social norms but is not necessarily regulated by legal authorities. Laws generally enforce public acts, but unethical acts may be done in private. Especially with the continuing advances in technology, legislation has a hard time keeping up with these advances, and even ethical norms have to be negotiated. Netiquette, online manners, exemplifies the idea of behaving ethically.

Furthermore, sometimes differentiating between legal and ethical behavior can be difficult. For instance, it is legal to have a book in the library that details how to make a bomb, but is it ethical? On the other hand, it might not be legal for librarians to make copies of items, but if a school has tossed out all VHS equipment, the librarian might have a library's VHS tape reproduced into a DVD so a teacher could play it in class. Such differences are more apparent for those institutions that do not receive U.S. federal funding and thus are not answerable to some regulations. For instance, nonpublic schools might not be required legally to provide digital citizenship training, but they would be ethically negligent if they failed to teach such skills.

Nevertheless, as information professionals *and* responsible adults, youth-serving librarians are in a unique position to model, practice, and instruct about legal and ethical management and use of information, especially as they provide R&I services.

FEDERAL LAWS AND REGULATIONS ABOUT MINORS

In that respect, laws for minors sometimes differ from laws for adults—individuals ages eighteen and older. For the general purposes of youth-serving libraries, R&I legal issues focus on those users who are minors (younger than eighteen years old). As such, they are bound by federal regulations such as Every Student Succeeds Act (ESSA), Family Educational Rights and Privacy Act (FERPA), Children's Online Privacy Protection Rule (COPPA), Children's Internet Protection Act (CIPA), and Individuals with Disabilities Education Act (IDEA), as well as possible state regulations. It should be noted that institutions that do not receive federal funds, which is often the case for private schools, typically have more flexibility as to how they address those laws.

ESSA, a federal law passed in 2015, basically reauthorizes the 1965 Elementary and Secondary Education Act (ESEA), which marks the federal role in K-12 public education. This most recent modification gives states more control in determining student academic standards. States still have to submit their goals, standards, and plans to meet those goals, and standardizing testing is still required. One aspect of ESSA was very encouraging: its increased support of school libraries, which can impact R&I services (ALA, 2022). School librarians can participate in school planning for digital literacy, they can be funded to support instructional services, they can get funding for collection development and professional development, and they can receive funds to facilitate integrating technology into learning activities. These provisions all support R&I services: from improving reference collections to providing technology-enhanced R&I services.

FERPA protects the privacy of students' educational records. It gives certain rights to parents (with written permission) and school officials to those records, and when a child becomes eighteen, those rights transfer over to that now-adult child or when that child attends a post-secondary school. Other parties might have access to those records under special conditions, such as judicial orders, accreditation entities, and approved researchers. Private schools, if they do not receive federal funds, are not covered by FERPA, nor are public libraries; however, joint school-public libraries typically are. The main issue for school librarians in general is determining whether library records about students are considered educational. The definition of an educational record is fuzzy, so school librarians need to develop privacy policies that cover student use of library resources, including online materials, and ensure that those policies are approved by the school board or other relevant policy-making body. Furthermore, school librarians should collect the minimum amount of personal information possible and delete any records after their usefulness (e.g., once an item is returned after borrowing it or website history). If possible, librarians should use data encryption to enhance privacy production; at the least, librarians should make sure that their integrated library management systems provide several administrative access levels so that individuals with only check-out privileges do not access to private information other than the name. This practice is particularly important if the library uses a union catalogue that includes circulation features. The issue of educational records also arises in conjunction with the Individuals with Disabilities Education Act as it applies to youth ages three to twenty-one.

On the other hand, The USA PATRIOT Act (Uniting and Strengthening America by Providing Appropriate Tools Required to Intercept and Obstruct Terrorism) expands law enforcement surveillance and investigative powers, including telecommunications. To a degree, this act countermands FERPA and can jeopardize intellectual freedom and privacy. The American Library Association (ALA) maintains a clearinghouse of useful resources to help deal with this act: https://www.ala.org/advocacy/patriot-act.

COPPA is particularly tricky to interpret. Commercial websites and online services directed at children constitute the target audience of COPPA, which addresses collecting, using, or disclosing information from children under the age of thirteen online. There is one caveat: the service provider must have actual knowledge that the children are younger than thirteen; ignorance "frees" them from liability. Technically, COPPA applies to libraries with public access online because they collect personal information for remote circulation services, might have public photos of minors, or offer public social media features that reveal personal information. Therefore, such parties have to post a clear, comprehensive online private policy about their practices; get parental consent (with limited exceptions) before collecting information; allow parents to see that information about their child; and maintain the confidentiality, security, and integrity of that information. In K–12 schools, which can act as loco parentis, those institutions have the right to act on behalf of parents who can give that consent. This decision to opt in may occur when subscribing to a learning management system or certain educational software, especially if it is cloud based. Additionally, large private schools may be impacted by COPPA fiscally if they are considered for profit. The Federal Trade Commission is the federal agency that enforces COPPA; their FAQ guide provides useful tips on compliance (https://www.ftc.gov/tips-advice/business-center/guidance/complying-coppa-frequently-asked-questions-0#A.%20General%20Questions).

It should also be noted that COPPA does not protect children from obscene or harmful content, such as pornography; the relevant law for that issue is the CIPA. This law applies to schools and libraries that receive discounted rates for Internet access through the E-rate program. CIPA does not apply to those institutions that receive discounts for telecommunications services alone. However, if schools or public libraries receive federal funds for computers or other Internet access, even if they do not receive E-rate discussion, they must comply with CIPA. To comply with CIPA, all of these institutions must have an Internet safety policy (which is usually covered by an acceptable use policy) that includes technology protection measures (which are usually covered by Internet blocking and filtering software)—even if the public library has no computer that youth can use (which would also raise an equity issue). Surprisingly, technology protection is only against visual depictions so if a browser is set to "text only," that action satisfies the requirement. These institutions must also teach minors about appropriate online behavior, including the use of social media (again, usually covered by requiring students to read the acceptable use policy). CIPA's technology protection measures, in effect, put restrictions on the Telecommunications Act, which requires schools and libraries to receive low-cost, accessible telecommunications services. Those measures also impact some Library Services and Technology Act (SLTA) grants; furthermore, CIPA does not fund the purchase of those technology protection measures.

IDEA was first enacted in 1974 as the Education for All Handicapped Children Act: a civil rights measure to provide equitable public education to this population. This act applies to youth from birth to age twenty-one, providing age-appropriate services: from early intervention services for children younger than three years old and their family to transition plans for teenagers. IDEA embraces universal design for learning (UDL), which affirms librarians' principle of inclusive practice. IDEA also helps to ensure that library videos are closed captioned or video described. IDEA has also funded several projects to support this population such as Bookshare's accessible online library collections and CAST (Center for Applied Special Technology)'s project for developing software that can adapt and customize digital materials for children with disabilities; these projects help to expand library access to resources than youth with disabilities share. In addition, long before IDEA, the National Library Service for the Blind and Print Disabled at the Library of Congress has provided books and magazines in braille and audio formats without charge via libraries.

Other federal acts that require appropriate resources and services to address individuals with disabilities include the Americans with Disabilities Act (ADA) and the Assistive Technology Act.

LIBRARY PROFESSION DOCUMENTS THAT SUPPORT LEGAL AND ETHICAL BEHAVIOR

Guiding principles for R&I librarians include equitable access, intellectual freedom, intellectual property, and privacy and confidentiality. Library organizations have developed a document to codify professional practice. Increasingly, these youth have been mainstreamed into public education while designing programs to meet individual needs.

Library Bill of Rights

These principles are codified by the ALA's Library Bill of Rights, which was first adopted in 1939 and most recently approved in 2019. It affirms "that all libraries are forums for information and ideas, and that the following basic policies should guide their services" (p. 1):

- Provide library resources that present all points of view for the community's information.
- Challenge censorship and resist curtailment of freedom of access and expression.
- Enable people to access and use the library, regardless of a person's origin, age, background, gender or sex, economic situation, disability, or view (including religion and politics).
- Advocate for privacy and confidentiality in library use.

The Bill of Rights has further clarified its interpretations, which include the following:

- Equity, diversity, inclusion. Librarians should support equity, diversity, and inclusion in all their library efforts.
- Diversity in collection development. Materials should represent a wide array of people and cultures in order to authentically reflect a variety of information.
- Challenged resources. Libraries should have a written collection development and promotion policy that includes procedures for challenged materials.
- Internet filtering. While Internet filtering is not recommended it may be legally required; librarians should have policies and procedures to minimize the negative impacts of filtering, such as unblocking needed content while maintaining user privacy. Nor should librarians expurgate library materials (e.g., deleting questionable words or drawing in clothing).
- Access to resources and services for minors. Access, including online activity, should not be restricted due to the users' age. School libraries, in especial, should promote intellectual freedom.
- User-generated content in library discover systems (e.g., ILMS). Libraries can provide opportunities for the user to generate content that engages with these systems. Libraries should note that such content could impact files, interface, and information flow.

Library Code of Ethics

As with other professions, librarians have a code of conduct, which describes their legal and ethical duty to their clients and to society. As with the Library Bill of Rights, the ALA Code of Ethics and its related codes can guide youth-serving librarians' decision-making process, particularly when they have to address situations that involve ethical conflicts. As an example, a librarian may try to find a work-around solution when a youngster cannot pay a library fine required for replacing a lost book.

As with the Library Bill of Rights, the ALA began talking about an ethical code in the early twentieth century, with the first code being adopted in 1939. Their core operational definition of ethics posits an "essential set of core values which define, inform, and guide our professional practice" (ALA, 2005). This Code of Ethics provides a framework to guide ethical decision-making. It includes statements about excellence in service, intellectual property and freedom, collegiality, conflict of interest, and professional growth. In 2021, ALA added another principle: "To confront inequity and oppression; to enhance diversity and inclusion; and to advance racial and social justice" (p. 1). The ALA Code of Ethics also has more detailed interpretations for specific issues, which impact R&I services.

- Copyright. Libraries support intellectual property by acquiring and promoting original creative endeavors, as well as informing their users about copyright and advocating for users' rights.
- Conflicts of interest. Librarian-vendor relations should avoid financial gain or undue influence, for instance.
- Ethics and social media. User education and user privacy extend to social media. Because the material is not only broadcast widely but hard to delete, librarians need to be particularly mindful about the accuracy, appropriateness, and intellectual property of materials that are created and shared on; they also have to honor their users' privacy and rights.

Furthermore, ALA takes a strong advocacy stance, which applies to R&I issues. For instance, ALA addresses censorship issues; supports library workers; fights for intellectual freedom; and fosters equity, diversity, and inclusion. ALA's advocacy webpage (https://www.ala.org/advocacy/) provides resources for standards, policies, programming, outreach, and workplace development.

Although the American Association of School Librarians (AASL) does not have a separate code of ethics, it has identified some common professional beliefs that impact ethical R&I service (AASL, 2018, p. 11).

1. The school library is a unique and essential part of a learning community.
2. Qualified school librarians lead effective school libraries.
3. Learners should be prepared for college, career, and life.
4. Reading is the core of personal and academic competency.
5. Intellectual freedom is every learner's right.
6. Information technologies must be appropriately integrated and equitably available.

AASL has also developed a series of position statements that address R&I ethical practice (https://www.ala.org/aasl/advocacy/resources/statements):

- Instructional Role of the School Librarian
- Labeling Practices

- Policy on Confidentiality of Library Records
- School Library Scheduling

While ALA's statements are laudatory in the eyes of library workers, they do not meet the test of law. Nevertheless, they can drive library policies that could have legal consequences.

BASES FOR MAKING LEGAL AND ETHICAL DECISIONS

Few librarians have legal expertise or credentials, but all libraries have some kind of legal counsel. Furthermore, libraries have approved policies and procedures to draw upon. Especially when legal and ethical challenges arise, being able to rely upon policies and procedures to address the issue minimizes unfair or arbitrary practices. If those documents themselves seem inequitable, librarians can confer with their supervisors or legal expert and can recommend reviewing those documents afterward to improve them. Particularly in light of recent political, social, and health issues, it makes sense for all libraries to review their policies and procedures in light of legal decisions as well as the revised ALA Bill of Rights and Code of Ethics.

In addition to the above legal and professional guidance, approaches and criteria have been developed to guide making ethical decisions.

The Markkula Center for Applied Ethics (2021) identified five approaches to ethical decision-making.

1. Rights approach. Are the rights of all stakeholders respected? Are some rights more important than others—and why?
2. Justice approach. Does the decision treat all stakeholders equally, equitably, or proportionately?
3. Utilitarian approach. Considering all stakeholders who would be affected, does the decision result in the most happiness and does the least harm and pain?
4. Common good approach. Considering all factors, does the decision best serve all the stakeholders as a whole, not just some of them?
5. Virtue approach. Does the decision help youth become a better person?

The center also developed a framework for ethical decision-making.

1. Identify the ethical issues. Who benefits and who is harmed? Is the impact uneven among the stakeholders? To what degree are the potential solutions good or bad? To what degree is the issue more than a legal one?
2. Get the facts. What are the facts? What information is unknown? What information can be gained? How much information is needed to make a decision? Who are the stakeholders? Have they all been consulted? What are the most important concerns—and according to whom? Why? Are there some creative solutions?
3. Evaluate alternative actions. What option best respects all stakeholders' rights? (Rights approach). What option is the fairest? (Justice approach). What option does the most good

and the least harm for the most stakeholders? (Utilitarian approach). What option best serves the community as a whole? (Common Good approach). What option makes me a better person? (Virtue approach).

4. Choose an option and test it. What was the result of the action? What was learned from this experience? What are the next steps, if any?

CURRENT TRENDS THAT INVOLVE LEGALITIES AND ETHICS

Technological Advances

Technological advances pose new ethical questions. Because of technology, copying and sharing are easier than ever; at the same time, getting permission to copy resources from one format to another because of wear-and-tear or loss has been difficult, although the Copyright Act (17 U.S. Code, Section 108) has given additional privileges to libraries and nonprofit educational institutions in this regard. It should be noted that such copies may not be distributed in that format beyond the physical site.

For certain, digital resources and platforms outrace copyright law. For instance, the Digital Millennium Copyright Act (DMCA) of 1998 prohibits any effort to circumvent technological protection measures, such as encryption. However, Section 1201, most recently ruled in 2021, enables persons with disabilities to use assistive technologies to bypass those measures as long as the resource has been lawfully obtained and creators have been remunerated or the material is a nondramatic literary work. In addition, because less than 10 percent of published materials are produced in a universally accessible format, a provision has been added to help access for individuals with print disabilities; the 2013 Marrakech Treaty to Facilitate Access to Published Words for Persons Who Are Blind, Visually Impaired or Otherwise Print Disabled (ratified by the United States in 2019) allows authorized institutions such as libraries to make a copy in an accessible format for such populations and to exchange those copies across borders.

Technological advances such as social media and the increasing prevalence of library makerspaces have expanded the creation and distribution of user-generated content. Can users add comments to library catalogues and social media that are disrespectful? Can users make a profit from selling products created with library 3D printers and supplies? What if disinformation, plagiarized, or other illegal content is made available through the library? Librarians should probably monitor such content or at least hold patrons accountable for noncompliance with acceptable use policies. A positive approach is educating youth about copyright and digital citizenship. Fortunately, Section 512 of the Copyright Act also protects information organizations from liability if a user stores infringing materials on the organization's computer system.

Despite these technological advances, the digital divide remains with respect to physical and intellectual access to information; this situation was starkly evident during the COVID-19 pandemic, especially disadvantaging youth with disabilities and youth in rural or lower socioeconomic situations. As societal information access safety nets, youth-serving libraries have an ethical responsibility to provide Internet access to their communities, at least on-site. With the advent of the COVID-19 pandemic, many schools and some public libraries are lending laptops to help young people access online information. These institutions have also worked with Internet providers such as cable companies to provide more wifi hotspots and offer connectivity discounts for needy households. Librarians have also been active in advocating for net neutrality: not interfering with Internet traffic (e.g., advantaging or blocking some websites and varying or interfering with network speed arbitrarily), which could jeopardize intellectual freedom.

Equity

Libraries need to ensure equitable physical and virtual access to R&I resources for youth. Young children, in particular, need explicit attention; for instance, can they read the library catalogue? Can they choose an appropriate book independently? Can they reach bookshelves? More fundamentally, minors often do not have the same access to information as adults because of circulation policies, fees associated with usage, literacy skills, and even transportation limitations.

Remember, too, that equality is not the same as equitable. As noted earlier, if everyone gets the same-sized keyboard, it may be equal, but it is not equitable for youngsters with small fingers; providing a smaller keyboard for children's computers results in a more even playing field to be able to use a keyboard to access online information. Similarly, providing a lower table for individuals in wheelchairs is an equitable action to ensure that everyone can access a desktop computer.

These examples point out the need for digital inclusion relative to equipment to access R&I sources. What about content? Are R&I online resources mobile-friendly? Websites should be accessible for individuals with vision or hearing impairments. Does the R&I collection have online material in all the languages reflected on your community's young people? Does the library provide easier websites for beginning readers and English language learners (ELLs)?

More fundamentally, librarians should help all young people learn how to use the Internet and other digital information tools effectively and efficiently, which may call for differentiated approaches and supports for diverse populations.

Cultural Responsiveness

Increasingly, the importance of cultural responsiveness has become apparent: the need to consider and act upon content and interaction from the user's cultural frame of reference (Cowden et al., 2021). Librarians need to manage R&I services that are culturally responsive for children and teens; this knowledge and mindset is a good ethical practice. This approach is especially important in an increasingly diverse and multilingual United States. Not only do different groups have rich cultural knowledge, but they may also manage information differently, which practices need to be respected in R&I interactions. Likewise, youth should have the opportunity to access R&I resources about different cultures to learn more about themselves and others.

Cultural responsiveness also constitutes one aspect of social equity and justice, for the goal is not only affirmation of youth and their culture but also youth cultural competence and resultant empowerment. In that respect, Paulo Freire's liberation theology underlies much of cultural responsiveness in that he linked education to socio-politics, and he asserted that educators (such as librarians) should act as facilitators to help learners develop a critical consciousness through reflection and action (Cowden et al., 2021).

Librarians and youth should also realize that culture can refer to many kinds of groups with a shared set of attitudes, values, and practices, such as people with disabilities, LGBTQ+ individuals, youth in military families, teen parents, and children of different religions. Moreover, a person can be a member of several cultures. Therefore, as a youth-serving librarian, the more that you know about the community of young people, the more effectively you can be in providing culturally responsive R&I collections and services. Such action starts from the very first interaction as introductions are very important. Likewise, you should vary your communication style to approximate the youth's paralanguage and engage the youth's strengths, be they in terms of a communication channel, individual or group preference, and hands-on or abstract. In terms of practice, if, for instance, you have library aides who practice Islam, you should let them have breaks to pray. You should also strive for authentic and situated learning; for example, you might provide special story hours for teen moms, where they can learn parenting skills along with participating in their children's library program activities. In that regard, doing one-shot class R&I instruction is not very conducive to such culturally responsive interaction; in such cases, librarians have to employ a UDL approach and provide choices in resources and interaction.

Such practices will not be successful if you, as a librarian, do not first build trust, gain and value cultural awareness, and model inclusive practices. Renee Wells (2020) developed an in-depth anti-racism self-assessment tool that can help youth-serving librarians reflect on their own attitudes and actions (https://unitedwayaddisoncounty.org/client_media/files/Renee-WellsAntiRacismSelfAssessmentTool.pdf). At the organizational level, the ALA Committee on Diversity (Harper, Franklin, & Williams, 2021) developed a diversity, equity, and inclusion (DEI) scorecard that can help in decision-making to improve R&I services in terms of organizational culture, professional development, staff, budget, and data practices (https://www.ala.org/aboutala/sites/ala.org.aboutala/files/content/2021%20EQUITY%20SCORECARD%20FOR%20LIBRARY%20AND%20INFORMATION%20ORGANIZATIONS.pdf).

ETHICAL ISSUES RELATED TO LIBRARY PRINCIPLES

Intellectual Freedom

One of the tenets of the Universal Human Rights is the right to information. Jaeger, Gorham, and Taylor (2019) stated:

> Increasingly, a central aspect of human rights is information. As information and related technologies have become increasingly essential to education, employment, social interaction, and civic participation, greater focus has been placed on the idea that information can be seen as a necessary human right. (p. 17)

The ALA defines intellectual freedom as "the right of library users to read, seek information, and speak freely as guaranteed by the First Amendment" (ALA, 2018, p. 1). Librarians hold intellectual freedom in the highest regard, even to the extent of accepting the freedom to seek and to hold fallacious ideas, even though the earth is two-dimensional. Basically, librarians promote the unfettered flow of information. At the same time, they select resources according to selection criteria such as accuracy, authoritativeness, and appropriateness developmentally. Librarians also try to help young people evaluate resources and content to determine their source, perspective, and content quality so they can make informed decisions.

One main facet of intellectual freedom is access. Censorship is the antithesis of intellectual freedom: restricting the flow of information. The censorship might consist of actions such as redacting, restricting, relocating, or removing information. Self-censorship can also occur, often out of fear of stakeholder pressure. The recent flurry of school library book-banning has had a chilling effect on material selection, including reference materials that might be considered controversial, such as medical manuals or religious texts.

Rubin and Rubin (2020) identified several factors that can affect intellectual freedom in terms of restricting access: personal values, community values, the desire to protect children, and concerns about library survival (e.g., withdrawing funding if undesirable R&I resources or programs are provided). As counterarguments, Rubin and Rubin also identified facts that can promote access: the need to educate young people, the duty to protect children's rights, and professional standards.

As is evident by now, intellectual freedom is under special scrutiny when it comes to children and adolescents. CIPA is a legal example. The underlying concept is that children are vulnerable to corrupting ideas; they do not have as much knowledge experience as adults to draw upon, and they are not emotionally mature to make wise decisions. To be fair, those limitations could also be applied to some adults. Nevertheless, some people think that certain subject matter, which might be included in reference collections, might negatively impact youth, such as sexual content, violence, and "offensive" language. Visual content is especially concerning as a young person does not have to be able to read in order to be exposed to certain controversial images, such as sodomy. One of the problems is over-generalizing the impact of content: the "slippery slope" of access to information. For instance, it is doubtful that any elementary school librarian would select books on human orgies (most likely because youngsters would not understand how and why people would perform such acts in a group), but should they reject a picture book that shows two girls holding hands?

Internet filtering (again referring to CIPA) is another slippery slope. The most basic issue is that no perfect filtering software exists: more specifically, no perfect algorithm exists (as witnessed in social media). Filters can block needed information, such as genocide, SuperBowls XXX to XXXVIII, or even sextants. Batch (2014) asserted that filters overblock legitimate websites about 17 percent of the time. Manually applied workarounds exist for most filtering software, but they may be applied arbitrarily; for instance, some school districts block any website that has at least one objection, while other school districts unblock any website that has one objection to its unavailability. This practice is especially problematic in K–12 school districts, where information about sexually transmitted diseases might be useful for a high school health course but not useful for kindergarteners (hopefully). Especially when filtering software needs to know about the user (as a possible solution for the immediate issue mentioned earlier), privacy guarantees are jeopardized. Furthermore, young people often figure out how to bypass filters, including using programs designed for just that purpose (even using a non-U.S. search engine can often "unlock" websites). The most obvious library solution is to teach young people how to evaluate information, if for no other reason than they gain skills that will help them when they graduate—and in the meantime when they access the Internet outside of school or libraries. Probably the trickiest situation occurs in public libraries, where a child might sit at a computer next to an adult viewing mature content on the adjacent computer. Usually public libraries have a separate section for children's computers, but it is also a good idea to have carrel-like computer stations to optimize privacy; there are also computer monitor overlay screens that prevent another person, at a different viewing angle, from seeing the online content.

Access is also an equity issue. In some areas, the library is the one place where youth can access R&I information. By law, librarians also need to make sure that resources are accessible to all individuals with disabilities. Even if no such law existed, it is an ethical responsibility to provide the greatest possible access to information for all youth, which was discussed earlier in terms of technological advances.

Several professional organizations offer valuable resources to guide youth-serving librarians to ensure intellectual freedom. The ALA has web pages that link to resources addressing intellectual freedom, including specifically censorship, (https://www.ala.org/advocacy/intfreedom/censorship) and tools to challenge censorship and other intellectual freedom rights. One of their web pages focuses on minors' intellectual freedom (https://www.ala.org/advocacy/intfreedom/minors).

The National Council of Teachers of English maintains an intellectual freedom center that provides relevant information (https://ncte.org/resources/ncte-intellectual-freedom-center/). More specifically, the National Coalition against Censorship discusses technology-related legal and policy issues of censorship in public libraries (https://ncac.org/resource/the-cyber-library-legal-and-policy-issues-facing-public-libraries-in-the-high-tech-era). Focusing on technology, the International Society for Technology in Society provides articles on digital equity (https://www.iste.org/explore/topic/digital-equity).

Intellectual Property

Freedom of information needs to be balanced with intellectual property. The World Intellectual Property Organization (WIPO) defines intellectual property as "creations of the mind, such as inventions; literary and artistic works; designs; and symbols, names, and images used in commerce" (p. 1). Intellectual property is protected by copyright, patent, and trademark law. As WIPO states, "By striking the right balance between the interests of innovators and the wider public interest, the IP system aims to foster an environment in which creativity and innovation can flourish" (p. 1).

Intellectual property encompasses a variety of laws. Copyright law is the most well-known legislation in the library world because it protects intellectual property in terms of the rights and compensation of intellectual creators balanced with the needs for access to information. The Copyright Act of 1976 is the driving statute; it codifies fair use as well as describes copyright rights and limitations. The Sonny Bono Copyright Act of 1998 extended copyright to seventy years after the creator's death, which impacted works about to be entered into the public domain; as of 2022, works published before 1927 now enter the public domain, which means that anyone can use the work without getting permission or even citing the original author, but no one can own it. The DMCA, also added in 1998, deals with technological issues, especially online material. It addresses digital presentation and limits database company liability as well. The technology practices can be very complex and restrictive, as these examples demonstrate:

- Images should not be altered or resized without explicit permission.
- If made public, photographs of recognizable people require written permission.
- Sharing scanned or digitized work publicly requires prior permission.
- Music and video downloads can be problematic, particularly as different producers may give different permissions for different products.
- Depending on the company's licensing agreement, computer program appearance, graphics, and sound might be covered by copyright.
- Online slander and libel, such as on social networks, have legal and possibly criminal consequences, even for minors.

Social media practice poses even more questions: Who is the author? For documents that are dynamic, such as wikis and blogs, what is copyrighted when compensation is considered? How are mash-ups copyrights? How are file-sharing entities handled? How does their copyright differ from traditional databases?

Fortunately, educational institutions enjoy more freedom in using copyrighted materials if the intent is teaching and personal research without market compensation. These fair use exemptions are listed in Section 107 of 17 U.S. Code 106:

1. the purpose and character of the use, including whether such use is of commercial nature or is for nonprofit educational purposes;
2. the nature of the copyrighted work;
3. amount and substantiality of the portion used in relation to the copyrighted work as a whole; and
4. the effect of the use upon the potential market for or value of the copyrighted work.

The TEACH Act of 2002 (Technology, Education and Copyright Harmonization) enables teachers to apply the same copyright practices to online learning environments as long as the resources are available only to the enrolled students for the period of the course.

When thinking about legalities, youth and the general public often consider librarians as the copyright police in their role as R&I providers and facilitators. Librarians probably know more about intellectual property and freedom issues than anyone else within the general populace, besides lawyers, and are more likely to interact with youth than lawyers.

For youth, intellectual property is most often addressed when they plagiarize or illegally duplicate electronic products such as music and software. Those practices may range from forgetting to use quotation marks out of ignorance or sloppiness, to making a profit from selling their own pirated video games. At the least, librarians should model and teach about intellectual property such as copyright law, including the fact that young people can take pride in their own work and even copyright it.

Intellectual property can come across as very restrictive and negative. Instead, librarians can suggest proactive ethical practices that comply with intellectual property, such as:

- taking notes from memory rather than taking a photo or copy-pasting text;
- learning how to paraphrase;
- creating images (e.g., drawing and photography) rather than copy-pasting from other sources; and
- citing accurately and completely.

Another good practice is the use of open education resources (OERs). These resources are publicly available for anyone to use, remix, modify, and redistribute, depending on the license applied. OERs are usually regulated by a Creative Commons license that stipulates how materials may be used. Typically, individuals can use and modify them as long as they credit the original authors. People are also encouraged to submit their modifications for others to use, crediting the changes. In this way, intellectual property is shared ethically and advances knowledge quickly. For instance, increasingly, librarians are developing repositories or data-bases of OERs that are generated in-house or within the library system or school district. These databases might include original works by the community, educational lessons and learning activities, data sets, and so forth. These recorded documents are also subject to copyright law, but increasingly, librarians and educators encourage the use of a Creative Commons Sample directories and repositories of OERs can be found at http://creativecommons.org.

As with other R&I issues, different cultures may have alternative attitudes and practices relative to intellectual property. This issue is especially important when dealing with new Americans and highlights the importance of respectful, ethical practice.

Several educational guidelines about copyright and fair use exist:

- ALA on copyright: https://www.ala.org/advocacy/copyright
- ALA for Information Technology Policy: https://alair.ala.org/handle/11213/23
- Copyright Advisory Office of Columbia University Libraries' Information Services: https://copyright.columbia.edu/index.html
- National Council of Teachers of English: http://www.ncte.org/positions/statements/fairuse medialiteracy and https://cccc.ncte.org/cccc/committees/ip/ipreports/transforming

- Library of Congress. Taking the Mystery Out of Copyright (website for teachers): http://www
.loc.gov/teachers/copyrightmystery/#
- Stanford University links on fair use: http://fairuse.stanford.edu
- University of Texas copyright crash course: https://guides.lib.utexas.edu/copyright
- The K–12 Internet Resource Center provides a student-friendly website on copyrights and
intellectual property rights: https://www.k12irc.org/development/policies/copyrights.php
- Media Education Foundation's "A Fair(y) Use Tale" is a fun video using Disney movies to
explain Fair Use: http://www.youtube.com/watch?v=4bK8AZSYtPU

Privacy and Confidentiality

Can parents, teachers, or even federal agents access individual library records? Is it OK to give
homeroom teachers a class list of students with overdue books or fees? Can library aides have
access to borrower records? How can librarians protect against third-party data collection of
online applications from library computers? These are just some of the scenarios that youth-
serving librarians might encounter. Librarians need to optimize data privacy and confidentiality, paying special attention to protecting children. ALA's website on privacy (https://www.ala
.org/advocacy/privacy) discusses core values; includes privacy and confidential FAQs; provides
guidelines, checklists, and privacy audits; notes laws and law enforcement inquiries; and has a
section specifically addressing minors. The Markkula Center for Applied Ethics' project "Your
Privacy Online" (https://www.scu.edu/ethics/privacy/) provides non-age-specific information
about data ownership, privacy loss impact, privacy protection, ethics, and case studies.

Adams (2013) suggested several actions to protect minors' privacy rights.

- Keep as few confidential records as possible (e.g., erase borrowing information once an item
is returned).
- Password-protect circulation and other sensitive programs. Establish levels of access to such
programs so that library workers, and volunteers, have access appropriate to their duties.
- Keep user questions, reserves, ILL information, and any fines/fees confidential.
- Discuss youth's library privacy rights and issues with site administrators and check how the
site complies with associated state and federal laws.
- Find out if the library's legal entity has a privacy policy, noting those circumstances when
a user's records can be released; help develop such a policy and have it approved if no such
document exists.
- Find out if the library's legal entity has a records retention policy; help develop such a policy
and have it approved if no such document exists.
- Train staff and other relevant stakeholders such as parents about privacy rights and policies,
including the need to keep library records confidential.
- Teach youth about online privacy settings, sharing of personal information, and other privacy protection actions—as well as respecting other people's privacy.

More recent issues about privacy examine the vendors' side. Increasingly, Internet and digital resource vendors can trace the data generated when people use digital technology (Hakimi, Eynon, & Murphy, 2021). For instance, GPS activity, the use of cookies, keystrokes, and even facial expressions can be captured. These data may be used internally (e.g., to see web searching history, track student's course progress, discover purchasing habits, or identify social influencers). They may also be shared, typically for profit, to other entities, often without users' informed consent. While companies such as Amazon, Apple, Facebook, Google, and Pearson are known for this kind of activity, extremist groups can also take advantage of data tracing for their own agenda. Analysis of such data helps marketers and other groups strategically target populations to influence their consumption and behaviors. Especially when large data sets are combined and disaggregated, supposedly anonymous data becomes personalized so that groups can monitor individual actions. Furthermore, data tracing can lead to biased and discriminatory algorithms, such as profiling, that perpetuate continued injustices. Thus, data tracing raises privacy issues as well as unethical influence and action. In addition, the question of who owns the data becomes both a legal and ethical question. For those reasons, librarians need to ask Internet, software, and hardware vendors direct questions about data tracing features and efforts to protect privacy and secure data. Librarians should also educate youth about data tracing, and means to control it, as part of digital safety and citizenship.

Several groups offer guidance that can help librarians' effort vis-à-vis privacy:

- ALA on privacy issues. https://www.ala.org/advocacy/privacy
- U.S. Department of Education on student privacy. https://studentprivacy.ed.gov
- Library Freedom Project on surveillance. https://libraryfreedom.org/
- Privacy Rights Clearinghouse. https://privacyrights.org/

Security and Authentication

Unfortunately, the security of library physical and digital resources has become increasingly problematic. Cybersecurity is now a significant industry, but it is hard to predict and outpace hackers and other data gatherers who might want access to data that they could capture, modify, or damage. While it would seem that libraries would have little to worry about security, library records contain personal information that could interest some parties, perhaps unscrupulously.

At the same time, some authorization and authentication processes can make it difficult for users to access the information needed, such as ways to retrieve or to change a password. Sometimes, out of compassion to help a young person, adults may share personal login in formation, only to find their own documents impacted.

For decades, schools have required acceptable use policies, which explain responsible and unacceptable online use and describe the consequences of noncompliance. Parents or guardians have to give consent for their minor children to use the Internet at school; young people age eighteen and older sign that policy themselves. Increasingly, public libraries are instituting acceptable use policies as well. These policies typically address aspects such as network accounts and network etiquette, cyberbullying and other harmful behavior, copyright guidelines, and privacy issues.

On their part, librarians have a responsibility to ensure data security, especially of personal information. All too often, third-party vendors of software can access individuals' data that they enter onto the computer and can trace program and browser-use history. Librarians need to review program and software license agreements carefully in terms of data security and possible use of any data accessed.

It should be noted that data security goes both ways. Those same vendors expect that libraries will keep program content secure as well from unauthorized access. Such precautions are easier to monitor when authorization is confined to static IP address, such as those designated within the physical library. In such cases, librarians might post the authentication information on the computer stations. However, most libraries provide and promote remote access to their web portal, including links to subscription databases. Such access requires authentication, usually consisting of an ID and a password; librarians typically work with their institution's IT department to set up these authentication terms (oftentimes consisting of the user's library card or student ID number and a self-generated password). School librarians may provide that information on the students' school ID card or school planner. A bad practice is to post the authentication information on the library web portal itself anyone to see if they can access school information, which is often the case; not only does this practice break the vendor's contract, but it also facilitates hackers' ability to access institutional computer systems and jeopardize data security.

ETHICAL ISSUES IN R&I COLLECTION DEVELOPMENT

R&I collection development constitutes the starting point in intellectual freedom; R&I resources have to be available in order for youth to access and use them. The Library Bill of Rights and Code of Ethics provide the ethical basis for selection. Selection policies, including criteria for digital resources, particularize the process in an equitable way. Special attention should be made to consider the community needs and the importance of diverse voices when selecting R&I resources, including issues of language and readability. To ensure optimum access to digital resources, librarians need to make sure that appropriate hardware and collectivity are available and accessible to all users. The ALA Office for Information Technology Policy (https://alair.ala.org/handle/11213/23) provides information on e-rate, ebooks, and digital content issues. Maintenance and deselection policies should also be employed to ensure that outdated materials are removed. Probably the trickiest ethical issue is possible self-censorship, be it based on personal or community values.

Ethical issues also arise in organizing R&I collections. How high are the shelves, especially for youngsters or individuals in wheelchairs? Are provisions made to access the materials, such as safe stepstools or pagers? Do reserves and e-reserves facilitate access rather than limit it? Librarians should avoid labeling materials by grade level, or marking items as "adults only." Are library catalogues child-friendly? Is the library web portal accessible and easy to navigate?

The other major ethical issue in R&I collection development involves vendor agreements. Librarians need to optimize budget decisions, ensure accessible resources for all youth, and ensure user privacy and data security. Librarians should not be afraid to change vendors if the quality of product or service is not satisfactory, assuming that another vendor is available. Librarians also need to avoid any possible conflict of interest, such as choosing a vendor because they benefit personally (e.g., get paid to be a spokesperson for the product). Even an attractive offer of the library getting a free set of encyclopedias if it promotes the sale of ten copies, or even states that the brand is the best one to buy, constitutes a conflict of interest.

The ALA Office for Literacy and Outreach Service (http://www.ala.org/offices/olos) focuses on ethical issues related to equitable access. They provide guidance for librarians to help provide R&I service for LGBTQ+ people, people of color, people with disabilities, poor and homeless people, and rural and tribal libraries.

ETHICAL ISSUES IN REFERENCE INTERACTION

RUSA's guidelines for R&I behaviors reflect professional and ethical standards. Librarians need to respect and show interest in youth and their information needs, and they need to provide youth with appropriate and accurate information in a timely manner. Rubin and Rubin (2020) listed some R&I interactions that would be considered unethical:

- Not listening, not helping to clarity the question, or not getting sufficient information to answer the question.
- Showing discomfort with sensitive topics.
- Excluding or shortcutting the user from the search process.
- Offering biased or lower-quality services to some populations.

Part of ethical behavior consists of modeling and teaching culturally responsive interaction. Such interaction considers students' cultural frames of reference and actively supports everyone's cultural competence and learning achievement. Especially as youth-serving librarians tend to be white middle-class females, they need to develop a critical consciousness that translates into shared power in R&I interaction.

R&I interactions offer a pro-active, preventative learning moment. For instance, when youth ask for help in finding an article in a subscription database aggregator, librarians can point out the citation feature, and make suggestion about ways to paraphrase the text. Librarians can also mention that access to the database costs money, and some of the money is given as royalty to the author. The cost of the subscription may also enable the user to download and keep the article legally. In effect, the library is facilitating young people's ethical access and use of information.

As they provide R&I service, librarians can also point out that some information on the Internet may well be illegal or unethical. While the First Amendment protects the rights of the website creators, youth should be aware of hurtful biases as well as credibility issues. For instance, librarians can use the Counter Extremism Project (https://www.counterextremism

.com/), which provides research and analysis on extremist groups to help understand and counter extreme ideology threats. Furthermore, librarians can alert young people that they may find that websites might include information plagiarized from another website or printed document. In some ways, these examples may cause a young person to think that such practices are permissible, but librarians need to point out that slander and plagiarism can lead to arrests, fines, and imprisonment. By complying with intellectual property laws, young people develop ethical values, and they can be proud of their own intellectual creations.

TEACHING YOUTH ABOUT ETHICAL BEHAVIOR

As realized by now, many ethical issues arise when accessing and using R&I services. As information professionals and responsible adults, librarians are uniquely trained and positioned to model and provide such ethical guidance. Particularly because young people are developing their moral values, they need help to know right from wrong, and to act ethically. Dealing with minors also adds another layer of legal issues and implies an additional ethical responsibility to model and teach ethical behavior so young people will experience and integrate such values.

There are many opportunities for librarians to teach young people ethical information use. In school settings, such instruction is usually best done in collaboration with a classroom teacher. However, public libraries serve as informal educational settings where ethical practice can be modeled and taught as well, especially in reference transactions. Any time that the librarian and a young person interacts is a potential learning moment.

In their set of learning standards (2018), the AASL shared foundation asserted that

> learners should follow ethical and legal guidelines for gathering and using information; . . . the school library serves as a context in which the school librarian ensures that the school community is aware of the guidelines for safe, ethical, and legal use of information; . . . the school library supports ethical processes for information seeking and use. (pp. 112–113)

Conducting Research Ethically

When youth conduct research, they should act ethically. Besides copyright compliance and the larger issue of intellectual property, the following ethical issues need young researchers' consideration (American Psychological Association, 2020). While these guidelines are directed to scholarly research and publication, the underlying principles apply to young persons' research efforts as well, and librarians should show students how their work draws upon the larger world of research.

- Pose ethical research questions. Questions should benefit society, not make conditions worse. For example, research should not be conducted in order to seek revenge on a colleague. Do not misrepresent the purpose of the research. Disclose any possible conflict of interest, such as personal gain. Get administrative approval for research that is conducted using the school community.

- Collect data ethically. Do not misrepresent the purpose of collecting data, unless conceal-ment or deception is justified for the research's value (e.g., the stated purpose is to determine which websites a student uses when in reality the study intends to determine the degree that youth share information about websites). Do not fabricate data. Do not use unethical means to arrive at an ethical result. Keep records safe and confidential.
- Make every effort to protect human and animal subjects and minimize any risk. Normally, research subjects should be voluntary and give informed consent about their responsi-bilities and obligations. Parents or guardians need to give consent for their children to be active research participants. In educational settings, explicit permission is not needed if the research involves normal educational practice, standard tests, anti-invasive surveys, observa-tion of public behavior, collection of preexisting data, and protection of individual identity. Get explicit permission for recording people's distinguishable voices and images.
- Maintain an ethical relationship with people who will be impacted by the research. Be sensi-tive to other people's concerns, such as student evaluations. Try to remain objective, and not favor one person over another. Do not play "spy" for the administration. If a person asks for some information to be "off the record," either keep that commitment or do not permit the person to share the information. Keep confidentialities unless there is imminent danger, such as violence or suicide.
- Analyze data ethically. Any personal biases and gains (such as getting money from a com-mercial database company) that impact interpretation should be openly acknowledged. Data should not be twisted to support some preexisting agenda or assumption. Clarify values that enter into the analysis or interpretation.
- Report the data ethically and in a timely manner. Do not misconstrue the data, findings, dis-cussion, or recommendations. Do not misrepresent data in statistical graphs. Acknowledge other sources of information.

Digital Citizenship

Digital citizenship constitutes a subset of ethics education. Digital citizenship may be defined as the ability and habit of using technology safely, responsibly, critically, productively, and pro-actively to contribute to society. Digital citizenship crosses curricular borders, just information and technology literacies do.

The following four-step process can guide youth in thinking about ethical behaviors, espe-cially in terms of digital citizenship and ways to act. In addition, several digital citizenship learning activities and informational sources can be found at https://csulblis.libguides.com/K12DigitalCitizenship

1. Awareness. Draw attention to young persons' personal digital informational needs and behaviors. How often do they use the Internet? What information do they search for? How do they ascertain the accuracy and value of information found? Use a survey to solicit youth's experiences with social networking and consequences, such as embarrassment, loss

of reputation, or cyberbullying. Ask them how they deal with their digital life in terms of privacy, identity, and social support.

2. Engagement. At this point, youth can learn about intellectual property and intellectual freedom laws as well as other legislation that impact information creation, dissemination, and use. Youth need to know both their rights and their responsibilities. Because technology keeps expanding and changing continuously, laws are behind practice, and even social norms of behavior are dynamic. Students can examine hoax information such as http://hoaxes.org and https://clark.libguides.com/web-misinformation; they can discuss how to evaluate information critically and posit possible consequences if someone acted on the false information. What responsibility should the hoaxer bear for real-life negative outcomes? When engaging with digital information from a legal or ethical standpoint, one of the most effective strategies is using case studies: librarians can share legal cases and current news (e.g., homeland security, wikileaks, National Security Agency surveillance) dealing with technology issues that arise in access to confidential information, broadcasting inappropriate information, social networking, file transfer, pirating or plagiarizing information, and other intellectual property issues. What are the underlying ethical issues? What are the consequences? What are alternative actions that could have been taken?

3. Manipulating information. Youth can develop their own scenarios to research. As young people self-identify inappropriate digital behaviors and impacts, they become more aware of the problem. When they are involved in developing ways to solve the problem, they gain more ownership and control, feeling empowered to cope themselves as well as to help their peers. Youth can also "produce" information by representing a given set of data: graphically, numerically, as a diagram, and as a lab report. Similarly, they can manipulate images through cropping/selection and filtering techniques. In doing these physical and psychological manipulations, students learn how different representations can be used to influence opinion in one way or the other.

4. Application. How does one act on the information? That is often the ultimate real-life goal, particularly as an ethical citizen. Perhaps by analyzing available information, one decides how to vote in an election. Librarians can facilitate this proactive application by having youth create position presentations for the local government or help a local group implement those recommendations, then that ethical learning can impact others. Other student-empowering activities that enable young persons to apply digital citizenship skills include reviewing digital sources, creating products for the community, capturing local oral and visual history, and training others in responsible technology use.

In addition to—or complementing—direct interactive instruction, youth-serving librarians can instruct "passively" through existing or in-house-created reference sheets, posters, online tutorials, podcasts, blogs, public service announcements, and articles in community publications.

Having a site-wide citizenship/ethics scope and sequence across curricular areas provides a systemic approach for teaching ethical behavior, including digital citizenship, that links to the overall intellectual framework (e.g., Mattson, 2021; Ribble, 2015). Public librarians can also provide digital citizenship learning opportunities. To support and reinforce digital citizenship education, libraries and their institutions need to model ethics/citizenship in their infrastructure and actions: providing equitable access to all formats of information, making provisions to ensure that their community is digitally safe, having a plan to secure and protect educational data in case of crime or disaster, maintaining privacy and confidentiality of individual records, creating and enforcing policies that product the digital rights of everyone, and training staff to keep them current in digital citizenship education themselves.

Food for Thought: R&I Equity in the School Library Case Study

The following case study, conducted by Yung Tran, exemplifies the ethical need to address the R&I needs of all students. The issue and the process are applicable to public library settings. As you read this study, consider the symbiotic relationship between the youth populations that you serve and the library's R&I? What next steps might you take as a result of reflecting on this case study?

A demographic profile of ABC Intermediate reveals a highly diverse, culturally rich image. The divisions are as follows: 351 students in grade seven and 301 students in grade eight from Orange County. Of this total, 41 percent are Limited English Proficient and 29 percent are Fluent English Proficient. The gender distribution is as follows: 349 male and 303 female. The ethnic distribution is as follows: American Indian 0.3 percent Asian 61.2 percent, Pacific Islander 0.2 percent, Filipino 1.1 %, Hispanic 18.5 percent, Black 0.9 percent, and White 17.8 percent. Students on free and reduced lunches make up 60 percent of the school. The school is high performing and is a California Distinguished school.

It is imperative that the school library must provide accommodations to serve different linguistic and cultural sub-groups. In this study, I address the needs of the English language learner (ELL) students, particularly the Vietnamese since they make up a huge bulk of the school population. I have analyzed the barriers and offered some solutions. Many of the recommendations might not become reality, but it is always good to know what is possible.

Student and Family Barriers to Information

Language:

- Mostly speak Vietnamese at home and even at school.
- The directions/signs/labels in the school library media center (LMC) are in English.
- To navigate and search for information require English.
- Most of the books in the LMC are in English.

Cultural:

- Students and family afraid to seek help from "the unapproachable authority" and when seeking help, "the teacher is regarded as the repository of all knowledge; no independent investigation is required, and it may in fact be strongly discouraged" (Bopp & Smith, 2011, p. 282).

- These ELL students tend to move in "flocks," that is, they need each other for assurance. If the LMC is full of the "other" kids, let say, Hispanic, these Vietnamese ELL students would not venture into the LMC.

Access:

- Not many students have computers at home. Even if they do, most of them would not have Internet services.
- Students lack computer skills.

LMC staffing:

- The LMC only has one school librarian (SL), who cannot be in several places at the same time.
- Teachers who bring their classes in are not very familiar with the services and design of the LMC to assist the SL.
- There are no library assistants who can speak the language.

Solutions

Language:

- Make Vietnamese language or bilingual materials available.
- Have LMC directions/signs/labels in Vietnamese.
- Have materials for teaching and learning English such as Vietnamese/English dictionaries.

Cultural:

- Create a "Vietnamese corner" in the LMC.
- Announce the newly arrived Vietnamese materials on the PA or in the ELL classrooms.
- Book talk in ELL classes.
- Find books that relate to their experiences such as the refugee camps or books about Vietnam to help the homesick.
- Smile.
- Have book lists in Vietnamese.
- Smile again.
- Ask for volunteers who speak Vietnamese to help out at lunch and break.
- Learn to say, "Have a good day" in Vietnamese.
- Allow students to post their Vietnamese experience work, for example, art or essays in the LMC so that they have the opportunities to share experiences.

Access:

- Have lists of Vietnamese websites for different topics.
- Increase orientation for ELL students to teach them how to navigate the LMC and on the computers (with bilingual aide if possible).
- Offer evening classes on technology for parents.
- Have the school website available in different languages.

- Ask parents to create Accelerated Reader (AR)/Scholastic Reading Counts tests for the books in Vietnamese.
- Purchase ELL software.

Staffing:

- Hire a library aide who can speak the language.
- Ask the counselor to assign more Vietnamese-speaking students to be in library practice.
- Do staff development services about access, especially in the Vietnamese area.
- Contact the public libraries or community services that have Vietnamese information services.
- Partner with the ELL teachers in their classroom projects/assignments.

Relevant policies:

I am not aware of any school or district policies on access for underserved groups. I am also not aware of any school or district policies on making these areas accessible for disabled students.

Evaluation of R&I Services

- Observation. How do students behave in the library from the first day to now? How long does it take for Vietnamese students to find relevant information? Do students walk to the school library door and then turn away? Do students avoid you when they need help? Can students perform searches independently after you show them the tools, and so on?
- Statistics. How many library users are Vietnamese? How many bilingual or Vietnamese books have been checked out? How much are reference materials used in-house by Vietnamese?
- Teachers' survey, especially the ELL teachers. Have the students found enough information to satisfy the requirements of the assignments? What should be deleted from orientation? What should be added to help their students navigate the school library?
- Informal student interview. What do you like to read? How difficult are reference books to read and understand? What online reference resources do you use? So you use online reference sources in Vietnamese; if so, how do you find or translate them?
- Form an advisory committee that looks at library R&I services periodically. Vietnamese students' and parents' involvement should be encouraged to participate.

ETHICS IS NOT EASY

As the chapter opening states, ethical issues abound when providing R&I services to young people. Fortunately, youth-serving librarians can draw upon legislation, school policies, and professional resources to help address these issues. Nevertheless, controversies remain. Here are a dozen legal and ethical conundrums to mull over. Often there is no one right answer; the solution has to be based on sometimes conflicting principles and practice, including one's own moral compass.

- You see a teenager posting a compromising picture of someone else online.
- You see an adult volunteer typing on a child-porn website.

- A youngster shows you his personal website, which has several Bugs Bunny figures.
- Should you allow cookies on the computers? The feature is sometimes required for access to the desired resource but captures personal information in the process.
- A preteen wants information on how to make beer.
- A parent wants you to remove a reference book on sexually transmitted diseases.
- A teacher gives one of her students her login and password information and then complains that her network directory has been compromised.
- A student and his parent have not signed the school's acceptable use policy; they demand equal access to information required for a course.
- You see a teacher's school website, which also publicizes his personal tutoring service.
- The principal asks you to make thirty photocopies of an article for a faculty in-service.
- You find that the newly purchased science software is not ADA-compliant.
- You collaborate with a teacher to study the impact of a proscribed reading program, which you dislike—and fear will negatively impact purchases for the library's reference collection. The study data finds that the reading program is very effective.

REFERENCES

Adams, H. (2013). *Protecting intellectual freedom and privacy in your school library.* ABC-CLIO.

American Association of School Librarians. (2018). *National school library standards for learners, school librarians, and school libraries.* American Library Association.

American Library Association. (2022). *Every student succeeds act.* American Library Association. https://www.ala.org/advocacy/advleg/federallegislation/schoollibraries/essa

American Library Association. Office for Intellectual Freedom. (2018). *Support for intellectual freedom; selection & reconsideration policy toolkit for public, school & academic libraries.* American Library Association. https://www.ala.org/tools/challengesupport/selectionpolicytoolkit/intellectualfreedom#:~:text=Intellectual%20freedom%20is%20the%20right,guides%20the%20defense%20against%20censorship

American Psychological Association. (2020). *Publication manual of the American Psychological Association* (7th ed.). American Psychological Association.

Batch, K. (2014). *Fencing out knowledge.* American Library Association.

Bopp, R., & Smith, L. (2011). *Reference and information services: An introduction* (4th ed.). Libraries Unlimited.

Cowden, C., Seaman, L, Copeland, S., & Gao, L. (2021). Teaching with intent: Applying culturally responsive teaching to library instruction. *Portal: Libraries and the Academy, 21*(2), 231–251.

Hakimi, L., Eynon, R., & Murphy, V. A. (2021). The ethics of using digital trace data in education: A thematic review of the research landscape. *Review of Educational Research, 91*(5), 671–717.

Harper, N., Franklin, K., & Williams, J. (2021). *Diversity, equity, and inclusion (DEI) scorecard for library and information organizations.* American Library Association. https://www.ala.org/aboutala/

sites/ala.org.aboutala/files/content/2021%20EQUITY%20SCORECARD%20FOR%20LIBRARY%20AND%20INFORMATION%20ORGANIZATIONS.pdf

Jaeger, P., Gorham, U., & Taylor, N. (2019). Human rights and information ethics. In J. Burgess & E. Knox (Eds.), *Foundations of information ethics* (pp. 17–24). American Library Association.

Markkula Center for Applied Ethics. (2021). *A framework for ethical decision making.* Santa Clara University. https://www.scu.edu/ethics/ethics-resources/a-framework-for-ethical-decision-making/

Mattson, K. (2021). *Ethics in a digital world: Guiding students through society's biggest questions.* International Society for Technology in Education.

Ribble, M. (2015). *Digital citizenship in schools* (3rd ed.). International Society for Technology in Education.

Rubin, R., & Rubin, R. (2020). *Foundations of library and information science* (5th ed.). American Library Association.

Wells, R. (2020). *Self-assessment tool: Anti-racism.* Middlebury College. https://unitedwayaddisoncounty.org/client_media/files/ReneeWellsAntiRacismSelfAssessmentTool.pdf

World Intellectual Property Organization. (n.d.). *What is intellectual property?* World Intellectual Property Organization.

FURTHER READING

Ferguson, S., Thornley, C., & Gibb, F. (2016). Beyond codes of ethics: how library and information professionals navigate ethical dilemmas in a complex and dynamic information environment. *International Journal of Information Management, 36*(4), 543–556.

Hughes-Hassell, S., & Stivers, J. (2015). Examining youth services librarians' perceptions of cultural knowledge as an integral part of their professional practice. *School Libraries Worldwide, 21*(1), 121–136.

Luo, L., & Trott, B. (2016). Ethical issues in reference: An in-depth view from the librarians' perspective. *Reference and User Services Quarterly, 55*(3), 189–198.

Shade, L. R., & Singh, R. (2016). "Honestly, we're not spying on kids": School surveillance of young people's social media. *Social Media+ Society, 2*(4), 2056305116680005.

SinhaRoy, S. (2021). Defenders of patron privacy. *American Libraries* (Sept.), 38–39.

University of British Columbia. Equity and Inclusion Office. (n.d.). *Equity, diversity, and inclusion committees: Getting started guide.* University of British Columbia. https://equity.ubc.ca/resources/activating-inclusion-toolkit/equity-diversity-and-inclusion-committees-getting-started-guide/

The Future of Reference for Children and Teens

Reference and information services should be a dynamic function, responding to changing information needs and behaviors as well as changing resources and emerging technologies. This chapter examines some of those emerging trends as they reflect and impact children's and youth's realities. Even as librarians respond to the changing environment, reference and information services have enduring values and roles that withstand the test of time, which is discussed in this chapter. The chapter ends with imagining possible scenarios for reference and information services in 2030.

WHAT IS NORMAL?

The preface noted the many changes over the last several years in terms of politics, techno-scientific realities, and societal issues. All of these factors have impacted library R&I services, including their application to young people. These changes also highlight the importance of library R&I service as a community service, which reflects their symbiotic relationship.

What, then, is in store for library R&I service? One could make a case that predicting the future is more futile than ever. Who would have suspected the pandemic or the Black Lives Matter, for instance? However, in looking back at those two issues, the signs were there for people to see: the encroachment of increasing human populations on wildlife, the growing economic and social gap between white billionaires and disenfranchised minorities, the threat of power recalibration, and the explosion of social media to share and manipulate opinion.

Some people may use a pendulum analogy to describe changes over time, going back and forth from one extreme to the other: the 1960s civil rights movement to the 1980s conservatism, from the 1990s boom and bust, the 2000s rise of xenophobia, and the late 2010s cry for social justice. The prejudicial talk went underground with "political correctness," later to emerge as open derision and violence, which called for "wokeness" and social action/reaction. This latter example of trends over time could also fit a spiral analogy, with the additional dimension of eventual change for the better (or worse). In that respect, it certainly feels as if the early 2020s are indeed a pivotal point in history.

Youth-serving librarians are grappling with this time of transition. Going back to the old normal is not an option for most librarians. Rather, as information professionals and lifelong learners, most librarians are trying to analyze the impact of change and how they have adjusted accordingly. What new practices should be embraced, such as leveraging and expanding online R&I service? What past practices should be improved, such as diversifying R&I collections and staffing? How should staffing be reallocated, for instance, adding an online specialist, sharing a staff person with another site, developing tiered R&I service, and adding a system instructional designer to create online reference tutorials?

Library R&I services should be dynamic, just as society changes. However, both society and libraries have enduring values such as Maslow's hierarchy of needs: safety and security, a sense of belonging, self-esteem, intellectual and aesthetic needs, and self-actualization. These needs are reflected in the Library Bill of Rights, as librarians try to help people meet their needs: from referring individuals to social agencies to facilitating career development, from providing a welcoming and community learning space to offering educational and cultural programs, and from facilitating interest groups to providing ways to contribute to the library. In that sense, the spiral analogy might be best imagined as a spiral staircase with a solid supporting core of values and practices. Normal can be both ever changing and enduring.

WHAT IS VALUABLE AND VALUED?

As youth-serving librarians look to the future, they should continue to ground themselves in their core values and leverage them as they work with others to provide effective R&I services to youth. As noted, the librarian profession as a whole has a number of core values, which are codified in the ALA Library Bill of Rights and the Library Code of Ethics. Youth-serving divisions within ALA also have core professional values:

- AASL: learning; innovation; equity, diversity, inclusion; intellectual freedom; and collaboration (2022).
- ALSC: collaboration, excellence, inclusiveness, innovation, integrity and respect, leadership, and responsiveness (2020).
- YALSA: accountability, collaboration, compassion, excellence, inclusion, innovation, integrity, professional duty, and social responsibility (2015).

In the United States, core values probably include democracy, freedom, equality, justice, individualism, unity, and diversity. More specifically, since libraries are fundamentally community-based, youth-serving librarians should then examine their stakeholders' values, including those that have gained more significantly since the pandemic. Of course, youth-serving librarians also need to align their values and practices with their own institution and system values and missions.

While most values have long-term importance, they exist within changing conditions, so that specific values may take a back seat to others, or even clash; currently, safety seems to be clashing against individuality. By finding and examining each entity's values and how they are prioritized, youth-serving librarians can build their library's future through collaborating with groups that have mutual values, concerns, and hopes.

In that examination process, librarians should also determine how those values are measured. Typical signs of value include budgets, staffing patterns and salaries, resource allocation, return on investment, ability to meet goals, usage, user satisfaction, outcomes and achievements, impact on users and the community at large, user reputation, and community support. Again, youth-serving librarians should find areas of agreement in terms of measuring how well values are supported as they plan for the future.

Food for Thought: A Planning Rubric for the Future

The following planning guide rubric helps youth-serving librarians align R&I services with institutional efforts and consider the implementation details needed to ensure success. Ideally, such planning should include all the stakeholders involved in serving youth, as well as the youth themselves. The planning guide also serves as a basis for assessing the effectiveness of the plan.

Table 10.1. R&I Planning Guide Rubric

	Target	Acceptable	Emerging
Planning process preparation	Includes logical key persons, clear and useful criteria, appropriate resources, thorough and feasible time frame, and valid and reliable assessment methods	Includes key persons, appropriate criteria, appropriate resources, feasible time frame, and valid assessment method	Lists few key persons, few and unclear criteria, inadequate resources, unrealistic time frame, and inadequate assessment method
R&I mission statement	Memorable and appropriate, involves key stakeholders, and aligns with and supports school mission	Clear and appropriate, involves other people, and aligns with the school mission	Unclear, done without input, and ignores school mission
R&I goals and objectives	Goals linked to assessment and library standards, effective objectives and strategies, and triangulated evaluation plan	Goals linked to assessment, reasonable objectives and strategies, and a valid evaluation plan	Goals not linked to assessment or standards, vague or unrealistic objectives and strategies, and inadequate evaluation plan
R&I action plan	Specific and clear plan of action, good alignment with prior work, reflects good use of time, and has good potential of impacting the library program and student success significantly	Clear plan of action, aligns with prior work, reflects good use of time, and has some potential of impacting the library program and student success	Unclear or sparse plan of action, reflects ineffective use of time, and has little potential of impacting the library program or student success
Supporting evidence and assessment	Includes strong evidence of the plan's implementation and assessment	Includes some evidence of the plan's implementation and assessment	Includes little evidence of the plan's implementation or assessment

BUILDING THE FUTURE THROUGH COMMUNITY

The past few years have soundly confirmed the importance of community. In times of crisis, when people join together for the benefit of the community as a whole, the outcome is more positive than when communities fall apart. More than ever, librarians need to know their communities and the individual youth within those communities, in order to provide the most effective R&I service. Especially now, with more alternative sources of information and the higher expectation for personalized interaction, librarians need to not only be respectful and responsive, but they need to collaborate with youth to optimize their experiences and their outcomes. To that end, libraries need to provide the resources and communication channels to facilitate user-librarian, librarian-librarian, user-user, librarian-community, and community-community connections.

Indeed, any R&I policy or major decision about its community's youth should solicit the perspectives of those youth and other youth-serving stakeholders such as families, home-schooler populations, formal and informal educational institutions, social and recreational centers, health care, economic sectors, and governmental agencies. Sometimes libraries are considered informational safety nets, but libraries need to have sustainable community partnerships that evolve into informational social networks. In that respect, librarians should not be just responsive and responsible R&I service providers, but rather they should also be R&I producers and leaders, embedded into the very core of their communities. Such directions may take librarians outside their comfort zone, be it because they are unfamiliar with certain groups or have not fully developed their leadership skills, but the efforts facilitate authentic professional development and increase the library and librarian's positive profiles.

Such partnerships require significant exchanges and coordination of information and resources such as community web portals, expanded philosophy and practice of inter-agency loan, co-sponsored informational programming, community-based professional development using community experience, and creative community-based funding and resource allocation. Certainly, technology needs to be forefront in these endeavors, including social media. Increasingly, library R&I services need to connect to facilitate wraparound social services such as health-care and socioeconomic supports. Communities as a whole need to support all their young people, giving them the informational tools for self-expression, self-improvement, and self-empowerment that can enrich the community as well. Fortunately, as informational professionals, librarians are uniquely positioned to identify potential community partners and to collaborate effectively with them to make a positive difference in young people's lives.

In 2016, the national advocacy organization All4Ed developed a Future School program and, more specifically, a Future Ready Librarians program to help school librarians provide innovative learning opportunities (https://futureready.org/thenetwork/strands/future-ready-librarians/). The website includes resources and strategies that are particularly useful in collaborating with leaders and show value in supporting schools. Driving this program is the Future Ready Librarians framework, which includes these elements: ensuring equitable access, designing collaborating spaces, supporting literacy, investing and curating digital resources, supporting student privacy and creations, building instructional and community partnerships, and leading beyond the library.

FUTURE LIBRARY R&I RESOURCES

By now, digital reference sources dominate R&I resources because of their potential timeliness and their relative ease of distribution. Authentication and security remain issues to contend with. The license agreement also continues to be problematic because of its potential proprietary status, fee base, and degree of accessibility. Open educational resources (OERs) have increased their status, and they need to be seriously considered and catalogued for convenient access. As mentioned in the collection development chapter, librarians should continue to seek opportunities to share resources and take advantage of group discounts; perhaps those information organizations can extend beyond library institutions.

To acknowledge more perspectives and youthful voices in information services, librarians might also incorporate young people's research into their in-house repositories, which are likely to be indexed and catalogued in the same way as other databases. Catalogue discovery tools can facilitate their ease of access. Especially as school librarians emphasize students' own curation and synthesis of information, this area of monitored reference resources can significantly empower and recognize young people's contribution to knowledge bases.

Youth-serving librarians will also need to be creative in addressing budgetary constraints, which have grown in the last few years and are likely to continue in the future. School librarians, in particular, have to fight for resources as resource allocation decisions increasingly occur at the local level, reflecting decentralized budgeting instead of federal decisions. Joint R&I services across libraries can be a money-saving strategy, although governance issues are sometimes a barrier.

R&I SERVICE AS EXPERIENCE AND DESTINATION

While there is still a need and expectation for "just the facts," most young people want a positive experience in the process. A library might have the greatest reference collection and the most knowledgeable staff, but if those staffs are unapproachable and the library environment is not accessible or inviting, then the library is, for all practical purposes, useless.

As noted earlier, youth have many choices for finding information. Young people might come to the library because no one else has the information they want. What makes the library the preferred destination for R&I, then? It should be the experience, not just the information goal, the journey rather than just the end of the road.

The R&I experience starts with access, as detailed in this book: from hours of operation face-to-face and real-time access to reference librarians to 24/7 access to the library portal, database, and e-resources. Next, the interface, be it physical or virtual, needs to be welcoming, inclusive, and appealing. The R&I presence should feel comfortable, safe, and secure. R&I service should be easy to find, and it should offer a sense of privacy; a "consult" cubicle or room is ideal. Likewise, the reference collection should be easy to find—with good signage: integrated into the general collection but also close to the R&I area with ready-reference—and quickly found as a separate heading in the library web portal. For on-the-fly R&I interactions, librarians can "float" through the library, tablet in hand, or make a Siri-like Q/A sessions available in different parts of the library. Both individual research study spaces, such as carrels with spacious surfaces, and glassed-in group study rooms with writing surfaces should be provided. In any case, spaces for R&I services will need to offer more flexible options, depending on young people's needs; for instance, some public libraries have a teens-only room, which can be customized by the teen users themselves. Online, librarians can consider virtual reality reference interactions. Although Second Life was a disappointing platform, a user-friendly virtual presence could attract new youth users to engage with R&I librarians. Librarians should also incorporate virtual reality experiences to provide authentic socially contextualized R&I applications.

CRYSTAL BALL GAZING

As youth-serving librarians assess and plan strategically, not just in response to current needs, they can systemically build top-notch R&I service that can weather temporary storms and provide a predictable vanguard condition for schoolwide achievement. Here are two possible scenarios.

The year is 2030. The tech-savvy credentialed school librarian manages a busy learning commons full time, supported by trained paraprofessional staff, adult volunteers, and student aides. A "cybrarian" provides virtual R&I services jointly for the school and public library. In the public library, middle schoolers are tutoring children who are English language learners (ELLs), and grade schoolers are creating digital stories to be posted on the library portal's storytelling web page. Some teenagers are screencasting oral histories with senior citizens, and their teen partners are getting ready to pin those stories on a local Google map. In both libraries, the R&I collection includes vetted young people's and community reference documents as well as other high-quality open source and commercial reference sources in various formats; the two library sites collaboratively develop these collections and hold joint workshops for youth-serving agencies to optimize the collections. At both sites, reference resources are projected on moveable small-group screens, and the libraries are bustling as young people collectively discover and curate knowledge to be uploaded onto the online national (or international) library R&I Creative Commons repository. The school community uses solar- and hand-powered mobile devices to access, create, and share information worldwide. A public library online club for preteens is collaborating with peers across the world on green technology projects. The school community also accesses school cybrarian subject specialists from around the world. The public library collaborates with health-care providers and psychologists to train teens as peer wellness mediators. Youth-serving librarians form virtual learning communities with classroom teachers to develop interest-based R&I expertise and produce digital reference products for their constituents. The two libraries also cosponsor a career development program for youth, which includes a range of R&I resources, volunteer database, college-created virtual reality tours of workplaces, and local industry sector representatives who serve as online speakers and mentors. All types of libraries and their institutions collaborate to provide seamless and relevant tiered R&I services for their communities' young people.

On the other hand, 2030 could look like the following scenario. Students access their textbooks from the cloud, accessed from their classroom computer tablets. Some students go to the media room to borrow a tablet from the volunteer clerk because the class set is short of working devices; those devices have to be returned at the end of the day. Other students, mainly white, are studying from home with the family's devices. The state curriculum provides the paced readings and tests, and teachers control classroom behavior while coaching students to meet state standards, which disadvantages students coming from other areas of the country. School library services are now provided only by public libraries, which have also become the community reading and technology safety net for students and the poor who do not have Internet access. The public library also has a small reference collection of old print books that date before reference books could be produced and accessed online by personal credit card. Public libraries are primarily staffed by technicians as this public service has been outsourced to private companies that hire one professional librarian to oversee each regional system and one other professional librarian to provide R&I services online. Young people who want to read for information download public domain or low-quality titles online, or families purchase ebooks from online vendors. Community volunteers create Little Free Libraries for neighborhoods that are information deserts, thanks to closed libraries.

What will be the future of library R&I services for youth? Future is up to you as a youth-serving librarian. The future will come, whether you plan for it or not. Strategically planning and assessing the effectiveness of your plans, taking proactive entrepreneurial steps to find innovative ways to engage youth, and advocating for—and collaborating with—community partners for effective R&I services—these approaches all help R&I services—and youth—to thrive in the future. The work may be hard, but it is good work—for the good of youth and their community.

REFERENCES

American Association for School Librarians. (2022). *AASL governing documents*. American Library Association.

Association for Library Service to Children. (2020). *ALSC strategic plan*. American Library Association. https://www.ala.org/alsc/aboutalsc/stratplan

Young Adult Library Services Association. (2015). *Core professional values for the teen services profession*. American Library Association. https://www.ala.org/yalsa/core-professional-values-teen -services-profession

FURTHER READING

Braun, L., & Peterson, S. (2017). *Putting teens first in library services: A road map*. American Library Association.

Crane, D. (2021, December 29). Gazing into the crystal ball. *Public Libraries Online*. http://public librariesonline.org/2021/12/gazing-into-the-crystal-ball/

Fallows, D., & Fallows, J. (2020). Our towns: The post-pandemic future of libraries. *Atlantic* (May). https://www.theatlantic.com/notes/2020/05/post-pandemic-future-libraries/611458/

Gaiman, N. (2020, October 15). Why our future depends on libraries, reading, and daydreaming. *Better Reading.* https://www.betterreading.com.au/kids-ya/neil-gaiman-why-our-future-depends-on -libraries-reading-and-daydreaming/

Kachel, D., & Lance, K. (2021). The status of state support of school library programs. *Teacher Librarian, 48*(5), 8–13.

Mouhanna, A. (2021, July). What's next for school librarians? *Perspectives on Reading.* https:// perspectivesonreading.com/whats-next-for-school-librarians/

School libraries 2021; Impact, obstacles, and the fight for the future. (2021, November 1). *School Library Journal.* https://www.slj.com/?detailStory=school-libraries-2021-impact-obstacles-and-the -fight-for-the-future

Tonini, S. (2020, June 24). 7 tips for future proofing school libraries. *eSchool News.* https://www .eschoolnews.com/2020/06/24/7-tips-for-future-proofing-school-libraries/

Bibliography

Abdullah, N., & Basar, S. K. R. (2019). How children gauge information trustworthiness in online search: Credible or convenience searcher? *Pakistan Journal of Information Management & Libraries, 21*, 1–19.

Abrahamson, J., Fisher, K., Turner, A., Durrance, J., & Turner, T. (2008). Lay information mediary behavior uncovered: Exploring how nonprofessionals seek health information for themselves and others online. *Journal of the Medical Library Association, 96*(4), 310–323.

Adams, H. (2013). *Protecting intellectual freedom and privacy in your school library.* ABC-CLIO.

Agosto, D., & Hughes-Hassell, S. (2005). People, places, and questions: An investigation of the everyday life information-seeking behaviors of urban young adults. *Library & Information Science Research, 27*(2), 141–163.

American Association for School Librarians. (2022). *AASL governing documents.* American Library Association.

American Association of School Librarians. (2018). *National school library standards for learners, school librarians, and school libraries.* American Library Association.

American Library Association. (2013). *ALA glossary of library and information science* (4th ed.). American Library Association.

American Library Association. (2021). *Code of ethics.* American Library Association.

American Library Association. (2022). *Every student succeeds act.* American Library Association. https://www.ala.org/advocacy/advleg/federallegislation/schoollibraries/essa

American Library Association; Office for Intellectual Freedom. (2018). *Support for intellectual freedom; selection & reconsideration policy toolkit for public, school & academic libraries.* American Library Association.

Association for Library Service to Children. (2020a). *ALSC strategic plan*. American Library Association. https://www.ala.org/alsc/aboutalsc/stratplan

Association for Library Service to Children. (2020b). *Competencies for libraries serving children in libraries*. Chicago: American Library Association.

Association of College and Research Libraries. (2012). *Diversity standards: Cultural competency for academic libraries*. American Library Association.

Bar-On, R. (2004). The bar-on emotional quotient inventory (EQi): Rationale, description, and summary of psychometric properties. In G. Geher (Ed.), *The measurement of emotional intelligence: Common ground and controversy* (pp. 115–145). Nova Science.

Batch, K. (2014). *Fencing out knowledge*. American Library Association.

Bates, M. (1989). The design of browsing and berrypicking techniques for the on-line search interface. *Online Review, 13*(5), 407–431.

Bennett, W. (Ed.). (2008). *Civic life online: Learning how digital media can engage youth*. MIT Press.

Bilal, D. (2007). Grounding children's information behavior and system design in child development theories. In D. Nahl & D. Bilal (Eds.), *Information and emotion: The emergent affective paradigm in information behavior research and theory* (pp. 39–50). Information Today.

Bopp, R., & Smith, L. (2011). *Reference and information services: An introduction* (4th ed.). Libraries Unlimited

Borgman, C. (1996). Why are catalogs still hard to use? *Journal of the American Society for Information Science, 47*(7), 493–503.

Buchanan, S., & Tuckerman, L. (2016). The information behaviours of disadvantaged and disengaged adolescents. *Journal of Documentation, 72*(3), 527–548.

Bulao, J. (2021, May 18). How much date is created every day in 2021? *Techjury*. https://techjury.net/blog/how-much-data-is-created-every-day/

Byström, K. (1999). *Task complexity, information types and information sources*. Doctoral diss., University of Tampere, Tampere.

Chatman, E. (1996). The impoverished life-world of outsiders. *Journal of the American Society for Information Science, 47*(3), 193–206.

Connaway, L. S., & Radford, M. L. (2007, March). Service sea change: Clicking with screenagers through virtual reference. In *Sailing into the future: Charting our destiny*; Proceedings of the Thirteenth National Conference of the Association of College and Research Libraries.

Cowden, C., Seaman, L., Copeland, S., & Gao, L. (2021). Teaching with intent: Applying culturally responsive teaching to library instruction. *Portal: Libraries and the Academy, 21*(2), 231–251.

Dahlgren, P. (2005). The Internet, public spheres, and political communication: Dispersion and deliberation. *Political Communication, 22*(2), 147–162.

Dervin, B. (1992). From the mind's eye of the user: The sense-making qualitative quantitative methodology. In J. Glazier & R. Powell (Eds.), *Qualitative research in information management* (pp. 61–84). Libraries Unlimited.

Dresang, E. T. (2005). Access: The information-seeking behavior of youth in the digital environment. *Library Trends, 54*(2), 178–196.

Dumler, M., & Skinner, S. (2008). *A primer on management* (2nd ed.). South-Western Pub.

Ellis, D. (1989). A behavioural approach to information retrieval system design. *Journal of Documentation, 45*(3), 171–212.

Erikson, E. (1968). *Identity: Youth and crisis* (No. 7). W. W. Norton & Company.

Etches, A. (2013). Know thy users: User research techniques to build empathy and improve decision-making. *Reference & User Services Quarterly, 53*(1), 13–17.

Eysenbach, G. (2008). Credibility of health information and digital media. In M. Metzger & A. Flanagin (Eds.), *Digital media, youth, and credibility* (pp. 123–154). MIT Press.

Ferrer-Vinent, I. (2010). For English, Press 1: International students' language preference at the reference desk. *The Reference Librarian, 51*, 189–201.

Fisher, K. E., Bishop, A. P., Fawcett, P., & Magassa, L. (2014). InfoMe: A field-design methodology for research on ethnic minority youth as information mediaries. In *New directions in children's and adolescents' information behavior research* (pp. 135–156). Emerald Group Publishing Limited.

Greene, G., & Kochhar-Bryant, C. (2003). *Pathways to successful transition for youth with disabilities.* Merrill.

Guinee, K., Eagleton, M. B., & Hall, T. E. (2003). Adolescents' Internet search strategies: Drawing upon familiar cognitive paradigms when accessing electronic information sources. *Journal of Educational Computing Research, 29*(3), 363–374.

Hakimi, L., Eynon, R., & Murphy, V. A. (2021). The ethics of using digital trace data in education: A thematic review of the research landscape. *Review of Educational Research, 91*(5), 671–717.

Hardof-Jaffe, S., Hershkovitz, A., Abu-Kishk, H., Bergman, O., & Nachmias, R. (2009). How do students organize personal information spaces? *International Working Group on Educational Data Mining.* https://files.eric.ed.gov/fulltext/ED539080.pdf

Harper, N., Franklin, K., & Williams, J. (2021). *Diversity, equity, and inclusion (DEI) scorecard for library and information organizations.* American Library Association.

Hicks, D., & VanScoy, A. (2019). Discourses of expertise in professional competency documents: Reference expertise as performance. *The Library Quarterly, 89*(1), 34–52.

Ingwersen, P. (1996). Cognitive perspectives of information retrieval interaction. *Journal of Documentation, 52*(1), 3–50.

International Council of Museums. (2004). *ICOM code of ethics for museums.* International Council of Museums.

Jaeger, P., Gorham, U., & Taylor, N. (2019). Human rights and information ethics. In J. Burgess & E. Knox (Eds.), *Foundations of information ethics* (pp. 17–24). American Library Association.

Johnson, P. (2018). *Fundamentals of collection development and management* (4th ed.). American Library Association.

Kuhlthau, C. (1985). A process approach to library skills instruction. *School Library Media Quarterly, 13*(1), 35–40.

Laretive, J. (2019). Information literacy, young learners and the role of the teacher librarian. *Journal of the Australian Library and Information Association, 68*(3), 225–235.

Luo, L., & Weak, E. (2013). Text reference service: Teens' perception and use. *Library & Information Science Research, 35*(1), 14–23.

Markkula Center for Applied Ethics. (2021). *A framework for ethical decision making.* Santa Clara University. https://www.scu.edu/ethics/ethics-resources/a-framework-for-ethical-decision-making/

Mattson, K. (2021). *Ethics in a digital world: Guiding students through society's biggest questions.* International Society for Technology in Education.

Montiel-Overall, P. (2005). A theoretical understanding of TLC. *School Libraries Worldwide, 11*(2), 24–48.

Nesset, V. (2016). A look at classification and indexing practices for elementary school children: Who are we really serving? *Indexer, 34*(3), 63–65.

Newsum, J. M. (2016). School collection development and resource management in digitally rich environments: An initial literature review. *School Libraries Worldwide, 22*(1), 97–109.

Overall, P. M. (2009). Cultural competence: A conceptual framework for library and information science professionals. *Library Quarterly, 79*(2), 175–204.

Powers, M., & Costello, L. (2019). *Reaching diverse audiences with virtual reference and instruction: A practical guide for libraries.* Rowman & Littlefield.

Rankin, C. (Ed.). (2018). *IFLA guidelines for library services to children aged 0–18.* International Federation of Library Associations and Institutions.

Reference and User Services Association. (2017a). *Guidelines for implementing and maintaining virtual reference services.* American Library Association.

Reference and User Services Association. (2017b). *Professional competencies for reference and user services librarians.* American Library Association.

Reference and User Services Association. (2017c). *Virtual accessibility.* American Library Association.

Reference and User Services Association. (2013). *Guidelines for behavioral performance of reference and information service providers.* American Library Association.

Reference and User Services Association; Cooperative Reference Service Committee. (2008). *Guidelines for cooperative reference services.* American Library Association.

Ribble, M. (2015). *Digital citizenship in schools* (3rd ed.). International Society for Technology in Education.

Rice, R., McCreadie, M., & Chang, S. (2001). *Accessing and browsing: Information and communication.* Cambridge, MA: MIT Press.

Rich, S., Bradley, D., Brennan-Wydra, E., Culler, T., Hanley, E., & Kalt, M. (2019). *Librarian role-playing as a method for assessing student information literacy skills.* Paper presented at the 82nd annual meeting of the Association for Information Science & Technology, Melbourne, Oct. 19–23. DOI: 10.1002/pra2.00018

Rubin, R., & Rubin, R. (2020). *Foundations of library and information science* (5th ed.). American Library Association.

Saponaro, M., & Evans, G. (2019). *Collection management basics* (7th ed.). Libraries Unlimited.

Sarkodie-Manash, K. (Ed.). (2000). *Reference services for the adult learner.* Haworth Press.

Shenton, A. K., & Pickard, A. J. (2014). Facilitating pupil thinking about information literacy. *New Review of Children's Literature and Librarianship, 20*(1), 64–79.

Sosulski, N., & Tyckoson, D. (2018). Reference in the age of disinformation. *Reference & User Services Quarterly, 57*(3), 178–182.

Subramaniam, M., Taylor, N. G., Jean, B. S., Follman, R., Kodama, C., & Casciotti, D. (2015). As simple as that?: Tween credibility assessment in a complex online world. *Journal of Documentation, 71*(3), 550–571.

Summey, T. (2017). Emotional intelligence: A framework for the competencies and traits of reference and user services librarians. In M. Matterson & S. Hines (Eds.), *Emotion in the library workplace* (pp. 127–142). Emerald Publishing.

Valenza, J. (2007). *Discovering a descriptive taxonomy of attributes of exemplary school library websites.* Doctoral diss., University of North Texas. http://digital.library.unt.edu/ask:/67531/metadc3911/ml/

VanScoy, A. (2019). Exploring reference and information service in a global information context. *ALISE 2019 proceedings* (pp. 219). Association of Library and Information Science Educators.

Webb, J. (2020). *Digital principle for photography.* Bloomsbury Visual Arts.

Wells, R. (2020). *Self-assessment tool: Anti-racism.* Middlebury College. https://unitedwayaddisoncounty.org/client_media/files/ReneeWellsAntiRacismSelfAssessmentTool.pdf

Wiley, D. A. (2021). Open educational resources: Undertheorized research and untapped potential. *Educational Technology Research and Development, 69*(1), 411–414.

Wilson, T. (1997). Information behaviour: An interdisciplinary perspective. *Information Processing & Management, 33*(4), 551–572.

Wittrock, M. (1974). Learning as a generative process. *Educational Psychologist, 19*(2), 87–95.

World Intellectual Property Organization. (n.d.). *What is intellectual property?* World Intellectual Property Organization.

Young Adult Library Services Association. (2017). *Teen services competencies for library staff.* Chicago: American Library Association.

Young Adult Library Services Association. (2015). *Core professional values for the teen services profession.* American Library Association. https://www.ala.org/yalsa/core-professional-values-teen-services-profession

Zipf, G. K. (1949). *Human behavior and the principle of least effort: An introduction to human ecology.* Addison-Wesley Press.

FURTHER READING

Abubakar, M. K. (2021). Implementation and use of virtual reference services in academic libraries during and post COVID-19 pandemic: A necessity for developing countries. *Library Philosophy and Practice*, 4951. https://digitalcommons.unl.edu/libphilprac/4951

Alvarez, B. (2015, January 2). Shelf life: The balancing act between physical and digital books. *Public Libraries Online*. http://publiclibrariesonline.org/2015/01/shelf-life-the-balancing-act-between-physical-and-digital-books/

American Library Association. (2013). *Virtual reference: A selected annotated bibliography.* American Library Association.

Anderson, K., & Cvetkovic, V. (2015). *Reinventing reference: How libraries deliver value in the age of Google.* American Library Association.

Bates, M. J. (2002). Toward an integrated model of information seeking and searching. *The New Review of Information Behaviour Research, 3*, 1–15.

Beak, J. (2014). *A child-driven metadata schema: A holistic analysis of children's cognitive processes during book selection.* Doctoral diss., University of Wisconsin–Milwaukee.

Bilal, D., & Beheshti, J. (Eds.). (2014). *New directions in children's and adolescents' information behavior research: Volume 10.* Emerald.

Braun, L., & Peterson, S. (2017). *Putting teens first in library services: A road map.* American Library Association.

Breeding, M. (2016). Refining digital strategies. *The Systems Librarian* (Jan.), 9–11.

Buchanan, S., & Tuckerman, L. (2016). The information behaviours of disadvantaged and disengaged adolescents. *Journal of Documentation, 72*(3), 527–548.

Buckland, M. (2017). *Information and society.* MIT Press.

Caputo, C. (2021). *Library services to homeschoolers: A guide.* Rowman & Littlefield.

Case, D. (2016). *Looking for information: A survey of research on information seeking, needs, and behavior* (4th ed.). Emerald Publishing Limited.

Cassell, K. (2021). *Public libraries and their communities: An introduction.* Rowman & Littlefield.

Cassell, K., & Miremath, U. (2018). *Reference and information services in the 21st century: An introduction.* American Library Association.

Cooke, N. (2016). *Information services to diverse populations: Developing culturally competent library professionals.* Libraries Unlimited.

Crane, D. (2021, December 29). Gazing into the crystal ball. *Public Libraries Online.* http://publiclibrariesonline.org/2021/12/gazing-into-the-crystal-ball/

Daul-Elhindi, C. A., & Owens, T. (2019). *Reference 360: A holistic approach to reference instruction.* University of Omaha. https://digitalcommons.unomaha.edu/cgi/viewcontent.cgi?article=1043&context=crisslibfacpub

Del Castillo, M., & Ball, M. (2018). *The myth of the declining reference statistics: Revealing dynamic reference services through digital analytics.* FIU Libraries. https://digitalcommons.fiu.edu/glworks/83/

Evans, A. (2014). How understanding teen brain development can help improve YA reference services. *Young Adult Library Services, 12*(3), 12–14.

Fabbi, J., Bressler, D., & Earp, V. (2007). *A guide to writing CMC collection development policies.* American Library Association.

Ferguson, S., Thornley, C., & Gibb, F. (2016). Beyond codes of ethics: How library and information professionals navigate ethical dilemmas in a complex and dynamic information environment. *International Journal of Information Management, 36*(4), 543–556.

Fraser, E. (2020). *Young adult nonfiction: A readers' advisory and collection development guide.* Libraries Unlimited.

Gaiman, N. (2020, October 15). Why our future depends on libraries, reading, and daydreaming. *Better Reading.* https://www.betterreading.com.au/kids-ya/neil-gaiman-why-our-future-depends-on-libraries-reading-and-daydreaming/

Getts, E., & Stewart, K. (2018). Accessibility of distance library services for deaf and hard of hearing users. *Reference Services Review, 46*(3), 439–448.

Goldsmith, F. (2016). *Crash course in contemporary reference.* Libraries Unlimited.

Goldsmith, F. (2015). *Crash course in weeding library collections.* Libraries Unlimited.

Gottfried, J., & Pennavaria, K. (2017). *Providing reference services: A practice guide for librarians.* Rowman & Littlefield.

Gregory, V. (2019). *Collection development and management for 21st century library collections: An introduction.* American Library Association.

Harisanty, D. (2018). Personal information management of urban youth. *Library Philosophy and Practice, 1944,* 1–9.

Hicks, D., & VanScoy, A. (2019). Discourses of expertise in professional competency documents: Reference expertise as performance. *The Library Quarterly, 89*(1), 34–52.

Hirsch, S. (2018). *Information services today: An introduction.* Rowman & Littlefield.

Hoffman, G., & Snow, K. (2021). *Cataloging and classification: Back to basics.* Routledge.

Houston, C. (2016). Reinventing your reference collection. In IASL Annual Conference Proceedings. https://journals.library.ualberta.ca/slw/index.php/iasl/article/download/7195/4194

Hughes-Hassell, S. (2020). *Collection management for youth: Equity, inclusion, and learning* (2nd ed.). American Library Association.

Hughes-Hassell, S., & Stivers, J. (2015). Examining youth services librarians' perceptions of cultural knowledge as an integral part of their professional practice. *School Libraries Worldwide, 21*(1), 121–136.

Jensen, K. (2020, October 26). Collection diversity audits. *Teen Librarian Toolbox.* https://www.teenlibrariantoolbox.com/2020/10/in-my-mailbox-questions-i-get-about-collection-diversity-audits/

Kachel, D., & Lance, K. (2021). The status of state support of school library programs. *Teacher Librarian, 48*(5), 8–13.

King, D. (2021). *Mobile technology in libraries.* American Library Association.

Lanning, S. (2014). *Reference and instructional services for information literacy skills in school libraries.* Libraries Unlimited.

Lanning, S., & Gerrity, C. (2022). *Concise guide to information literacy* (3rd ed.). Libraries Unlimited.

Lee, S. (2019). *Electronic resources and collection development.* Routledge.

Lee, T. H., & Choi, I. (2019). Multilingual access support evaluation guideline in the website of public library. *iConference 2019 Proceedings.* https://www.ideals.illinois.edu/bitstream/handle/2142/103329/Lee_Choi_Poster.docx?sequence=1

Luo, L., & Trott, B. (2016). Ethical issues in reference: An in-depth view from the librarians' perspective. *Reference and User Services Quarterly, 55*(3), 189–198.

Mandal, S. (2018). Development of multilingual resource management mechanisms for libraries. *Library Philosophy and Practice, 1768.* https://digitalcommons.unl.edu/libphilprac/1768

Mardis, M. (2020). *The collection program in schools: Concepts and practices* (7th ed.). Libraries Unlimited.

Mehra, B., & Davis, R. (2015). A strategic diversity manifesto for public libraries in the 21st century. *New Library World, 116*(1/2), 15–36.

Mnzava, E. (2020). Twitter library account: Highlights for the users and librarians. *Library Hi Tech News.* https://www.emerald.com/insight/content/doi/10.1108/LHTN-07-2020-0064/full/html

Moore, C. L. (2016). A study of social media and its influence on teen information seeking behaviors. *The Serials Librarian, 71*(2), 138–145.

Moran, B., & Morner, C. (2017). *Library and information center management* (9th ed.). Libraries Unlimited.

Mouhanna, A. (2021, July). What's next for school librarians? *Perspectives on Reading.* https://perspectivesonreading.com/whats-next-for-school-librarians/

Newsum, J. M. (2016). School collection development and resource management in digitally rich environments: An initial literature review. *School Libraries Worldwide, 22*(1), 97–109.

Nutefall, J. (2016). *Service learning, information literacy, and libraries.* Libraries Unlimited.

Nylen, B., & King, S. (2021). Video models and the transitioning of individuals with developmental disabilities: A systematic literature review. *Education and Training in Autism and Developmental Disabilities, 56*(3), 341–353.

Orr, C. (2014). *Crash course in readers' advisory.* Libraries Unlimited.

Pattee, L. (2020). *Developing library collections for today's young adults: Ensuring inclusion and access* (2nd ed.). Rowman & Littlefield.

Polger, M. (2021). *Library signage and wayfinding design: Communicating effectively with your users.* American Library Association.

Posner, B. (2016). *Library information and resource sharing: Transforming services and collections.* Libraries Unlimited.

Powers, M., & Costello, L. (2019). *Reaching diverse audiences with virtual reference and instruction: A practical guide for librarians* (Vol. 59). Rowman & Littlefield.

Puckett, J. (2015). *Modern pathfinders: Creating better research guides.* American Library Association.

Radford, M. L., Costello, L., & Montague, K. (2021). Surging virtual reference services: COVID-19 a game changer. *College & Research Libraries News, 82*(3), 106–107.

Readers' advisory. (2021). *Library training and learning hub.* http://librarylearn.org/reders-advisory

Reference and User Services Association. (2021a). *Children with disabilities.* American Library Association. https://www.ala.org/rusa/children-disabilities

Reference and User Services Association. (2021b). *Virtual accessibility.* American Library Association. https://www.ala.org/ursa/virtual-accessibility

Reference and User Services Association. (2019). *Assistive technology.* American Library Association. https://www.asgcladirect.org/wpcontent/uploads/2017/06/

Reference and User Services Association. (2007). *Measuring and assessing reference services and resources: A guide.* American Library Association.

Reference & User Services Quarterly. https://journals.ala.org/index.php/rusq

The Reference Librarian. https://www.tandfonline.com/journals/wref20

Reference Services Review. https://www.emeraldgrouppublishing.com/journal/rsr

Reisig, J. (2018). *Access: Unlocking the power of research: A guide to library services and information literacy.* CreateSpace Independent Publishing Platform.

Riedling, A., & Houston, C. (2019). *Reference skills for the school librarian: Tools and tips* (4th ed.). Libraries Unlimited.

Rod-Welsh, L. (2019). *Improving library services in support of international students and English as a second language learners.* American Library Association.

Ross, C., Nilsen, K., & Radford, M. (2018). *Conducting the reference interview* (3rd ed.). American Library Association.

School libraries 2021; Impact, obstacles, and the fight for the future. (2021, November 1). *School Library Journal.* https://www.slj.com/?detailStory=school-libraries-2021-impact-obstacles-and-the-fight-for-the-future

Shade, L. R., & Singh, R. (2016). "Honestly, we're not spying on kids": School surveillance of young people's social media. *Social Media+ Society, 2*(4), 2056305116680005.

Shenton, A., & Pickard, A. (2014). Facilitating pupil thinking about information literacy. *New Review of Children's Literature and Librarianship, 20*(1), 64–79.

SinhaRoy, S. (2021). Defenders of patron privacy. *American Libraries* (Sept.), 38–39.

Smallwood, C., & Becnel, K. (2013). *Library services for multicultural patrons: Strategies to encourage library use.* Scarecrow Press.

Sowards, E., & Chenoweth, J. (Eds.). *The reference librarian's Bible: Print and digital reference resources every library should own.* Libraries Unlimited.

St. Jean, B., Gorham, U., & Bonsignore, E. (2021). *Understanding human information behavior.* Rowman & Littlefield.

Summey, T. (2017). Emotional intelligence: A framework for the competencies and traits of reference and user services librarians. In S. Hines & M. Matteson (Eds.), *Emotion in the library workplace* (pp. 129–146). Emerald Publishing Limited.

Tonini, S. (2020, June 24). 7 tips for future proofing school libraries. *eSchool News.* https://www.eschoolnews.com/2020/06/24/7-tips-for-future-proofing-school-libraries/

University of British Columbia, Equity and Inclusion Office. (n.d.). *Equity, diversity, and inclusion committees: Getting started guide.* University of British Columbia.

Upson, M., Reiter, H., Hall, C., & Cannon, K. (2021). *Information now: A graphic guide to student research and web literacy* (2nd ed.). University of Chicago Press.

Vadnais, A. (2019). Reaching out and giving back: Academic librarian works with grade K–12 students. *Reference & User Services Quarterly, 59*(2), 113–119.

VanScoy, A. (2019). Conceptual and procedural knowledge: A framework for analyzing point-of-need information literacy instruction. *Communications in Information Literacy, 13*(2), 3. https://pdxscholar.library.pdx.edu/cgi/viewcontent.cgi?article=1348&context=comminfolit

Walz, J., Jones, A., McCoy, E., & Rice, A. C. (2018). Annotated bibliography: The reference desk: Grand idea or gone down the river?. *The Christian Librarian, 61*(2), 8. https://digitalcommons .georgefox.edu/cgi/viewcontent.cgi?article=2024&context=tcl

Wilkinson, F., Lewis, L., & Lubas, R. (2015). *The complete guide to acquisitions management*. Libraries Unlimited.

Wisconsin Department of Public Instruction Public Library Development Team. (2019). The inclusive services assessment and guide for Wisconsin public libraries. Wisconsin Department of Public Instruction.

Wong, M., & Saunders, L. (2020). *Reference and information services* (6th ed.). Libraries Unlimited.

Zwierski, J., McCroskey, M., & Fountain, J. (Eds.). (2021). *Cataloging correctly for kids: An introduction to the tools and practices* (6th ed.). American Library Association.

Index

About the Author

Dr. Lesley Farmer has been a librarian educator, teacher, and librarian for over forty years. She has authored over thirty-five books, edited journals, and written blogs for professional library organizations. As professor of Library Media at California State University (CSU) Long Beach, she coordinates the Teacher Librarian program and was named as the university's Outstanding Professor. She also manages the CSU ICT Literacy Project. Over the years, she has worked as a librarian in school, public, academic, and special libraries. She earned her MS in Library Science at the University of North Carolina at Chapel Hill and received her doctorate in Adult Education from Temple University. Dr. Farmer chaired the IFLA's School Libraries Section and is a Fulbright scholar. A frequent presenter and writer for the profession, she won several honors, including American Library Association's Phi Beta Mu Award for library education and the Ken Haycock Leadership Award, the International Association of School Librarianship Commendation Award, and the AASL Distinguished Service Award. Dr. Farmer's research interests include school librarianship, international librarianship, digital citizenship, information and media literacy, and data analytics.

Made in the USA
Middletown, DE
16 May 2024

54424811R00130